Enterprise J2ME™

Developing Mobile Java™ Applications

Michael Juntao Yuan

PRENTICE
HALL
PTR

Prentice Hall PTR
Upper Saddle River, NJ 07458
www.phptr.com

A Cataloging-in-Publication Data record for this book can be obtained from the Library of Congress.

Editorial/Production Supervision: *Faye Gemmellaro*
Cover Design Director: *Jerry Votta*
Cover Design: *Talar Boorujy*
Cover Photography: *Karen Strelecki*
Manufacturing Manager: *Alexis R. Heydt-Long*
Executive Editor: *Gregory G. Doench*
Editorial Assistant: *Brandt Kenna*
Marketing Manager: *Jennifer Lundberg*

7th Printing   December 2006

ISBN 0131405306

Pearson Education Ltd.
Pearson Education Australia Pty., Limited
Pearson Education Singapore, Pte. Ltd.
Pearson Education North Asia Ltd.
Pearson Education Canada, Ltd.
Pearson Educación de Mexico, S.A. de C.V.
Pearson Education—Japan
Pearson Education Malaysia, Pte. Ltd.

To my parents and my dear wife Ju

About Prentice Hall Professional Technical Reference

With origins reaching back to the industry's first computer science publishing program in the 1960s, and formally launched as its own imprint in 1986, Prentice Hall Professional Technical Reference (PH PTR) has developed into the leading provider of technical books in the world today. Our editors now publish over 200 books annually, authored by leaders in the fields of computing, engineering, and business.

Our roots are firmly planted in the soil that gave rise to the technical revolution. Our bookshelf contains many of the industry's computing and engineering classics: Kernighan and Ritchie's *C Programming Language*, Nemeth's *UNIX System Administration Handbook*, Horstmann's *Core Java*, and Johnson's *High-Speed Digital Design*.

PH PTR acknowledges its auspicious beginnings while it looks to the future for inspiration. We continue to evolve and break new ground in publishing by providing today's professionals with tomorrow's solutions.

Contents

Foreword

The U.S. Department of Commerce published a report "Education and Training for the Information Technology Workforce" in August 2003. It points out that innovations that can drastically improve productivity will continue to be developed by U.S. companies and that the developer community must be prepared to leverage these innovations. The key question is to identify the technologies that manifest these innovations and focus on those that drive revenue.

Enterprise mobility has been identified as a very promising answer technology as it enables extensions to existing IT solutions. These extensions include support for alternate form factor devices like PDAs and Smart Phones, as well as extended operational characteristics such as sporadically connected operations over low bandwidth networks with potentially high latency and sparse geographic coverage.

Many of today's solutions for financial traders, sales agents, factory floor engineers, warehouse managers, and health care professionals still rely on pen- and pencil-based solutions when they are out there in the field because they either don't have network coverage, cannot use a PC-based form factor, or both. The overall business efficiency is often limited by these "in the field" bottlenecks. As more companies look into mobility extensions to improve efficiency, which directly affects the bottom line, developers who lead this field of IT-based solution extensions for mobility will have ample job opportunities in the global economy.

The best enterprise mobility strategy is *not* to re-invent the wheel. Rather, it should take advantage of existing infrastructure, standards, and developer skills to extend a consistent architecture that incorporates everything from powerful backend servers to laptop computers to PDAs and to the smallest smart phones.

The author of this book, Michael Yuan, has worked extensively with engineers from IBM and many other enterprise mobility solution providers. This book is a very comprehensive technical guide to today's enterprise mobility landscape. It covers architectural design patterns, best practices, and real-world innovations. Important mobile paradigms and architectures such as smart clients, end-to-end managed services, synchronized data access, and content-based security are discussed in detail. What I like the most about this book is that it not only covers the pros and cons of certain architectures but also walks you through concrete solutions using sample applications.

A consistent architectural solution is most valuable when it is based on open standards. This enables solution integrators to make technology selections from multiple providers with minimal impact on integration cost. This book is a comprehensive guide to many of these real-world innovations from multiple providers. The unbiased and technical discussions not only allow readers to make informed choices but also illustrate real-world design approaches.

Enterprise mobility is one of the most promising and cutting-edge fields in the IT industry. If you are an experienced developer looking to modernize your skill set and move up the value chain, I highly recommend this book.

Jim Colson

IBM Distinguished Engineer
Chief Architect, IBM Pervasive Computing Division

Austin, Texas
August, 2003

About this Book

Target Audience

This book targets all mobile software developers and business decision makers. It focuses on end-to-end architectural patterns, best practices, key innovations, and real-world design approaches. For different readers, this book offers different benefits:

- *Managers and entrepreneurs*: This book is a comprehensive guide to mobile enterprise applications and the Java 2 Micro Edition (J2ME). It covers the capabilities, limitations, common best practices, and commercial solutions of the state-of-the-art mobile Java technologies. It helps you decide which mobile Java profile and products are the best for your business.

- *Experienced mobile developers*: This book skips the basic MIDP API tutorial materials and goes straight to the more advanced and more useful topics. It uses several complete sample applications to illustrate common architectural patterns and coding best practices in mobile enterprise applications. For developers who are looking for specific solutions (e.g., messaging, database, XML, and security), the technical discussions on leading third-party J2ME tools and libraries will prove useful. Those real-world innovations also serve as prime examples of how you should design and implement your own solutions for similar tasks.

- *Experienced Java developers*: For experienced Java enterprise developers (J2EE developers), the move to mobility is about leveraging existing skills. This book walks through familiar design patterns and best practices and shows developers how to apply them in mobile applications. Lightweight mobile versions of enterprise Java APIs (such as JDBC, Java servlet, JMS, and Java Cryptography Extension) are discussed. Those are excellent examples of how to scale down enterprise solutions for mobility while still preserving core functionalities. With a few notes on mobile-specific issues, it is the fastest path to add mobility to existing enterprise infrastructure.

Prerequisites

To fully understand the technical content in this book, the readers should be familiar with the basic Java 2 Micro Edition, Mobile Information Device Profile (J2ME/MIDP) APIs and development tools. A quick MIDP programming guide is provided in Appendix A.

To run the end-to-end sample applications, you will need to deploy the serverside components to your own Java application server and run the clientside components on the desktop emulator or real devices. Please refer to the product manuals of your tools for step-by-step instructions.

Although serverside Java is not the focus of this book, familiarity with basic Java 2 Enterprise Edition (J2EE) concepts such as servlets, Java DataBase Connectivity (JDBC), Java Messaging Service (JMS), Java XML processing and Enterprise JavaBean (EJB), will help you understand various topics in this book.

Contents

This book is divided into six parts:

- Part I is the introductory material for mobile commerce, mobile enterprise applications, and J2ME. It covers the overall architecture, current status, and future roadmaps of J2ME.

- Part II is the heart of this book. It presents several example applications to illustrate the smart client mobile application paradigm, common architectural patterns, and best practices. It covers how to run container-managed applications (e.g., servlets) on PDA devices. It also presents a useful advanced HTTP client library for J2ME clients.

- Part III is about mobile messaging. In the mobile world, messaging clients are easy to use and fit into the mobile lifestyle. In the enterprise world, messaging is the best way to build loosely coupled applications that have guaranteed quality-of-service (QoS). This part of this book seeks to combine the best of the two worlds. It covers email and

SMS-based end-to-end applications as well enterprise mobile messaging servers.

- Part IV discusses mobile databases that are core to occasionally connected and synchronization-based applications. This part covers commercial and open source innovations for mobile databases, synchronization engines, and legacy database connectivity. Two sample database applications from PointBase are presented.

- Part V covers how to integrate mobile clients into the enterprise Web services infrastructure. It discusses existing and emerging J2ME XML and SOAP toolkits, specifications and showcases several complete sample applications.

- Part VI is all you need to know about J2ME mobile security solutions. It goes way beyond the simple connection-based end-to-end solutions such as the HTTPS. This part covers open source and commercial cryptography toolkits for J2ME. Due to the complexity of cryptography APIs, API tutorials for each important toolkit are provided.

- There are two appendices to this book. One of them uses a simple end-to-end MIDP application to illustrate the whole development and deployment cycle. The other appendix introduces the IBM WebSphere Studio Device Developer IDE and provides un-documented instructions on how to install IBM J2ME runtimes on PocketPC devices.

Code Examples

This book uses complete example applications to demonstrate design patterns, best practices, and important API usages. Since this book discusses a wide range of technologies, innovations and application scenarios, it is impractical to cover everything within a monolithic example. Instead, I decided to develop several small to midsize samples, each focusing on a particular topic. This approach allows the readers to partition the learning task and read one part of this book at a time.

The source code is presented in easy-to-digest segments that are relevant to the discussion text. Nonessential parts of the code (e.g., exception handling, importing packages) are often deliberately omitted from the listings for clarity. Hence, the printed listings are sufficient for understanding the ideas but are not directly runnable code. For readers who want to test and play with the code, the complete source code packages and build instructions are available for download from this book's Web sites: http://www.enterprisej2me.com/book/code/ and http://authors.phptr.com/yuan/. Sample applications used in this book are as follows:

- *iFeedBack*: The grand prize winner of the NexTel/Motorola/Sun wireless application contest in 2002 (Chapter 3).

- *Echo*: A GUI client and a service running in an OSGi clientside container (Chapter 4).

- *Pizza Order*: An example included in the IBM Service Management Framework download. It demonstrates how to build smart clients with HTTP front ends (Chapter 4).

- *Smart Ticket*: The Sun Wireless Blueprints application v2.0 early release code (Chapter 5).

- *HttpClient*: The code for the advanced HTTP library we develop in this section (Chapter 6).

- *Mail*: An MIDP email client based on the Mail4ME v1.0 library (Chapter 8).

- *WMATester*: A simple messaging application that illustrates the use of Wireless Messaging API v1.0 (Chapter 9).

- *ContactManager*: A mobile address book based on the PointBase v4.5 library (Chapter 11).

- *ContactManagerSync*: A synchronized mobile address book based on the PointBase v4.5 library (Chapter 13).

- *AmazonExample*: An kXML client for Amazon Web services using both kDOM and XmlPull APIs (Chapter 15).

- *PeekAndPick*: A RSS reader for mobile phones developed by Jonathan Knudsen (Chapter 15).

- *Google*: A simple client for the Google Web services API. Both kSOAP v1.2 and v2.0 versions are available (Chapter 16).

- *SmartPhrases*: An integrated Google search and online dictionary application (Chapter 16).

- *MapPoint AxisFacade*: An Apache Axis facade for MapPoint v3.0 Web services (Chapter 18).

- *MapPoint AxisClient*: Personal Profile and MIDP clients for the Map-Point facade (Chapter 18).

- *MobileSecurity*: A collection of small applications that demonstrate the correct usage of cryptography APIs (Chapter 20).

- *SimpleDemo*: A simple MIDP application to illustrate key concepts and APIs in MIDP programming (Appendix A).

Commercial Products

This book covers and compares more than 30 toolkits and libraries from more than a dozen third-party vendors. The descriptions and API usage examples of those products are intended to give the readers a solid technical ground to make informed comparisons and decisions. They also serve as real-world examples for API and tool designs. However, they *do not* substitute for the formal product documentation from the vendor. I strongly encourage interested readers to obtain the latest evaluation package and documentation from the vendor to investigate further.

Related Publications

Some of the materials used in this book are loosely based on articles I published previously on several online magazines.

- The Sun Smart Ticket blueprint discussed in Chapter 5 is also covered in *"End-to-End J2ME Application Development by Example,"* published on the Sun Wireless Java Web site in June 2003.

- The first half of Chapter 9 is also covered by *"Mobile P2P messaging, Part 1,"* published on IBM developerWorks in December 2002.

- Examples in Part IV are adapted from *"High-availability mobile applications,"* published on JavaWorld in June 2003.

- Chapter 16 is based on *"Access Web services from wireless devices,"* published on JavaWorld in August 2002.

- The example in Chapter 18 is adapted from *"Let the mobile games begin, Part 2,"* published on JavaWorld in May 2003.

- Part VI is loosely based on *"Data security in mobile Java applications,"* published on JavaWorld in December 2002.

Production Notes

This book is produced by the LaTeX typesetting system on a 1GHz Apple PowerBook running Mac OS X—the best consumer operating system ever produced. Microsoft Word is used for collaborative editing and reviewing. The figures are made with Microsoft Visio, OmniGraffle, GIMP, and the ImageMagick utilities.

The example applications are developed using a variety of development tools, including VI, JEdit, IntelliJ IDEA, and the WebSphere Studio Device Developer IDE. Apache Ant is used to build the applications. Mobile clients are tested on many vendor SDKs, including those from Sun Microsystems (the J2ME Wireless ToolKit), IBM (the WebSphere Micro Environment), Nokia, and Motorola. Real device testing was conducted on Motorola i95cl, Nokia 7210, Nokia 6800, and PocketPC Phone devices.

Acknowledgments

The biggest challenge for writing a cutting-edge technical book on a fast-evolving topic is to keep learning new things. When I started writing this book a year ago, the world of enterprise mobility looked very different than it is today. This massive learning and writing project is not possible without the help and guidance of many individuals.

Professor Andrew B. Whiston started this all by introducing me to the wonderful world of mobile commerce. As the director of Center for Research in Electronic Commerce at the University of Texas at Austin, Andy's vision and guidance proved crucial to the successes of all the researcher fellows and graduate students in the Center.

Developers in IBM Pervasive Computing Division reviewed and provided technical support for the IBM tools covered in this book. IBM's distinguished engineer and chief architect in device software Jim Colson oversaw the IBM review effort and wrote the foreword to this book. Senior engineer and OSGi fellow B. J. Hargrave provided valuable feedback on Chapter 4. Robert Elliott, the lead in Device Software Partner Program, helped me locate tutorial materials and handled many logistics issues. Thanks, Bob, it is a pleasure to work with you!

Individuals from many other companies have contributed valuable comments to the manuscript and the sample applications at various stages of the development. I would like to acknowledge Martyn Mallick, Bryan Stevenson, Kevin Gilhooly, Les Arnold, Norbert Runge, Alec Beaton, Esakki Sankaran, Ray Ortigas, Sean Sheedy, Jonathan Knudsen, Gary Adams, Jacob Christfort, David Hook, Jon Eaves, Oscar Batyrbaev, Kurt Dietrich, Stefan Haustein, Michael Yaffe, Michael Cox, Roger Sullivan, Sal Danna, and Carl Sayres.

I am grateful to the fine professionals at Prentice Hall PTR. Executive editor Greg Doench is the driver behind this project. He patiently guided me through the entire publishing process, helped define the scope and depth of the book, and yet allowed me to write freely. The production staff and freelance contractors are very helpful. I thank Brandt Kenna for reviews and other logistics, Lisa Iarkowski and Faye Gemmellaro for production management, Carol Lallier for copy editing, Debby Van Dijk for marketing management, Lori Hughes for LATEXhelp, and many others who worked behind the scenes. I also would like to thank my technical reviewers: Steve Jones, Sandeep Garg, Enrique Ortiz, and Angus McIntyre. Steve Jones also provided the mobile database sample applications used in Chapters 11 and 13.

Finally, this book would not have been possible without the support from my family. My mother Ming Zhang and late father ChengChang Yuan inspired me to be all I can be, and they have always supported my choices of career paths. I am deeply in debt to my dearest wife Ju Long for all the support and encouragement she has given me during the past several years. Ju has shouldered most of the tedious housework despite her own busy schedule as a Ph.D. candidate in Management Information Systems. *In addition*, her professional expertise and insights have proven essential to this book. Ju is the true hero behind the scenes, and she deserves all the glory.

Part I

Introduction

Chapter 1

Mobile Commerce: Visions, Realities, and Opportunities

CHAPTER OVERVIEW

- Mobile Commerce Value Propositions

- Mobile Technology Adoption

- The Search for Killer Mobile Applications

- Mobile Commerce Revenue Models

- Emerging Mobile Commerce Business Models

Moore's law states that computer capabilities double every 18 months. Meanwhile, prices for key computer components drop by halves. When cheap personal computers became powerful enough for most common tasks and graphic user interfaces, they were massively adopted by average home users and enterprises. Together with Internet technology, the personal computer is widely credited as a key enabler of the electronic commerce *New Economy* revolution of the 1990s.

Ten years later, Moore's law still holds. Today, computer devices are everywhere in our lives. Those small and cheap devices have processing power beyond the high-end PCs of only a few years ago. When coupled with mobile communication devices and the mobile Internet, new-generation pervasive devices empower us to access information anywhere, anytime.

International Data Corporation (IDC) has projected that by year 2007, two-thirds of the U.S. workforce will be mobile workers. We are entering a new era of mobile commerce. The freedom to access information without constraints of landlines and bulky PCs will create great business opportunities and improve our quality of life for years to come. The *freedom economy* is "what's next."

However, knowing the path is different from walking the path. To seize future mobile commerce opportunities, developers and business managers have to understand the value creation process and have solid business plans. In the first chapter of this book, we study basic concepts of mobile commerce and look at the business cases.

1.1 Mobile Commerce Value Propositions

A lesson we learned from the bust of dot-com bubbles is that a cool technology itself does not automatically translate into business success. Successful business models leverage new technology to create values and profits from ultimate customer satisfaction. So, what new values or cost savings can mobile technology create?

Unlike the PC-centric electronic commerce, mobile commerce is focused on personal experiences. A person carries a pervasive mobile device and gets information anytime, anywhere, from anyone. For the first time in history, a person's information access can be disassociated from her environment. For example, a traveler does not need to be in her office at a specific time to get ticket information. That unprecedented freedom of information could fundamentally affect all business categories. The next several sections provide a brief overview with examples.

1.1.1   Business to Consumer (B2C)

From a consumer's perspective, mobile commerce provides extreme convenience, speed, and personalization to access information services. Let's use a hypothetical stock trader example to illustrate how mobile commerce can change the way we consume information. A mobile stock trader can access markets around the world anytime, anywhere. He can take advantage of the 24/7 continuous global markets and never miss any profit opportunities. Mobile services store the trader's portfolio and target price information. Relevant news and price alerts are pushed to the trader at real time regardless of his location. Using personalized smart mobile agents, the trader can focus on stock researches and use his time more efficiently. As a result, he now spends more time with his family and enjoys life. In this case, mobile commerce creates value by saving time, improving efficiency, reducing opportunity loss, and improving the quality of life for its consumer. In fact, the financial services industry has been a major adopter of mobile commerce technologies. Almost all major banks, credit card companies, and trading firms have offered mobile interfaces to their informational and even transactional services. According to IDC, mobile banking has grown tenfold in western Europe from 1999 to 2001 and is expected to reach $334 million during 2003 in western Europe alone.

In addition to improving existing services, the freedom of information enables new breeds of consumer information services. For example, with smart in-home monitoring devices, patients may now stay with their families instead of in hospital observation rooms. Phase Forward is one of many firms in this emerging market. Another example is customized marketing application. Marketing firms can take advantage of the human desire for instant gratification and design more effective product promotion schemes based on consumers' real-time experiences. Avantgo is a leading company that provides mobile marketing solutions. Those new applications improve our lives directly and represent huge opportunities of profits for mobile commerce firms.

1.1.2   Business to Business (B2B)

From a business's perspective, mobile commerce could create value by improving efficiency. A good example is mobile supply chain management. Today's business supply chains consist of multiple suppliers and sellers at multiple levels from multiple countries. A poorly managed supply chain can create redundant inventories or insufficient supplies (and hence market share losses). In highly competitive business sectors, such as the PC business, efficient supply chain management can determine the survival of a firm. PC business leader Dell excels in supply chain management. As a result, Dell can make profits even when competitors are taking huge losses.

In a mobile supply chain management system, warehouse workers and truck loaders use mobile devices to track inventory and shipment data. The data is uploaded into enterprise backend systems at real time. Managers make timely decisions based on the most up-to-date supply chain information. Real-time information also allows the management team to quickly identify and correct bottlenecks in supply chains. Purchase authorization, billing, and payment are also completed by field agents at real time, streamlining the whole process and reducing turnaround time for both goods and information. Supply chain management innovation is often custom done inhouse. A commercial product that enables real-time supply chain management using mobile technology is Savi Technology's Smart Chain solution.

Better managed and more transparent supply chains can ultimately benefit a business's bottom line by increasing customer satisfaction at the end of the supply chain. Mobile technology enables vendors to ship goods faster and to better predict the availability or arrival dates. UPS and FedEx's package-tracking services have became hugely popular. In a world of mobile commerce, real-time order tracking would be the norm of retail business. Highly visible supply chains allow customers to adjust their schedules to meet the product delivery time.

1.1.3   Business to Employee (B2E)

Mobile commerce allows firms to reduce operational costs for their mobile employees, including sales force, field agents, and factory floor workers.

Pharmaceutical companies rely on physicians to sell new medicines. Pharmaceutical sales representatives and doctors often meet at lunchtime outside of the doctor's office—it is easier to make personal connections during an informal lunch. However, it is difficult to hook up a networked computer on a dining table. If the doctor wants to make a purchase, the sales representative has to come back later with price and inventory quotes—a lengthy and costly process. Companies like AvantGo and XcelleNet develop mobile sales management and automation suites for big pharmaceutical companies. With the help of mobile commerce, the salesperson can quote prices and close the deal right on the dining table, and the doctor can then track the shipment. Of course, mobile sales automation can go far beyond the pharmaceutical industry. Combined with leading CRM (customer relationship management) software, companies of all sizes, such as IBM, NexTel, SAP, and Numeric Computer Systems, offer a range of mobile sales solutions.

Like sales representatives, field agents also need to access their company's enterprise information system on the run. Endurable equipment vendors from Xerox to Otis equip their field service technicians with mobile devices. They can check technical information as well as conduct asset management on customer sites.

Even for factory workers who do not work outside the company, mobile information access can still be very useful. Boeing has huge plants to build commercial jet airliners. It is impossible to wire the plant with Ethernet cables, since there are so many moving parts. Technicians working inside a plane often need to make little trips to a nearby computer terminal to check digital blueprints. That is not only inefficient but also error prone—humans can recall wrong details even after a short walk. Mobile information devices make it possible for technicians to check blueprints inside the plane right at the problem spot, improving efficiency, reducing error, and hence saving operational costs.

1.1.4   Public Services and Safety

Government sectors are among the first to adopt sophisticated mobile applications. Police officers need to check driver's license, license plate, and vehicle identification numbers whenever they stop a driver. Emergency medical workers at an accident scene need to check drug conflicts and other life-critical information, and emergency response systems have to be coordinated wirelessly. The military requires real-time updates from soldiers and commanders in the battlefield.

The events of September 11, 2001, in the United States revealed successes and failures in government mobile information systems. When all the fixed-voice and data lines were knocked off by the terrorist attacks, the cell network was still functional. Cell phone calls and wireless email messages became the last words we heard from many people in the World Trade Center and in the hijacked planes. However, the emergency response wireless networks proved fatally flawed. Many firefighters in the Towers never received the evacuation orders. The information gathered by police helicopter pilots about the imminent danger of building collapse never reached the fire department information system. Reliable mobile information systems are crucial to public safety in the 21st century.

1.2   Mobile Technology Adoption

To take advantage of mobile commerce, businesses and consumers must adopt state-of-the-art mobile technology. The diffusion of innovations usually goes through five stages: visionary, missionary, ordinary, commodity, and maturity. The characteristics of each stage are listed below (see Figure 1.1).

- *Visionary*: The technology has just come out. Few people see its business value. The technology proponents in the visionary stage base their arguments on advocacy rather than on solid value propositions. A famous advocacy slogan is "You need this. You just do not know it yet." In this stage, few companies except infrastructure builders can make money.

- *Missionary*: Business practitioners start to see the value of the innovation. Pioneer companies or employees become early adopters of the new technology and start to profit from it.

- *Ordinary*: The value of the technology is well accepted by the mainstream business executives, and most companies have developed plans to implement solutions based on the new technology. In this stage, the developers and enablers of the new technology make the bulk of profits.

- *Commodity*: In this stage, the adoption of the technology becomes common practice. The technology has started to generate profits industrywide. However, since implementations have been standardized, the barrier of market entry becomes substantially lower, which results in intense competition in the enablers sector.

- *Maturity*: In a mature market, most commodity technology suppliers are consolidated to a few dominant players.

On a typical innovation diffusion curve, the transition period between missionary and ordinary stages are associated with explosive growth of adoptions and a limited number of technology firms who have the expertise to implement viable solutions. The unbalanced demand and supply creates golden opportunities for developers and technology firms to make money. We have seen this pattern repeated throughout history.

At the time of writing (Fall 2003), the value of mobile commerce has been well accepted by industry leaders and business executives. Leading companies in financial services, information services, transportation, and manufacturing sectors have already started to implement their mobile commerce strategies. Other companies will soon follow suit. All these signs indicate

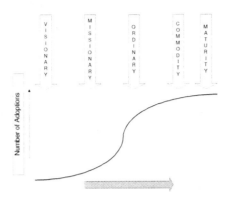

Figure 1.1. Technology adoption curve.

that mobile commerce is currently at late missionary stage and is moving toward the ordinary stage.

Although mobile commerce poses to bring tremendous opportunities, we have to be cautious and understand the risks. Historically, technology adoption was never a smooth or linear process. As we have seen in the recent rise and fall of dotcoms, the expectations of technology adoption are often exaggerated; the relationships between the new and old business models are often distorted. Those unrealistic expectations have resulted in severe consequences for those failed dotcom companies and their employees. Nevertheless, adoption of e-commerce as a whole is steadily moving on. I expect the mobile commerce adoption will experience similar up and downs. Many of the heavily hyped, first-generation mobile companies may not ultimately survive. The final winners might still be steady and effectively managed blue chip companies.

1.3   The Search for Killer Mobile Applications

The value of mobile commerce is ultimately realized through successful applications. A popular application can jump-start the technology adoption process and make a lot of profit for its inventor. The search for mobile "killer applications" has started from the beginning days of mobile commerce. In this section, we will discuss application ideas and trends.

1.3.1   Mobile Entertainment

The most mature consumer markets for mobile commerce are in the Asia-Pacific region and Northern/Western Europe. In those markets, mobile entertainment applications are hugely successful. A good example is Japan's DoCoMo. However, in the United States, mobile entertainment has yet to take off. U.S. consumers are less subject to crowded public transportation systems and have easy access to superior wired voice and data networks. The individualistic culture of the U.S. society makes community and messaging-based games less attractive to American consumers. Mobile entertainment might never be a killer application in the United States.

However, mobile entertainment represents only a small part of the consumer commerce. Mobile commerce's application is much broader than personal entertainment.

1.3.2   From Toys to Tools

Although mobile entertainment can grow huge businesses, it provides nonessential toys to consumers. Enterprise mobile applications that enable essential business tools are more likely to be killer applications for future mobile commerce. For example, mobile games allow travelers to kill time when waiting in long lines in airports. In contrast, a mobile ticketing and scheduling application allows travelers to go directly to gates and avoid the lines altogether.

According to a study released by the IDC, the number of mobile workers in the United States will reach 105 million by year 2006. That is almost two-thirds of the total U.S. work force. Those mobile workers perform complex and essential tasks. Their workflows must be fully integrated into the IT infrastructure through enterprise mobility solutions.

In reality, enterprise mobile applications are quickly gaining momentum, especially in the United States. Although the public wireless network in the United States is not as advanced as many Asian and European countries, U.S. companies have seen the value of enterprise mobile applications and have invested a lot of money to build high-speed corporate wireless networks using technologies such as WiFi. The leading mobile commerce applications in the United States are not games but business applications.

1.3.3   The Enterprise Mobility Eco-system

The mobile commerce revolution goes much deeper than a single killer application. It is about the freedom of information access. For example, mobile workers can access email and synchronize with calendar applications; securely read and write company files and databases; get price and inventory quotes from live application servers; and respond to customer service requests anytime, anywhere. Mobile enterprise applications change the ways consumers, employees, and companies conduct their businesses.

Enterprise mobility will become a driving force behind the mobile commerce revolution and form an eco-system nobody can live without. This collection of killer mobile business tools and applications provides great opportunities for businesses and developers.

1.4   Mobile Commerce Landscape

The previous sections explained the rationales and values behind enterprise mobile applications. After a company develops a mobile strategy, the natural next step is to implement it. Given the complexity of a mobile commerce solution, it requires collaborations from many different application and infrastructure service providers. Mobile commerce provider firms can generate revenues from hardware, software, or services sales.

1.4.1   Mobile Device Manufacturers

There is a wide range of mobile devices, including many kinds of cell phones, PDAs, consoles, and auto-mounted devices. Since mobile devices are to become pervasive personal belongings, they pose some unique design and technical challenges to manufacture. Successful mobile devices should have the following features.

- Small size

- Rich multimedia presentation capabilities

- Fast response time

- Large memory for data and applications

- Long battery life

- Fashionable and personalizable

Billions of dollars have been invested in mobile hardware research by leading companies such as Intel, Nokia, Motorola, and Qualcomm; they have produced many competing chipsets and handset designs.

1.4.2   Mobile Internet Service Providers

Mobile commerce requires mobile devices to be connected to data networks. Mobile Internet Service Providers (MISPs) are often wireless network carriers such as SprintPCS and AT&T. Those carriers build radio towers across the country and buy expensive radio spectrum licenses. They provide national cell phone voice and data services and often bundle Internet services in wireless access packages. Companies can also partner with wireless carriers to provide mobile Internet access to their customers under their own brand name. An example of an independent MISP is Palm.net.

If your mobile application is internal to your company, you may not need a national MISP. You can set up your own local corporate wireless network. Provision stations around your building or campus connect your wireless network to your internal network and then connect to the general Internet through your company firewalls. This way, you act as your own MISP.

1.4.3   Mobile Software Platform Providers

Given the diversity of mobile hardware, there are many mobile device operation systems. Examples include PalmOS, Symbian OS, Windows CE, and Embedded Linux. The OS SDKs (Software Developer Kits) often lack advanced programming language support and important libraries for business functions.

So, on top of operating systems, there are also application software platforms. Those platforms run on a variety of mobile devices and provide advanced sets of development tools and features. Examples of such platforms include WAP microbrowsers, Java, and Microsoft .NET Compact Framework. Java mobile application platform is one of the major focuses of this book.

1.4.4   Mobile Application Service Providers

Since mobile devices have very limited processing power and poor network connections, they often rely on backend servers to conduct sophisticated tasks. Mobile Application Service Providers (MASP) provide middleware and backend services. Examples of MASPs are 247 Solutions, JP Mobile, AGEA, Avantgo, and many others.

Companies looking for customized inhouse enterprise solutions can become their own MASPs. This book is targeted to MASP developers in both outsource and inhouse firms. We discuss mobile commerce-specific backend and middleware solutions in detail in the rest of this book.

1.5 Summary

The *freedom economy* and *mobile commerce* are truly revolutionary ideas that would transform the way we do business. The "killer applications" in this mobile revolution are enterprise applications that streamline business processes and improve efficiencies. Developers who enter the game early would benefit from high profit margins and lasting job security. In the rest of this book, we introduce an array of cutting-edge mobile technologies and related tools. Developers can learn their uses through concrete examples and avoid pitfalls through best practice advice. Business managers can read about application scenarios and understand the capabilities and limits of the current technology.

Resources

[1] *The Freedom Economy: Gaining the mCommerce Edge in the Era of the Wireless Internet.* Ron Mackintosh, Peter G. W. Keen, and Mikko Heikkonen. McGraw-Hill Osborne, June 2001.

[2] *M-Business: The Race to Mobility.* Ravi Kalakota and Marcia Robinson. McGraw-Hill, September 2001.

[3] *Mobile and Wireless Design Essentials.* Martyn Mallick. John Wiley and Sons, March 2003.

Chapter 2

J2ME: Is Mobile Java Ready for Enterprise?

CHAPTER OVERVIEW

- The Java Advantages

- The Java Community Process

- The Java 2 Micro Edition

- J2ME Configurations

- J2ME Profiles

- J2ME Optional Packages

- .NET Compact Framework and BREW

The Java technology is emerging as one of the most important enablers for mobile enterprise solutions. An October 2002 research survey, published by the Zelos Group, estimated that more than 44 million Java-enabled handsets were sold worldwide in year 2002: That is 11 percent of all handset shipments in that year. The survey projects that in 2007, Java handset shipments will reach more than 450 million, constituting 74 percent of all handset shipments. Java mobile devices will soon surpass Wintel PCs and become the dominant information access clients.

All major mobile device vendors, including Nokia, Motorola, Siemens, Samsung, Fujitsu, Inventec, LG Electronics, Mitsubishi, NEC, Panasonic, Psion, RIM, Sharp, and Sony, have adopted Java as part of their core strategy for future smart devices. Major wireless carriers such as NexTel, SprintPCS, and AT&T have committed to support Java devices and applications on their networks.

What is the big deal about the mobile Java platform? In this chapter, we first discuss why Java technology is perfectly suited for mobile development. Then, we look at the architecture, components, and newest trends of the Java 2 Micro Edition. We also briefly survey mobile Java competitors.

2.1   Why Java?

Before Java was called *Java*, it was *Oak*—a programming language designed for TV set-top boxes and other devices (see "Resources"). Considering its deep roots in devices, there is no surprise that many philosophies and designs behind the Java technology are perfectly suited for mobile applications. The advantages of the Java technology are as follows.

- *Cross platform*: This is very important in the diversified mobile device market. In a heterogeneous enterprise environment, the ability to develop and maintain a single client for all devices results in huge savings.

- *Robust*: Since Java applications are completely managed, the bytecode is verified before execution, and memory leaks are reclaimed by garbage collectors. Even if a Java application does crash, it is contained within the virtual machine. It will not affect other sensitive applications or data on the device.

- *Secure*: The Java runtime provides advanced security features through a domain-based security manager and standard security APIs.

- *Object oriented*: The Java language is a well-designed, object-oriented language with vast library support. There is a vast pool of existing Java developers.

- *Wide adoption at the back end*: It is relatively easy to make Java clients work with Java application servers and messaging servers. Due to the wide adoption of Java 2 Enterprise Edition (J2EE) on the server side, mobile Java is the leading candidate for enterprise frontend applications.

However, technical merits are not the only factors that determine the success of a technology. The business values are just as important. In particular, the vendor's ability to address the concerns of the developer and user community is key to the technology's adoption. Now, let's have a look at how the Java community influences the evolution of the technology.

2.2 The Java Community Process

The concept of open interfaces is core to the Java technology. It works as follows: For a given computing task, a set of standard APIs is defined by a standards committee. Individual vendors then provide competing libraries that implement those APIs. The application code using the API is completely decoupled from the specific implementation provider. That approach minimizes the developer's learning cost and improves code portability. Yet, it also protects the freedom of choosing vendors. The Java Community Process (JCP) is an effort to develop standard Java API specifications.

JCP Executive Committees (ECs, see Table 2.1) consist of industry leading companies. Anyone in the general public can submit a new Java Specification Request (JSR) for a new API. The appropriate EC decides whether to accept this new JSR. Once approved, the JSR lead can recruit more companies or individuals to develop the API specification together. Every specification goes through multiple stages of community and public reviews before it becomes an official Java standard.

The JCP ensures that all interested parties can express their concerns. As a result, the final APIs are supported by industry consensus. All standard mobile Java APIs are developed democratically through the JCP.

Now, let's look at the most trends in the Java world and how they relate to mobility.

Table 2.1. J2ME Executive Committee			
BEA	Cisco	Ericsson	IBM
Insignia	Matsushita	Motorola	Nokia
Palm	Philips	RIM	Siemens
SONY	Sun	WindRiver	Zucotto

2.3 Java Everywhere

The conference theme of the 8th JavaOne conference in 2003 is "Java Everywhere." Beyond the buzz and the hype, the Java Everywhere vision signals a departure from Java's traditional focus on "Write Once Run Anywhere" (WORA). Instead, it promotes a single consistent architecture, compatible APIs and easy skill migration for developers. Java Everywhere will have profound impacts on Java-based mobility solutions.

2.3.1 The Single Architecture Solution

Although cross-platform compatibility is a key concept behind the Java philosophy, Java designers also realize that portability has its limits. Portability is only meaningful among similar OSs and hardware platforms. Today, the Java platform is partitioned into three editions, all of which have significant roles in mobility. The overall architecture of the Java platform is shown in Figure 2.1.

- *The Java 2 Standard Edition (J2SE)*: The J2SE is the basis of the Java platform. It defines the JVMs and libraries that run on standard PCs and workstations. In the mobility world, J2SE is the ideal choice for wireless laptop-based applications.

- *The Java 2 Enterprise Edition (J2EE)*: The J2EE is J2SE plus a large number of serverside APIs, containers and tools. It aims to implement complex application servers. J2EE application servers can drive browser-based (e.g., WML and xHTML) mobile applications and become service end-points for smart mobile clients.

- *The Java 2 Micro Edition (J2ME)*: J2ME is a Java platform that is designed for small devices. It contains specially designed, lightweight virtual machines; a bare minimum of core-class libraries; and lightweight substitutes for standard Java libraries. J2ME is the ideal mobile client platform for wireless PDAs and enhanced mobile phones.

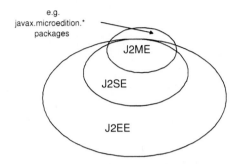

Figure 2.1. The Java 2 platform architecture.

Applications for each of the Java editions can follow similar architectures. That allows companies to leverage existing developer talent, cut cost and build more maintainable products.

2.3.2   Opportunities for J2EE Developers

The single architecture approach benefits existing Java developers the most. As the serverside technologies reach maturity, consolidation and outsourcing become the trend. According to a U.S. Department of Commerce study, in year 2002, the IT employment in the United States fell for the first time in history. Many J2EE development projects have been moved to cheaper offshore locations.

Enterprise developers have to keep up with the need of their customers and stay on top of the innovation value chain to stay employed. As more companies look for IT solutions to improve mobile workers' productivity, enterprise mobility is a natural next step for developers. Fortunately, with the Java Everywhere architecture, it is easy for experienced J2EE developers to migrate their skills to the mobile arena. For example,

- Common J2EE design patterns can be applied to end-to-end applications with little change.

- Mobile enterprise messaging, data access, integration and security solutions are parallel to their serverside counterparts.

- Lightweight editions of popular J2EE frameworks are already available on J2ME.

In the rest of this book, we will discuss the above topics in detail.

2.4   Java 2 Micro Edition Explained

Although enterprise mobility solutions can be implemented over J2SE laptops and J2ME devices, the J2ME solutions have significantly lower costs. A Gartner 2002 study concluded that the TCO (Total Cost of Ownership) of smart phones is only one-tenth of wireless laptops and one-fourth of wireless PDAs. The sheer number of J2ME devices makes J2ME the most important enterprise mobility platform. We will focus on J2ME in this book.

2.4.1   J2ME Architecture

Merely distinguishing J2ME from J2SE does not solve all our compatibility problems. There is a huge variety of mobile devices, designed for different purposes and with different features. The "lowest common denominator" does not work. For example, applications on an automobile mounted system are much more complex than those on a cell phone. Even among similar devices, such as high-end and low-end cell phones, portability can cause underutilization of resources on one device and strain on another.

To balance portability with performance and feasibility in the real world, J2ME contains several components known as configurations, profiles, and optional packages (Figure 2.2). Each valid combination of a configuration and a profile targets a specific kind of device. The configurations provide the most basic and generic language functionalities. The profiles sit on top of configurations and support more advanced APIs, such as a graphical user interface (GUI), persistent storage, security, and network connectivity. The optional packages can be bundled with standard profiles to support specific application needs.

2.4.2   J2ME Components

The two most important J2ME configurations are as follows.

- The Connected Limited Device Configuration (CLDC) is for the smallest wireless devices with 160 KB or more memory and slow 16/32-bit processors. The CLDC has limited math, string, and I/O functionalities and lacks features such as the JNI (Java Native Interface) and custom class loaders. Only a small subset of J2SE core libraries is supported by the CLDC virtual machines (known as KVMs or Kilobyte Virtual Machines). The most recent version of the CLDC is version 1.1. It was developed by the JSR 139 and released in March 2003.

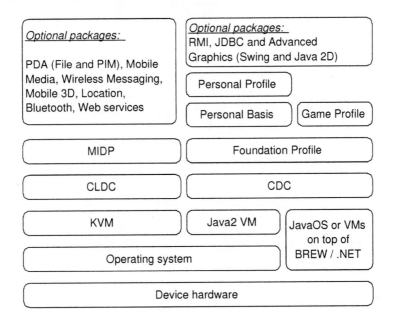

Figure 2.2. J2ME components.

- The Connected Device Configuration (CDC) is for more capable wireless devices with at least 2 MB of memory and 32-bit processors. Unlike the CLDC, the CDC supports a fully featured Java 2 VM and therefore can take advantage of most J2SE libraries. The CDC v1.0 was developed by the JSR 36 and it became available in March 2001. The new CDC v1.1 is currently being developed by the JSR 218 and is expected before the end of year 2003.

The most important and successful J2ME profile is the Mobile Information Device Profile (MIDP), based on the CLDC. The MIDP targets the smallest devices, such as cell phones. It is already deployed on millions of handsets. However, the MIDP v1.0 lacks some important features, such as security and advanced UI controls. As a result, device vendors often supply their own MIDP extensions to provide advanced custom features. Vendor-specific extensions undermine the portability of J2ME applications. Many problems with the MIDP v1.0 have been fixed in the MIDP v2.0, which came out of JCP in August 2002. Table 2.2 lists MIDP-compatible optional packages. Most of those optional packages run on CDC profiles as well. The profiles and optional packages based on the CDC are listed in Tables 2.3 and 2.4.

| Table 2.2. MIDP Optional Packages |

Name	Description
PDA Optional Package	It is designed for PDAs such as the Palm series products. It adds more PDA-specific APIs, such as Personal Information Managers (PIM), to the MIDP. The public review came out in July 2002. For more details, see Chapter 8.
Mobile Media API	It supports audio/video controls and streaming media. The v1.0 specification was finalized in June 2002.
Wireless Messaging API	It supports wireless messaging, including SMS messages. The Wireless Messaging API (WMA) v1.0 specification came out of JCP in August 2002. WMA v2.0, currently under development in JSR 205, will include Multimedia Message System (MMS) capabilities. For more details, see Chapter 9.
Location API	It supports location tracking for wireless devices. The v1.0 final release came out in September 2003. For more details, see Chapter 18.
J2ME Web Services API	It supports Web Services-related XML processing. For more details, see Chapter 17.
Bluetooth API	It supports the Bluetooth communication protocol. It is already available.
Security and Trust API	It allows a Java phone to interact with its security smart card. This API should be available in late-2003.
Mobile 3D Graphics API	It supports 3D graphics. This API is still under JCP development.
SIP API for J2ME	It provides support for the Session Initiation Protocol (SIP), which is commonly used in multimedia and VoIP applications. A public review draft of this API was released by the JSR 180 expert group in May 2003. The final specification release is expected before the end of 2003.
Presence and IM APIs	These are J2ME versions of bigger JAIN packages. They are developed by JSRs 164/165 and 186/187. They leverage SIP to provide presence and IM support for mobile devices.

Note

According to the roadmap published by the JSR 185 (Java Technology for the Wireless Industry [JTWI]), the Mobile Media API must be present on JTWI-compliant devices if they expose video/audio capability to Java applications.

Table 2.3. CDC-Based Profiles

Name	Description
Foundation Profile (FP)	It is designed for devices with reliable network connections. The FP provides a rich Java network environment, including support for multiple communication protocols and security. The FP does not support GUIs. It is used on network devices that do not require direct user interactions. The FP came out of JSR 46 in March 2002.
Personal Basis Profile (PBP)	It adds GUI support on top of the FP. The PBP targets high-end PDAs, such as Compaq iPaq and Sharpe Zaurus, and Internet appliances. PBP's GUI API is a subset of J2SE Abstract Windowing Toolkit (AWT). The PBP became a formal specification in June 2002.
Personal Profile (PP)	It is built on top of the FP and the PBP. It targets the same device category as the PBP. However, PP devices tend to be more powerful (2.5 MB RAM is required for the PP as opposed to 2 MB for the PBP). The PP was released by the JCP in September 2002.
Game Profile	It targets high-end consumer game devices (game consoles). The Game Profile is still under JCP development, but it has not been active since June 2001.

Table 2.4.   CDC-Based Optional Package

Name	Description
RMI Optional Package	It includes lightweight RMI APIs to support interoperability with RMI-based J2SE and J2EE applications. This package enables Jini technology for distributed device networks. This package became available in June 2002.
JDBC Optional Package	It provides a subset of JDBC v3.0 APIs to support direct database access from mobile devices. This package was approved by the JCP in December 2002.
Advanced Graphics and UI	This package provides Swing, Java 2D, Image I/O, and the Input Method Framework APIs for more capable mobile devices. It includes new classes defined in J2SE 1.4.1. This optional package is currently being developed under JSR 209.

The JCP at work

When JSR 209 (Advanced Graphics and UI Optional Package for J2ME) was proposed, there were some doubts about the wisdom of supporting the large Swing/Java 2D libraries in J2ME. Some were concerned about the fragmentation of the Swing API, while others argued that if a device is powerful enough to support those APIs, it should probably run J2SE instead of J2ME. But most EC members agree that Swing is a nice-to-have feature if it is completely optional. Then, in JSR 216 to 219, Sun Microsystems proposed to prepare the next-generation (version 1.1) CDC/FP/PP for Swing and Java 2D support, which would result in added baggage for vendors who do not plan to support the optional JSR 209. That caused a major revolt among J2ME EC members. A vast majority of EC members voted against the new JSRs and sent them back for reconsideration, which demonstrates the democratic JCP process at work.

2.5   Competing Technologies

Finally, it is worth noting that J2ME is not the only technology that enables mobile commerce. Leading competing technologies are as follows.

- *WAP/WML*: WAP/WML is a platform for thin client applications (i.e. microbrowser-based applications). The thin client paradigm is completely different from the smart client paradigm enabled by the J2ME (Chapters 3 and 4). J2ME smart clients are likely to replace WAP/XML applications in the future.

- *BREW*: Qualcomm's Binary Runtime Environment for Wireless (BREW) is a technology that supports rich client development and provisioning. BREW applications are written in C/C++ and run natively on BREW-enabled phones. However, only a limited number of phones support BREW. Although BREW native applications can be heavily optimized, they are not executed in managed environments and therefore are prone to programming errors. J2ME applications could run on BREW devices through a J2ME runtime for BREW (e.g., the BREW MIDP runtimes from IBM and Insignia).

- *.NET Compact Framework (.NET CF)*: Microsoft's .NET CF is the closest competition to the J2ME. Like J2ME, it targets smart-managed mobile clients development. It has a strong focus on enterprise applications. However, the .NET CF runs only on high-end Windows CE and PocketPC devices. For a detailed analysis of the .NET CF and J2ME, please refer to the articles in the "Resources" section.

2.6   Summary

In this chapter, we discussed the advantages of the Java 2 Micro Edition as a mobile commerce platform. We introduced the basics of J2ME philosophy, architecture, and components, including new specifications currently in JSR development. J2ME technologies and their applications on enterprise mobile applications are the focus of the rest of this book.

Resources

[1] *Wireless Java: Developing with J2ME, 2nd ed.* Jonathan Knudsen. Apress, 2003.

[2] *Core J2ME Technology and MIDP.* John W. Muchow. Prentice Hall PTR, 2002.

[3] Zelos Group Mobile Handset Survey.
http://www.microjava.com/articles/perspective/zelos

[4] The Early History of Java.
http://java.sun.com/features/1998/05/birthday.html

[5] The Connected Limited Device Configuration (CLDC) v1.1.
http://www.jcp.org/en/jsr/detail?id=139

[6] The Connected Device Configuration (CDC) v1.0.
http://www.jcp.org/en/jsr/detail?id=36

[7] The CDC v1.1 development JSR.
http://www.jcp.org/en/jsr/detail?id=218

[8] The Mobile Information Device Profile (MIDP).
http://java.sun.com/products/midp/

[9] The PDA Profile (PDAP). http://www.jcp.org/en/jsr/detail?id=75

[10] The Foundation Profile. http://java.sun.com/products/foundation/

[11] The Personal Basis Profile (PBP).
http://java.sun.com/products/personalbasis/

[12] The Personal Profile (PP).
http://java.sun.com/products/personalprofile/

[13] The Game Profile. http://www.jcp.org/en/jsr/detail?id=134

[14] The Mobile Media API. http://java.sun.com/products/mmapi/

[15] The Mobile 3D API. http://www.jcp.org/en/jsr/detail?id=184

[16] The Wireless Messaging API.
http://wireless.java.sun.com/midp/articles/wma/

[17] The Location API. http://jcp.org/en/jsr/detail?id=179

[18] The J2ME Web Services API. http://www.jcp.org/en/jsr/detail?id=172

[19] The Java API for Bluetooth. http://www.jcp.org/en/jsr/detail?id=82

[20] The Security and Trust Services API.
http://www.jcp.org/en/jsr/detail?id=177

[21] The SIP API for J2ME. http://www.jcp.org/en/jsr/detail?id=180

[22] The JAIN SIMPLE Presence API.
http://www.jcp.org/en/jsr/detail?id=164

[23] The JAIN SIMPLE Instant Messaging.
http://www.jcp.org/en/jsr/detail?id=165

[24] The JAIN Presence. http://www.jcp.org/en/jsr/detail?id=186

[25] The JAIN Instant Messaging. http://www.jcp.org/en/jsr/detail?id=187

[26] Java Technology for the Wireless Industry (the Road Map).
http://www.jcp.org/en/jsr/detail?id=185

[27] The RMI Optional Package. http://java.sun.com/products/rmiop/

[28] The JDBC Optional Package. http://java.sun.com/products/jdbc/

[29] Advanced Graphics and User Interface Optional Package for the J2ME
Platform. http://www.jcp.org/en/jsr/detail?id=209

Part II

End-to-End Enterprise Applications

Chapter 3

The Smart Client Paradigm: iFeedBack

CHAPTER OVERVIEW

- Benefits of Smart Clients

- The iFeedBack Application

- Distributed Authentication

- The UI Call Model

- The Thread Model

- Implementation Walk Through

J2ME represents a new mobile application paradigm: smart clients. Smart clients, especially Java smart clients, have many advantages over competing solutions such as WAP/WML. In this chapter, I use a sample application, iFeedBack, the grand prize winner of 2003 NexTel/Sun/Motorola University Wireless Developer Contest, to illustrate the power of smart clients and the basic end-to-end architecture. We will focus on the overall design and briefly walk through the implementation.

Since this book targets advanced Java developers, I assume that you already have knowledge of J2ME application development and deployment. If you need to refresh your memory, a quick start guide is available in Appendix A. A list of entry level J2ME books and tutorials can also be found in the "Resources" section. Although the implementation details of the J2EE serverside components are not the focus of this book, knowledge on servlet, JDBC, JMS, JAX-RPC and EJB will greatly help you understand the sample applications. To run the sample applications, you also need to know how to deploy J2EE applications to your application server.

3.1 Benefits of Smart Clients

Microbrowser-based thin client technologies (e.g., Wireless Application Protocol, WAP) were instrumental in bringing mobile Internet to masses in the early days of mobile commerce. But WAP-based mobile commerce has never been very popular due to the lack of usability on the client side. The new generation of smart client mobile technology (e.g., J2ME and Microsoft's .NET Compact Framework) promises to bring feature-rich clients to mobile applications. The benefits of smart clients over thin clients include the following.

- Smart clients have richer and more pervasive user interfaces. In particular, the judicial use of threads can drastically improve user perception of the application performance.

- Smart clients can be more easily personalized. Extreme personalization is one of the most touted benefits of the freedom (mobile) economy.

- On-device data storage reduces network traffic, especially unnecessary round trips; enables transactions; supports the "offline" mode when the network is temporarily unavailable; and hence improves overall performance, reliability, and availability of mobile applications.

- Smart clients can leverage device extensions. For example, a smart client program can talk with the device's built-in (or attached) GPS module and bar-code scanners. A smart client can also integrate with device-specific software (e.g., email and messaging clients) to improve the user's workflow.

- Smart clients support more powerful and flexible security schemes, such as content-based security and distributed single sign-on.

- Smart clients support advanced integration technologies. They are easy to plug into existing corporate infrastructure. Supports for asynchronous messaging and XML Web Services are crucial for reliable and maintainable mobile solutions.

The focus of this entire book is to introduce technologies, architectures, and tools that maximize those benefits. The iFeedBack example in this chapter presents a bird's eye view of the smart client paradigm through a concrete application.

3.2   Introducing iFeedBack

In order to tap J2ME smart clients' potential in emerging markets and seek new ideas of killer applications, NexTel, Sun Microsystems, and Motorola jointly sponsored the University Wireless Developer Contest in the United States. My contest entry "iFeedBack: A Single Sign-on Mobile Survey Tool for University Students" won the grand prize of $20,000. In the rest of this chapter, I use iFeedBack as an example to illustrate what can be done with managed smart clients. The complete source code of the iFeedBack application can be downloaded from this book's Web site (see "Resources").

3.2.1   The Problems to Solve

A big "business problem" we had for a long time in the higher education enterprise (i.e., universities) was the lack of communication channels between knowledge producers (professors) and consumers (students). College students in large universities usually have little interaction with professors. The lack of feedback on course advances and teaching techniques is one of the major factors that impede effective learning. Course evaluation surveys at the end of the semester often are the only way a student can convey his or her opinions of the teaching to the professor. But there are two problems with such delayed instructor surveys: They are too late for the students to remember earlier incidents, and they are too late for the professor to take corrective measures.

An open, real-time, and convenient communication channel between professors and students will benefit both parties. iFeedBack is a mobile survey application that allows questionnaires to be presented and answered anytime, anywhere. It is not only suitable for frequent instructor surveys, but can also be used in in-class quizzes and homework assignments.

3.2.2 Architecture

The overall architecture of iFeedBack is illustrated in Figure 3.1.

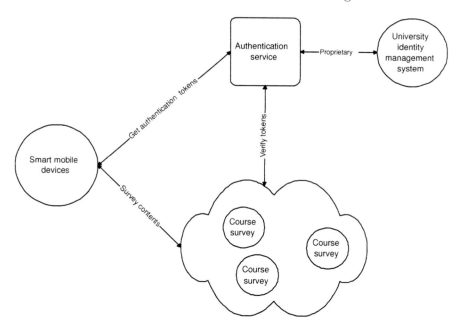

Figure 3.1. The iFeedBack architecture.

There are three major components in an iFeedBack deployment:

- Each class has its own survey site that feeds current questions to mobile clients and receives time-stamped answers over the HTTP. The professor and teaching assistants have administrative access to that site.

- The university provides a single sign-on service. This server authenticates students and issues time-limited access tokens to survey sites. The student uses tokens to access class survey sites. Class sites also connect to the authentication server to verify the tokens. To ensure interoperability with potentially large numbers of different clients, this single sign-on service is provided via an XML Web Services interface.

- The smart MIDP client provides user interface and temporary storage for time-stamped answers. It also manages authentication credentials and maintains a list of endpoint URLs for classes the student is attending.

Why Single Sign-On Tokens

The single sign-on server provides authentication services to all class survey sites. Single sign-on and on-device credential management are crucial features to make this application usable. Imagine the hassle if the student has to manually enter a username and password for every class survey she uses. Another benefit of the single sign-on scheme is that it separates the user identity from the surveys she completes. The professor sees only anonymous survey results. That encourages students to tell the truth.

3.2.3   Real-World Deployment

iFeedBack is a prototype application that is designed to sell to universities rather than to individual students. The backend services are deployed into the university IT infrastructure: The single sign-on services should be linked with the existing electronic ID systems; the class surveys could be integrated with existing campus-wide course Web sites, such as the blackboard system. The two serverside components I provided with the sample application are for proof-of-concept demonstration only.

3.3   iFeedBack Usage Scenarios

Before we dive into the code, let's see how iFeedBack works from a user's perspective. To test run the application, we have to build and deploy it first.

3.3.1   Build and Deploy

The application download package has three subdirectories, each containing an application component. You can use the ANT build.xml script in each directory to build and deploy the component.

Directory surveyserver contains a sample survey server application. After running ANT, a file bin/iFeedBackSurvey.ear is generated. It can be deployed to any J2EE-compliant server (J2EE v1.3 RI is tested). If this is the first time you deploy it, you need to run the sql/Init.sql script against your default database.

Directory singlesignon contains an example single sign-on token service. Currently, all usernames and passwords are hardcoded into the source code for simplicity. Obviously, in real-world deployment, it must be hooked up with campus identity databases. File deployable.war is produced by the ANT script and can be deployed to the Java Web Services Developer Pack v1.0 engine.

Directory wireless contains the MIDP mobile client. Command ant builds the JAR file in the bin directory. Command ant run runs the client in the J2ME Wireless Toolkit device emulator. In the default setting, the MIDP client assumes that both the class survey server and single sign-on server reside on a computer at IP address localhost.

Note

> Once you build the JAR files for the J2ME and J2EE components, you can deploy them to any compatible emulators, devices and servers. For details on how to set up your device emulator and server environment, please refer to your product manual.

3.3.2 Try It Out!

Now, you can follow these steps to test and run the application. Figure 3.2 shows the screen shots.

1. Start up the MIDlet.

2. Choose Update Token and put in username/password pair test01/pass01. Then click UPDATE. The MIDlet will contact the single sign-on server and obtain a new authentication token for future use.

3. Choose Add Course. Add in a new class survey nickname and endpoint URL. You can just accept the suggested values.

4. Now you should see CS 301 available for selection under the Choose Course menu item. If you want to add more class surveys, you can repeat the last step.

5. Choose a course. iFeedBack will fetch the current question and display it for you.

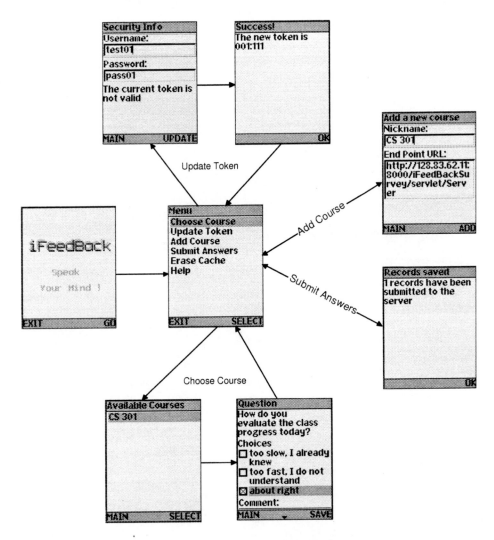

Figure 3.2. The iFeedBack application: The screen in the middle is the main menu. The surrounding screens show how different menu actions work. The application workflow is described in the text.

6. Choose the appropriate answer and put in any comments. Then click **SAVE** to save the time-stamped answer to the on-device persistent cache.

7. You can repeat the last two steps multiple times for different questions from different courses.

8. From the main menu, click Submit Answers to submit all cached answers to their corresponding endpoints. All successfully submitted answers will be deleted from the cache.

9. Now you can view the uploaded answers from the class survey server. Just point your HTML browser to the URL http://host:8080/iFeedBackSurvey/servlet/Server.

We have seen how iFeedBack works. It is now time to look under the hood!

3.4   Implementation Walk Through

In this section, we use sample code snippets to illustrate the overall structure of the implementation. We focus on the J2ME smart client.

3.4.1   The Call Model

The MIDP application contains multiple screens interconnected by menu selection and soft button actions. I decided to make each screen an independent functional unit with its own event handlers, transparent data models, and UI view generator. Each screen is represented by a class derived from abstract class MVCComponent (Listing 3.1). The relationship of classes in the UI model is illustrated in Figure 3.3.

Listing 3.1. The MVCComponent abstract class

```
public abstract class MVCComponent implements CommandListener {

  // Set from outside at beginning
  public static Display display;

  // Returns the screen object from the derived class
  public abstract Displayable getScreen();

  public Displayable prepareScreen () throws Exception {
    if ( getScreen() == null ) {
      initModel();
      createView();
    } else {
      updateView();
    }
    getScreen().setCommandListener ( (CommandListener) this );
```

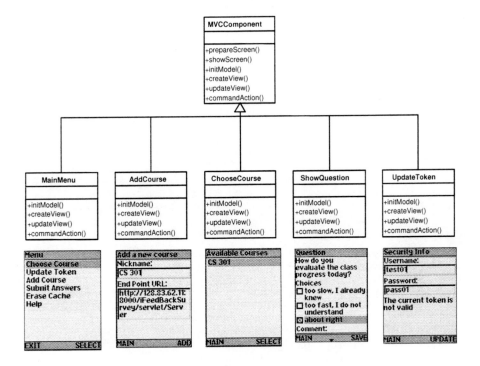

Figure 3.3. UML model for the UI component.

```
    return getScreen ();
}

public void showScreen() {
  try {
    display.setCurrent( prepareScreen() );
  } catch (Exception e) {
    e.printStackTrace();
    Alert a = new Alert("Error");
    a.setTimeout(Alert.FOREVER);
    display.setCurrent(a);
  }
}

// Initialize. If a data member is not backed by RMS,
// make sure it is null before you put in values.
protected abstract void initModel () throws Exception;

protected abstract void createView () throws Exception;
```

```
   protected abstract void updateView () throws Exception;

   public abstract void commandAction(Command c, Displayable s);
}
```

Using the UpdateToken object as an example, code Listing 3.2 illustrates how to make a new screen object from the MVCComponent class.

Listing 3.2. Example implementation of MVCComponent

```
public class UpdateToken extends MVCComponent {

   // MIDP UI components: Commands, TextFields etc.
   // ... ...
   // Model parameters
   private static String username;
   private static String password;
   private static String token;
   private static String endPointURL;

   // Bean-style methods to access data members

   // Event handler
   public void commandAction(Command c, Displayable s) {
     try {
       if (c == backCommand) {
         (new MainMenu()).showScreen();
       } else if (c == updateCommand) {
         username = usernameField.getString();
         password = passwordField.getString();
         UpdateTokenTask t =
           new UpdateTokenTask(endPointURL, display);
         t.go();
       }
     } catch (Exception e) {
       // Show some alerts
     }
   }

   public Displayable getScreen () {
     return screen;
   }
```

```
// In initModel(), first check whether the
// the data model is persistently saved.
//
// The use of persistent store is transparent
// to this class's users.
protected void initModel() throws Exception {
  try {
    securityInfoStore =
      RecordStore.openRecordStore("securityInfo", true);
    RecordEnumeration re =
      securityInfoStore.enumerateRecords(null, null, false);
    ByteArrayInputStream bais =
      new ByteArrayInputStream( re.nextRecord() );
    DataInputStream din = new DataInputStream(bais);
    username = din.readUTF();
    password = din.readUTF();
    token = din.readUTF();
    din.close();
    bais.close();
    securityInfoStore.closeRecordStore();
  } catch (Exception e) {
    username = Start.UsernameSugg;
    password = Start.PasswordSugg;
    token = "-1:-1";
  }
}


// createView() creates a view from the current
// model into the screen object
protected void createView() throws Exception {
  backCommand = new Command("MAIN", Command.SCREEN, 2);
  updateCommand = new Command("UPDATE", Command.SCREEN, 1);
  usernameField = new TextField("Username:",
                  username, 40, TextField.ANY);
  passwordField = new TextField("Password:",
                   password, 40, TextField.ANY);

  screen = new Form("Security Info");
  ((Form) screen).append( usernameField );
  ((Form) screen).append( passwordField );
  ((Form) screen).append( "Current Token is " + token );
  screen.addCommand( backCommand );
  screen.addCommand( updateCommand );
}
```

```
// updateView() updates the screen object when
// the model changes.
protected void updateView() throws Exception {
  // display updated username and password
  usernameField.setString( username );
  passwordField.setString( password );
  // Deletes the old token display
  ((Form) screen).delete(2);
  if ( "-1:-1".equals(token) ) {
    ((Form) screen).append("The current token is not valid");
  } else {
    ((Form) screen).append("Current Token is token");
  }
}
}
```

Using the UpdateToken screen is very simple. All you need to do is set up the model data and then call the showScreen() method.

3.4.2   The Threading Model

An important feature of iFeedBack is its use of worker threads during lengthy network operations to improve the perceived performance. The threading model of iFeedBack includes a worker thread, an animation thread, and a UI frontend thread (see Figure 3.4).

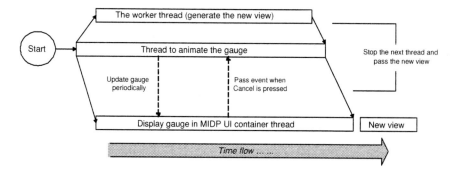

Figure 3.4. Execution flow: iFeedBack's worker threads.

All worker threads are derived from abstract class BackgroundTask (Listing 3.3; see Figure 3.5).

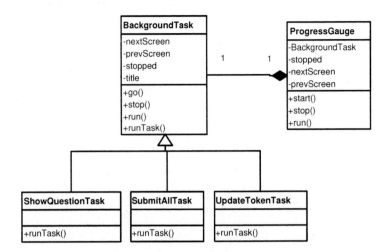

Figure 3.5. Classes in the iFeedBack thread model.

Listing 3.3. The BackgroundTask is the base for all thread tasks

---

```
public abstract class BackgroundTask extends TimerTask {
  private Thread th;
  private boolean stopped;

  // Could be set in derived class

  // If the task is successfully completed
  protected Displayable nextScreen;
  // If the task is aborted
  protected Displayable prevScreen;
  // Display to draw-on
  protected Display display;
  // The gauge screen title
  protected String title;

  // Do we need to display an alert before
  // moving to the nextScreen?
  protected boolean needAlert = false;
  protected Alert alertScreen;

  public BackgroundTask (Display d) {
    display = d;
```

```
    th = new Thread(this);
  }

  public void go () {
    stopped = false;
    th.start();
  }

  public void stop () {
    stopped = true;
    th.setPriority(Thread.MIN_PRIORITY);
  }

  public void run() {

    ProgressGauge pg = null;
    try {
      pg = new ProgressGauge(this, title, display, prevScreen);
      runTask ();
    } catch (Exception e) {
      // elaborate error handling using alerts
    } finally {
      // Since pg could callback and reset
      // "stopped" when its
      // Cancel key is pressed on Gauge.
      if (!stopped) {
        if ( needAlert ) {
          pg.setNextScreen(alertScreen, nextScreen);
        } else {
          pg.setNextScreen(nextScreen);
        }
        pg.stop();  // notify progress gauge to quit
      }
    }
  }

  // template method.
  public abstract void runTask () throws Exception;
}
```

The ProgressGauge object starts a foreground thread that displays an animated gauge. It features a Cancel button. If the Cancel button is pressed, the ProgressGauge displays the prevScreen screen, instructs the BackgroundTask not to update the display when finished, and stops. For more information, please refer to the ProgressGauge source code.

In your derived class for a specific task, you only need to implement the runTask(). Upon completion of the task, the runTask() updates the nextScreen variable. Listing 3.4 shows the runTask() method in the Update-TokenTask class.

Listing 3.4. The UpdateTokenTask implementation

```
public class UpdateTokenTask
       extends BackgroundTask {

  private String endPointURL;

  public UpdateTokenTask (String url, Display d) throws Exception {
    super (d);
    endPointURL = url;
    prevScreen =
      (new UpdateToken()).prepareScreen();
  }

  public void runTask () throws Exception {
    String username = UpdateToken.getUsername ();
    String password = UpdateToken.getPassword ();
    String token = getToken(username, password);

    if ( "-1:-1".equals(token) ) {
      needAlert = true;
      alertScreen = new Alert("Cannot update token");
      alertScreen.setString(
          "Authentication failed!");
      alertScreen.setTimeout(Alert.FOREVER);
      nextScreen = prevScreen;
    } else {
      UpdateToken.setAll( username, password, token );
      needAlert = true;
      alertScreen = new Alert("Success!");
      alertScreen.setString("The new token is token");
      alertScreen.setTimeout(Alert.FOREVER);
      nextScreen = (new MainMenu()).prepareScreen();
    }
  }
  // ... ...
}
```

To invoke the worker thread, you only need to call its **go()** method (Listing 3.2). The threading model presented here is rather simplistic. For more advanced threading control examples, please refer to the Smart Ticket example (Chapter 5).

3.4.3   Data Exchange

The MIDP client communicates with the class survey server via a pre-agreed binary format over the HTTP. In the wired world, generic binary data are passed through TCP/IP sockets. Higher-level protocols such as HTTP are used to transport application specific data, which require additional semantic structures (e.g., HTTP headers). However, in the J2ME world, access to raw TCP/IP sockets is not ubiquitous. In fact, HTTP is the only protocol mandated by the MIDP v1.0 specification. Therefore, J2ME developers often use HTTP to transport generic binary data.

Convenience I/O methods in the **DataInputStream** and **DataOutputStream** classes are extensively used to pack or unpack application data to or from the stream. For example,

1. The **writeUTF()** method writes a data string with leading bytes indicating the string length and encoding into the stream.

2. The **readUTF()** method at the other end of the stream reads the length and encoding bytes first, and then reads the specified number of bytes from the stream and reconstructs the correctly encoded string.

There is a pair of convenience read/write methods for every primitive Java data type. Those methods have greatly simplified our work. Listing 3.5 shows the relevant code segments from the **SubmitAllTask** class, which retrieves the cached answers from the RMS store and submits them to the remote HTTP server. As we can see, the I/O convenience methods are also extensively used to access unstructured RMS record data. Interested readers can refer to Chapter 12 for advanced tools and techniques that build structured and easy-to-manage storage structures on top of the RMS.

Listing 3.5. The binary I/O in the SubmitAllTask class

```
public class SubmitAllTask extends BackgroundTask {

  public SubmitAllTask (Display d) throws Exception {
    // Set up screens
  }
```

```
public void runTask () throws Exception {

  RecordStore answerStore =
      RecordStore.openRecordStore("answer", true);
  RecordEnumeration re =
      answerStore.enumerateRecords(null, null, false);
  int recordNum = 0;
  while ( re.hasNextElement() ) {
    recordNum++;
    int recordid = re.nextRecordId();
    ByteArrayInputStream bais =
      new ByteArrayInputStream( answerStore.getRecord(recordid) );
    DataInputStream din = new DataInputStream(bais);
    String url = din.readUTF();
    int qid = din.readInt();
    long timestamp = din.readLong();
    String answer = din.readUTF();
    String comment = din.readUTF();

    HttpConnection conn = null;
    DataInputStream hdin = null;
    DataOutputStream hdout = null;
    try {
      conn = (HttpConnection) Connector.open( url );
      conn.setRequestMethod(HttpConnection.POST);
      hdout = conn.openDataOutputStream();
      hdout.writeInt(1); // Submit opcode
      hdout.writeUTF( UpdateToken.getToken () );
      hdout.writeLong( timestamp );
      hdout.writeInt( qid );
      hdout.writeUTF( answer );
      hdout.writeUTF( comment );
      hdout.flush();

      hdin = conn.openDataInputStream();
      boolean authsucc = hdin.readBoolean();
      if (authsucc) {
        boolean updatesucc = hdin.readBoolean();
        if ( updatesucc ) {
          answerStore.deleteRecord( recordid );
        } else {
          // Server error. Show alert
        }
        nextScreen = prevScreen;
```

```
      } else {
        // Auth error. Show Auth token screen
      }
    } finally {
      // Close all connections
    }
  }
  re.destroy();
  answerStore.closeRecordStore();

  // Setup the next screen and show the number of
  // records submitted
 }

}
```

The binary data exchange formats are efficient, but they are proprietary and result in tightly coupled data producers and consumers. For services that require open interfaces, such as the authentication server, binary protocols are not sufficient. We implemented the iFeedBack authentication server using Sun's Java Web Service Developer Pack (v1.0). The server exposes its services through the SOAP (Simple Object Access Protocol) XML API and publishes the API specification in an open WSDL (Web Services Definition Language) document. On the mobile client side, we use the kSOAP library to assemble and parse the SOAP data. For more information on kSOAP and mobile Web Services, please refer to Part V of this book.

3.5   Summary

Using the iFeedBack application as an example, we demonstrated the capabilities and basic programming models of mobile smart clients. Programming topics covered in this section include the UI call model, the threading model, and the custom data exchange protocol. All those techniques serve a central purpose: to improve user experiences. Some topics in this chapter will be further elaborated on in Chapter 5 when we discuss patterns in the Sun Smart Ticket blueprint.

Resources

[1] *Wireless Java: Developing with J2ME, 2nd ed.* Jonathan Knudsen. Apress, 2003.

[2] *Core J2ME.* John Muchow. Sun Microsystems Press, 2002.

[3] *J2ME in a Nutshell.* Kim Topley. O'Reilly and Associates, 2002.

[4] The iFeedBack application download and documentations.
http://www.enterprisej2me.com/book/code/

[5] The J2EE Reference Implementation (v1.3 is used in the example).
http://java.sun.com/j2ee/download.html

[6] The Java Web Services Developer Pack (v1.0 is used in the example).
http://java.sun.com/webservices/webservicespack.html

[7] The J2ME Wireless Toolkit.
http://java.sun.com/products/j2mewtoolkit/

[8] The Motorola J2ME SDK.
http://www.motocoder.com/motorola/pcsHome.jsp

[9] The Nokia Developer's Suite for J2ME. http://www.forum.nokia.com/

[10] The kSOAP J2ME SOAP parser. http://www.ksoap.org/

Chapter 4

Managed Smart Clients

CHAPTER OVERVIEW

- Container-Managed Mobile Clients

- OSGi Containers

- OSGi Bundle Interactions

- IBM Service Management Framework

- A Simple Echo Service Example

- Smart Client with HTTP Front End

- The Pizza Order Example

- Mobile Gateways

In Chapter 3, we discussed the smart client paradigm. However, for complex mobile applications, monolithic clients with intertangled code segments are very hard to develop and maintain. We need a framework to develop modularized application and service components. In this chapter, we introduce the concept of managed smart clients—self-contained components inside software containers. The container provides common crosscutting services and a framework for components to communicate with each other. The industry standard for lightweight mobile containers is the OSGi (Open Services Gateway initiative) specification. Using several example OSGi applications running on IBM Service Management Framework, we explain how OSGi-managed smart clients work in real-world applications. In addition to supporting managed clients, OSGi applications can also deliver mobile gateway services. We will cover the gateway architecture near the end of this chapter.

4.1   Container-Managed Applications

In the field of software engineering, the term *container* refers to specialized software that runs other software. For example,

- The MIDP Application Management Software (AMS) is a container that installs, starts, pauses, stops, updates, and deletes MIDlet applications. In the CDC Personal Basis Profile, the Xlet programming model also features container-managed life-cycle methods.

- A Java servlet engine is a container that invokes servlets and provides access to the HTTP context.

- The Java Virtual Machine (JVM) itself is a container. It monitors Java applications for proper memory usage (garbage collector) and security.

In the next two sections, we will discuss the features and benefits of mobile containers.

4.1.1   Container Features

As mobile enterprise applications become mainstream, the complexity of smart clients grows. For example, fully commercial applications often require features such as user login, logging, transaction, and transparent data access. Without proper tools for code and service reuse, mobile developers have to duplicate those functionalities for every smart client. Wasting time reinventing the wheel is not only inefficient but also causes error-prone code.

Containers in J2EE

Containers are central to the serverside Java technologies (J2EE). For example, the core value proposition of the popular Enterprise JavaBean (EJB) technology lies in EJB containers that automatically take care of security, transaction, logging, synchronization, persistence, and many crosscutting application concerns. The EJB developers can focus on coding the value-added core business logic. The result is much better software and drastically improved developer productivity. Years of intensive research in J2EE have developed many advanced techniques to design and implement software containers.

Hence, it makes sense to make those common features available as services in software containers that run on mobile devices. An advanced container usually provides the following functionalities.

- *Self-contained applications*: Applications run inside the container are self-contained with portable code and necessary configuration files. The interdependence of applications and library components could be managed by the container. Examples are the WAR files for servlet containers and EAR files for EJB containers.

- *Life-cycle management*: By calling the life-cycle methods defined in the container framework and implemented by all applications, the container can install, start, stop, update, and delete any application programmatically or through an interactive console.

- *Application services*: The container provides services that are common to all applications. For example, an authentication module in the container could allow all applications to authenticate against a single password database.

- *Custom services:* The container should also allow its applications to offer services to each other. That encourages code reuse and prompts architectures for layered and modularized applications.

In this book, we use the term *container* rather loosely. Our containers do not impose arbitrary boundaries for API usages. Applications installed inside the container can transparently access any Java or native API available on the device. These containers are often known as *frameworks*. The container architecture on J2ME mobile devices is illustrated in Figure 4.1.

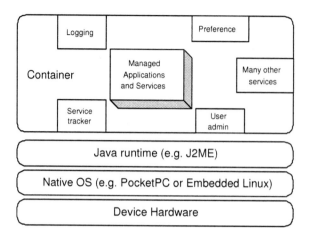

Figure 4.1. The container architecture for J2ME smart clients.

4.1.2 Benefits of Containers

The above container features translate to real benefits in mobile development projects:

- *Reduced code redundancy*: Since the common services are not repeatedly implemented, we can reduce overall footprint and potential number of errors while improving the developer productivity.

- *Managed update*: When we fix a bug or add a new feature in a service, all applications that use it automatically get the update. Some containers support service versioning for more refined controls.

- *Support for multitiered application models*: Services in a container offer natural separations between application tiers (e.g., the presentation and business layers).

- *Simplified application provisioning*: Self-contained applications can be easily deployed to any container. That enhances Java's value proposition of "write once, run anywhere."

Given these benefits, containers or frameworks are widely used in mobile Java application development. In the next section, we introduce a standard container specification for lightweight mobile devices: the OSGi specification.

Note

Every MIDP device comes with the AMS container for provisioning,
security, and life-cycle management. However, the MIDP platform
is too resource-constrained to run any more advanced containers.
As a result, the containers we discuss in this chapter require at least
J2ME/CDC or PersonalJava runtimes.

4.2 OSGi Containers

The OSGi Alliance is an industry consortium that creates open standard
specifications for network-delivered services. Founded in March 1999, OSGi
is a nonprofit organization with open membership. Its board of directors
includes Acunia, BMW, Deutsche Telekom, Echelon, Gatespace, IBM, Motorola, Oracle, Philips, ProSyst, Samsung, Sun and Telcordia. The OSGi
specification defines the mobile container framework and standard container
services as Java APIs that span from J2ME to J2SE to J2EE.

The OSGi Service Platform Release 2 specification was released in October 2001. It has been widely adopted by vendors and has many implementations. The OSGi Service Platform Release 3 specification was made
available in March 2003. The IBM Services Management Framework (SMF)
v3.5 is targeted to be OSGi R3 compatible. It is available for free evaluation
from the IBM Web site (see "Resources"). We discuss both Release 2 and 3
in this chapter. However, all examples are written for and tested on Release
2 containers.

Note

Despite the term *Gateway* in its name, the OSGi specification does
not define any particular kind of gateway servers. It defines a framework for service components delivery and execution. The OSGi container provides the runtime environment for those services. Gateway
server is only one of OSGi's application areas.

4.2.1 Bundles

OSGi applications are packaged as *bundles*, which are just standard JAR
files. The OSGi bundle is completely self-contained with all the necessary
metadata in its manifest file. The OSGi container completely manages the
bundle life cycle:

- Install, update, and uninstall the bundle.

- Start and stop the bundle.

- Register, unregister, and track services in the bundle.

The bundle management interfaces are defined in the org.osgi.framework package. Since the bundles can be deployed to the container dynamically without restarting the container, the OSGi platform is an ideal choice for mobile application provisioning clients. It allows applications to be managed, tracked, and updated throughout its lifetime.

4.2.2   Standard Services

The OSGi container provides common crosscutting services such as device drivers, user preferences, and logging to all its bundles. Table 4.1 lists the OSGi services defined in OSGi Service Platform Release 2 specification. The new OSGi Service Platform Release 3 specification defines more services, some of which are of great importance to mobile applications. Those new services are listed in Table 4.2.

4.2.3   Bundle Interaction and Custom Services

The OSGi framework provides powerful ways for bundles to interact with each other. This encourages code reuse and makes it easier to architect complex multilayer applications. For example, the OSGi container on a stock trader's PDA might be provisioned with services bundles from major exchanges. Each bundle knows how to run real-time queries and execute trades in a specific exchange market, and it makes those functionalities available to other bundles. The trader can then deploy the actual trading client bundle, which provides a user interface, supports custom trade logic, and executes the query/trade through the individual service bundles. The possible interactions among bundles are as follows.

- *Static sharing*: The OSGi container runs on a single JVM instance but has a different classloader for each bundle. That means bundle namespaces are separate. We cannot directly access objects or classes in another bundle by default. However, a bundle can explicitly export some of its Java packages through the Export-Package attribute in its manifest file. It can also import Java packages exported by others using the Import-Package manifest attribute. The export and import features allow direct sharing of Java packages.

Table 4.1.   OSGi Services in OSGi Service Platform Release 2 Specification (org.osgi.*)

Java package	Description
service.http	The HTTP service responds to HTTP requests. The service listens on ports specified in the container configuration. It dispatches each HTTP request to a handling servlet based on an URL-to-servlet mapping table registered by individual bundles. Finally, it returns the servlet's response to the HTTP requester. The service also handles HTML content without the help of a servlet.
service.device	The device service manages custom device adaptors. It allows bundle developers to plug in device drivers and develop algorithms to match devices to drivers. This service allows the OSGi bundles to respond to many different types of client devices.
service.prefs	The preference service manages a hierarchical collection of preference data resembling the JDK v1.4 preference API. It is much more advanced than simple Java property files.
service.useradmin	The user administration service provides role-based authorization service. It manages user credentials and user groups.
service.permissionadmin	The permission service allows operators to manage bundle permissions.
service.packageadmin	The package administration service manages Java packages exported by bundles (see Section 4.2.3 for exported packages).
service.metatype	The metatype service provides a mechanism for bundles to expose their configuration metadata.
service.cm	The configuration manager service administrates bundle configurations.
service.log	The logging service logs messages during the bundle execution. We can extend the basic logging service interface for custom logging needs.
util.tracker	The ServiceTracker class in this package provides easy ways to use and manage the container's service registry.

Table 4.2. New OSGi Services in OSGi Service Platform Release 3 Specification (org.osgi.*)

Java package	Description
service.startlevel	A policy service that allows the developer to specify the startup and shutdown sequence of bundles.
service.url	This service allows bundles to register URL schemes with content types and provide content handlers for the registered types.
util.xml	This is a utility service that allows bundles to use JAXP, SAX, and DOM XML parsers. Each parser interface can have multiple implementations.
service.wireadmin	It supports a convenient way to connect data producers and consumers. Two utility classes are commonly used with the wireadmin service to handle measurement-related (e.g., error calculation and unit conversion) and position-related (location, speed, orientation) data.
service.io	This service allows bundles to handle arbitrary network protocols using the J2ME Generic Connection Framework (GCF). Since the GCF is a layered and abstract framework, bundles only need to extend the abstract connection factory to return the correct connection class based on the URL string format.
service.upnp	This service makes OSGi bundles transparently available to universal plug-and-play networks.
service.jini	This service allows OSGi bundles to interact with Jini network services.

- *Dynamic services*: In addition to standard services provided by the container, any bundle can consume and provide services from/to other bundles at the same time:

  1. A bundle can dynamically register (or unregister) services with the container. The bundle needs to register the service interface with a concrete implementation class. Any change to the service (register, modify, unregister) will result in framework events that could be captured and processed.

2. Another bundle finds the service reference through a lookup API in the framework. It calls a framework method to obtain the service implementation object from the service provider bundle. The service object is now ready to use.

The interacting bundles allow us to deliver reusable services to any OSGi node, from the high function grid to pervasive devices.

4.2.4 OSGi Runtime Requirements

Currently, different OSGi vendors have different requirements for their products. The required execution environments range from PersonalJava v1.1 to J2SE. This has created considerable confusion in the developer community. In an effort to standardize the runtime requirements, the OSGi Service Platform Release 3 specification formally defines the following runtime environments:

- *The Java 2 Micro Edition*: All OSGi implementations should run under the CDC v1.0 plus Foundation Profile v1.0 runtime environment.

- *The OSGi minimum execution environment*: The specification also defines a subset of CDC/FP APIs, which allows devices not powerful enough for the CDC/FP (e.g., Palm PDAs) to run the OSGi framework. The OSGi minimum execution environment is defined to be a proper subset of CDC/FP and J2SE.

The standard execution environments make it easier for developers, especially resource-conscious mobile developers, to choose the right OSGi product.

4.3   A Simple Echo Service Example

In this section, we first introduce a J2ME-compatible OSGi implementation from IBM. Using a simple echo example, we demonstrate how to implement bundles and share services among them.

4.3.1   The IBM Service Management Framework

The IBM SMF is a readily available OSGi implementation. It has a memory footprint of 3 MB and runs on both execution environments defined in the OSGi Service Platform Release 3 specification. IBM supports the J2ME environments through WME (WebSphere Micro Environment JVM) and the minimum execution environment through WCE (WebSphere Custom Environment JVM) products. It can be tightly integrated into IBM's WebSphere Studio Device Developer IDE. The SMF product versions we cover in this book are v3.1 for OSGi R2 and v3.5 for OSGi R3.

The SMF installation process varies among devices. It generally involves the following steps.

1. Download and unpack the SMF toolkit from IBM.

2. Copy the following directories and files to the target device (or to a local execution directory, if you want to run SMF on a desktop computer). For my PocketPC device, I put all four items under the device root directory.

    - The jarbundles directory contains installed bundles.
    - The smf.jar file provides implementation classes for the OSGi specification.
    - The smfconsole.jar file provides a command-line management console for the container.
    - The smf.properties file specifies the runtime configuration.

3. Make sure that the com.ibm.osg.smf.bundledir property in the smf.properties file points to the correct bundle directory. For example,

```
com.ibm.osg.smf.bundledir=jarbundles
```

4. Now we can start the SMF console using the following command (in one line) or its equivalent on the device platform.

```
java -classpath "smf.jar:smfconsole.jar"
com.ibm.osg.smf.SMFLauncher -console "launch"
```

For my PocketPC device with IBM WebSphere Micro Environment preinstalled, I use the following command (in one line). Please refer to the Appendix B for the steps to install the IBM J2ME runtimes on PDA devices.

```
"\WSDD\j9.exe" -jcl:foun
"-Xbootclasspath:\WSDD\lib\jclFoundation\classes.zip;
\smf.jar;\smfconsole.jar" "com.ibm.osg.smf.SMFLauncher"
-console "Launch"
```

After the SMF console is started, it loads all currently installed bundles into the container and presents the user a command-line interface for management tasks. For a complete list of management commands, please refer to the SMF manual. Figure 4.2 shows the command-line console on desktop and PocketPC devices. Table 4.3 lists some of the most frequently used commands.

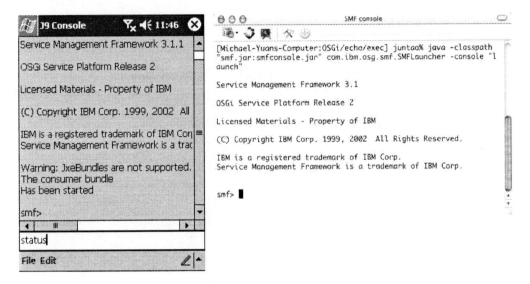

Figure 4.2. The SMF console on desktop and PocketPC devices.

In the next two sections, we describe how to create and deploy two OSGi bundles: The EchoService bundle exposes an echo service; the EchoUIConsumer bundle presents a simple GUI client and uses the EchoService in the container to echo user input. Figures 4.3 and 4.4 show the two bundles in action in J2SE and J2ME OSGi containers. Figure 4.5 shows user interactive OSGi bundles.

4.3.2   The EchoService Bundle

The EchoService bundle demonstrates how to implement and register a service in an OSGi bundle. The service itself is extremely simple: It only defines one method that does nothing more than echo a string input. The steps to create the bundle are as follows.

1. Define the service interface as a Java interface (Interface EchoService, Listing 4.1).

Command	Description
	Table 4.3. Common Commands Available in the SMF Console
Command	Description
install url	Installs a bundle from a URL and returns a bundle ID. The URL could point to files on the local file system, such as file:/path/bundle.jar.
update id	Updates the package from the same URL as specified by the install command.
uninstall id	Uninstalls the bundle.
start id	Starts the bundle.
stop id	Stops the bundle.
bundle id	Displays information about an installed bundle.
status	Displays all installed bundles and registered services.
packages	Displays the imported and exported packages for each bundle.
close	Shuts down the container and exits the console.

2. Create an implementation class for the interface (Class EchoserviceImpl, Listing 4.2).

3. Create a BundleActivator class that implements the required OSGi life-cycle methods and registers the service with the container upon startup (Class EchoActivator, Listing 4.3).

4. Create a manifest file that specifies the BundleActivator class for this bundle and exports the service interface package (Listing 4.4). The OSGi container uses the manifest to find the entry point of the bundle and collect necessary configuration data.

5. Package the compiled classes and manifest file into a standard Jar file.

Listing 4.1. The EchoService interface

```
package com.enterprisej2me.osgi.echoservice;

public interface EchoService {
  public String echo (String s);
}
```

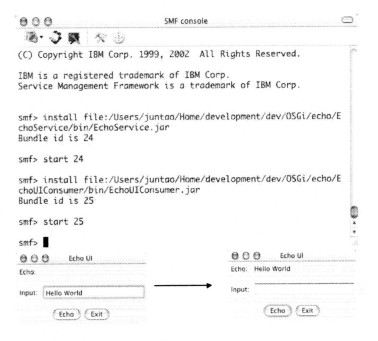

Figure 4.3. The echo bundles in action in J2SE.

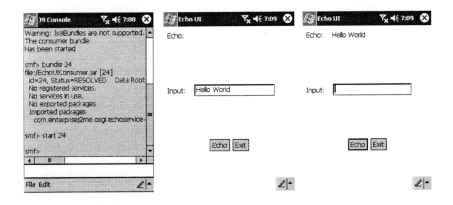

Figure 4.4. The echo bundles in action in J2ME.

Listing 4.2. The EchoServiceImpl class

```
package com.enterprisej2me.osgi.echoserviceimpl;
```

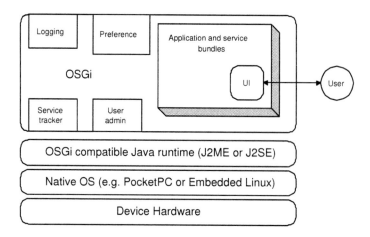

Figure 4.5. OSGi bundles with UIs.

```
import com.enterprisej2me.osgi.echoservice.*;

public class EchoServiceImpl implements EchoService {

  EchoServiceImpl () { }

  public String echo (String s) {
    return s;
  }

}
```

Listing 4.3. The EchoActivator class

```
package com.enterprisej2me.osgi.echoserviceimpl;

import org.osgi.framework.*;
import com.enterprisej2me.osgi.echoservice.*;


public class EchoActivator implements BundleActivator {

  private ServiceRegistration reg;

  public EchoActivator () { }
```

```
public void start (BundleContext context) throws Exception {
  EchoServiceImpl impl = new EchoServiceImpl ();
  reg = context.registerService (
      EchoService.class.getName(), impl, null);
}

public void stop (BundleContext context) throws Exception {
  reg.unregister ();
}
}
```

Listing 4.4. The JAR manifest for the echo service bundle

```
Manifest-Version: 1.0
Bundle-Name: Echo service
Bundle-Description: Echo the input
Bundle-Activator: com.enterprisej2me.osgi.echoserviceimpl.EchoActivator
Import-Package: org.osgi.framework; specification-version=1.1
Export-Package: com.enterprisej2me.osgi.echoservice
Export-Service: com.enterprisej2me.osgi.echoservice.EchoSerivce
```

Now, we can install and start the package in our SMF console.

4.3.3   The EchoUIConsumer Bundle

The EchoUIConsumer bundle is created to demonstrate how to use the echo service through the framework:

1. Create a BundleActivator implementation as the entry point to the bundle (Class EchoUIConsumer, Listing 4.5).

2. In the EchoUIConsumer.start() method, create and open a ServiceTracker object to track the echo service we started.

3. Create the UI frame class EchoFrame (Listing 4.6) and pass the ServiceTracker object and the current bundle (i.e., the echo consumer bundle) to EchoFrame.

4. The EchoFrame object obtains the EchoService object from the ServiceTracker and uses the EchoService to echo any user input. When we hit the Exit button in the UI frame, the AWT event handler calls

the bundle's stop() method and triggers the container to invoke the EchoUIConsumer.stop() method. For more details, refer to method actionPerformed() in Listing 4.6.

5. In the EchoUIConsumer.stop() method, dispose the UI frame and close the ServiceTracker (Listing 4.5).

6. Create the manifest file (Listing 4.7). We import the package containing the EchoService interface here.

7. Package and deploy the JAR bundle.

Tracking the Services

In the service consumer bundles, we could manually look up the service objects from the framework. Then, we would have to register event listener and callback methods to handle situations when other bundles or the container itself changes those services (e.g., removes the service). This could be a tedious task. Instead, we take a shortcut and use a pair of ServiceTracker objects to automatically track those services.

The ServiceTracker object tracks a list of services meeting certain criteria passed to it in the constructor. It provides default event handlers for the services it tracks.

The ServiceTracker object can be instantiated with a ServiceTrackerCustomizer object. When a service in the tracker is added, modified, or deleted, the appropriate method in its associated ServiceTrackerCustomizer is called. For more usage examples of the ServiceTracker class, please refer to Section 4.4.

Listing 4.5. The EchoUIConsumer class

```
package com.enterprisej2me.osgi.echouiconsumer;

import org.osgi.framework.*;
import org.osgi.util.tracker.*;
import com.enterprisej2me.osgi.echoservice.*;

public class EchoUIConsumer implements BundleActivator {

  ServiceTracker echoTracker;
  EchoFrame frame;

  public EchoUIConsumer () { }
```

```
public void start (BundleContext context) {
  echoTracker = new ServiceTracker (context,
              EchoService.class.getName(), null );
  echoTracker.open ();
  frame = new EchoFrame(250, 250, echoTracker, context.getBundle());
}

public void stop (BundleContext context) {
  frame.dispose ();
  echoTracker.close();
}
}
```

Listing 4.6. The EchoFrame class

```
package com.enterprisej2me.osgi.echouiconsumer;

import java.awt.*;
import java.awt.event.*;
import org.osgi.framework.*;
import org.osgi.util.tracker.*;
import com.enterprisej2me.osgi.echoservice.*;

public class EchoFrame extends Frame
    implements WindowListener, ActionListener {

  private TextField entryText;
  private Label echoedText;
  private Button submit;
  private Button exit;
  private Panel content, top, bottom, middle;
  private ServiceTracker echoTracker;
  private Bundle echoUIConsumerBundle;

  public EchoFrame (int width, int height,
                  ServiceTracker t, Bundle b) {
    super ("Echo UI");
    setBounds(0, 0, width, height);
    echoTracker = t;
    echoUIConsumerBundle = b;

    entryText = new TextField (20);
```

```
    echoedText = new Label ("  ");
    submit = new Button ("Echo");
    exit = new Button ("Exit");
    submit.addActionListener (this);
    exit.addActionListener (this);

    top = new Panel ();
    middle = new Panel ();
    bottom = new Panel ();
    top.setLayout(new FlowLayout(FlowLayout.LEFT));
    top.add(new Label("Echo: "));
    top.add(echoedText);
    middle.setLayout(new FlowLayout(FlowLayout.LEFT));
    middle.add(new Label("Input: "));
    middle.add(entryText);
    bottom.setLayout(new FlowLayout(FlowLayout.CENTER));
    bottom.add(submit);
    bottom.add(exit);

    content = new Panel ();
    content.setLayout(new GridLayout(3, 1));
    content.add(top);
    content.add(middle);
    content.add(bottom);

    add (content);
    addWindowListener(this);
    pack ();
    setVisible (true);
  }

public void actionPerformed (ActionEvent e) {
    if ( e.getSource() == submit ) {
      top.remove (echoedText);

      // Obtain the echo service object
      EchoService echoObj = (EchoService) echoTracker.getService();
      // Use the echo service to echo a string
      echoedText = new Label ( echoObj.echo(entryText.getText()) );

      top.add (echoedText);
      entryText.setText("");
      setVisible (true);
    } else if ( e.getSource() == exit ) {
      // see note
```

```
    // echoUIConsumerBundle.stop();
    dispose ();
  }
}

public void windowClosing(WindowEvent e) {}
public void windowOpened(WindowEvent e) {}
public void windowClosed(WindowEvent e) {}
public void windowIconified(WindowEvent e) {}
public void windowDeiconified(WindowEvent e) {}
public void windowActivated(WindowEvent e) {}
public void windowDeactivated(WindowEvent e) {}


}
```

Listing 4.7. The manifest file for the echo consumer bundle

```
Manifest-Version: 1.0
Bundle-Name: Echo UI consumer
Bundle-Description: Consume the echo service
Bundle-Activator: com.enterprisej2me.osgi.echouiconsumer.EchoUIConsumer
Import-Package: com.enterprisej2me.osgi.echoservice,
 org.osgi.framework; specification-version=1.1,
 org.osgi.util.tracker; specification-version=1.1
Import-Service: com.enterprisej2me.osgi.echoservice.EchoSerivce
```

Limitations of the Bundle State-Change APIs
Note that when we exit the EchoFrame UI, it merely disposes the UI window but does not stop the underlying bundle. That is because the synchronous state-change APIs in the current OSGi specification do not allow a bundle to change its own state safely. This limitation is being addressed by the OSGi expert group. When it is resolved in a future OSGi edition, the EchoFrame exit event handler can simply call the echoUIConsumerBundle.stop() method to dispose the window and stop the bundle.

The Espial DeviceTop

The Espial DeviceTop is an OSGi implementation running on PersonalJava platforms. In addition to standard OSGi services, it provides an *application* service that supports bundles with GUIs. The bundle's BundleActivator class can extend the espial.devicetop.refui.Application class, which automatically takes care of the interactions between the UI frame and the bundle itself. With Espial's proprietary Espresso UI library, we can create sophisticated mobile UI applications on the DeviceTop framework.

4.4   Smart Client with HTTP Front End

The managed GUI bundle uses only a fraction of the power provided by the OSGi container. Through its services, the OSGi container supports external applications and devices over the network. To use a separate program to render the UI, we can more effectively separate the business and presentation layers.

The "pizza order" example application distributed with the SMF illustrates the use of HTTP services in the OSGi framework. After starting the bundle from the SMF console, we can launch the device's built-in HTML browser (Internet Explorer for PocketPC or the Opera browser for Embedded Linux) and point the URL to http://localhost/pizza. An HTML page of a dummy pizza store appears. We can fill out the pizza order form, submit the form, and get response from a servlet running inside the bundle. The screen flow is shown in Figure 4.6.

This design allows us to build a simple UI very quickly, using HTML without messaging with complex event handlers in AWT code. It also allows the vast majority of serverside Java developers to transfer their skills and make use of their familiar patterns, such as the Model-Viewer-Controller pattern. The overall architecture of the smart client with HTTP front end is illustrated in Figure 4.7.

4.4.1   The Pizza Order Bundle

The PizzaBundle class (Listing 4.8) implements the BundleActivator interface. This bundle does not register or provide any new services. It customizes the container HTTP service to serve pizza order HTML content at a specified URL. It also uses the container logging services to record activities inside the bundle. If no logging service has been registered for this bundle, it logs to the standard output.

Start the Pizza
HTTP service

Access the service from
Pocket IE

Figure 4.6. The pizza order application in action.

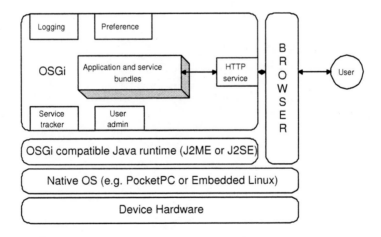

Figure 4.7. The smart client with HTTP front end.

1. The bundle **start()** method instantiates trackers for **LogService** and **HttpService**. The bundle then invokes their **open()** methods.

2. When the **ServiceTracker** for the **HttpService** is opened, it obtains all registered **HttpService** references from the container, adds them into the tracker, and invokes the corresponding **ServiceTrackerCustomizer**'s **addingService()** method for each added reference.

3. The addingService() method obtains the HTTP service object from
   the container and customizes it with the pizza order servlet and other
   resources.

4. When the bundle stops, its stop() method calls the close() methods
   of the two ServiceTrackers. The HttpService tracker in turn calls the
   removedService() method, which unplugs the servlet from the HTTP
   service.

Listing 4.8. The PizzaBundle class

```
public class PizzaBundle implements
  BundleActivator, ServiceTrackerCustomizer {

  /** BundleContext for this bundle */
  protected BundleContext context;

  /** Log Service wrapper object */
  protected LogTracker log;

  /** Http Service tracker object */
  protected ServiceTracker tracker;

  /** HttpContext for HTTP registrations */
  protected HttpContext httpContext;

  // ... ...

  public PizzaBundle() { }

  // Methods in BundleActivator
  public void start(BundleContext context) throws Exception {
    this.context = context;
    httpContext = new HttpContext() { ... ... };
    log = new LogTracker(context, System.err);
    tracker = new ServiceTracker(context,
        HttpService.class.getName(), this);
    tracker.open();
  }

  public void stop(BundleContext context) throws Exception {
    tracker.close();
    log.close();
```

```
}

// Methods for ServiceTrackerCustomizer
public Object addingService(ServiceReference reference) {
  HttpService http = (HttpService)context.getService(reference);
  if (http != null) {
    try {
      http.registerServlet(servletURI,
          new Pizza(), null, httpContext);
      http.registerResources(servletURI+imagesURI,
                      imagesURI, httpContext);
      log.log(log.LOG_INFO, "Pizza Servlet registered");
    } catch (Exception e) {
    // handle the exception
    }
  }
  return http;
}

public void modifiedService(ServiceReference
              reference, Object service) {
}

public void removedService(ServiceReference
              reference, Object service) {
  HttpService http = (HttpService) service;

  http.unregister(servletURI);
  http.unregister(servletURI+imagesURI);

  context.ungetService(reference);
  log.log(log.LOG_INFO, "Pizza Servlet unregistered");
}
}
```

4.4.2   The Pizza Order Servlet

In the addingService() method, we use a servlet Pizza (Listing 4.9) to provide
the custom HTTP service (the application logic). This is just a standard Java
servlet that reads from HttpRequest and writes HTML data to HttpResponse
objects. Those HTTP context objects are provided by the container.

Listing 4.9. The Pizza servlet

```java
import javax.servlet.*;
import javax.servlet.http.*;
import java.io.*;
import java.util.*;

public class Pizza extends HttpServlet {
  protected void doGet(HttpServletRequest req,
                       HttpServletResponse res)
          throws ServletException, IOException {
    // Generate some output
    res.setContentType("text/html;" + "charset=iso-8859-1");
    PrintWriter out = res.getWriter();
    out.print(" ... ... ");

    // Get query parameters
    String queryString = req.getQueryString();

    // any pizza order logic
    // ... ...

    out.println("</body></html>");
  }
}
```

4.4.3   The Logging Service

A container can have multiple logging services. For example, one service implementation could log messages to a disk file while another could send the critical message as Instant Message alerts to administrators. The OSGi framework provides a common LogService interface for all logging services. Implementations of the LogService interface are provided and shared by individual bundles. In our pizza example, the LogTracker (Listing 4.10) object is a ServiceTracker object that tracks all available logging services from the container registry and makes sure each message is logged by all services.

1. The LogTracker.open() method is invoked in the bundle start() method to initiate the tracker.

2. LogTracker.open() calls its base class's open() method, which obtains all LogService references in the container.

3. When the bundle needs to log a message, it calls the LogTracker.log() method, which iterates through the current list of tracked LogService references. It obtains the service object for each reference and pushes the message to all available logging services.

4. If the container does not have any registered logging service (the reference list size is zero), the LogTracker object will call its noLogService() method to log to the standard output.

Note

The LogTracker class does not register any new LogService to the container.

Listing 4.10. The LogTracker class

```
public class LogTracker
      extends ServiceTracker implements LogService {

  protected final static String clazz =
        "org.osgi.service.log.LogService";
  protected PrintStream out;

  public LogTracker(BundleContext context, PrintStream out) {
    super(context, clazz, null);
    this.out = out;

    open();
  }

  // Implements various log() messages with
  // different signatures.
  // ... ...

  public synchronized void log(ServiceReference reference,
        int level, String message, Throwable exception) {
    ServiceReference[] references = getServiceReferences();

    if (references != null) {
      int size = references.length;
      for (int i = 0; i < size; i++) {
        LogService service = (LogService) getService(references[i]);
        if (service != null) {
```

```
          try {
            service.log(reference, level, message, exception);
          } catch (Exception e) { }
        }
      }
    return;
  }
  noLogService(level, message, exception, reference);
}

protected void noLogService(int level, String message,
    Throwable throwable, ServiceReference reference) {
  if (out != null) {
    synchronized (out) {
      switch (level) {
        case LOG_DEBUG: {
          out.print("Debug: ");
          break;
        }
        case LOG_INFO: {
          out.print("Info: ");
          break;
        }
        case LOG_WARNING: {
          out.print("Warning: ");
          break;
        }
        case LOG_ERROR: {
          out.print("Error: ");
          break;
        }
        default: {
          out.print("Unknown Log level[");
          out.print(level);
          out.print("]: ");
          break;
        }
      }
      out.println(message);
      if (reference != null) {
        out.println(reference);
      }
      if (throwable != null) {
        throwable.printStackTrace(out);
      }
```

```
      }
    }
  }
}
```

4.4.4 Rich UI Clients for the HTTP Service

Although the pizza order example supports clearly separated application layers, the drawback is that it does not really take advantage of the rich UI capability of smart clients. There are several ways to create rich UI clients for the HTTP service.

- *Rich browsers*: Instead of plain HTML content, the servlet can provide rich content such as Java Applet and Flash for capable browsers.

- *Standalone GUI*: We can also replace the browser completely with a standalone GUI application. The OSGi HTTP service can serve binary or XUL (XML User Interface) content and allow the standalone GUI front end to decide how to render it.

4.5 Mobile Gateways

In the previous sections, we discussed service and application bundles in clientside OSGi containers. Besides clientside containers, another major application area of the OSGi framework is to deploy and execute services on mobile gateway devices that do not have UI front ends. Small, pervasive devices delegate computationally expensive tasks to the more powerful gateway. In the gateway configuration, the OSGi powered hub provides services to a variety of devices:

- The Jini service (service.jini) allows us to incorporate an OSGi-based gateway into a Jini network. For example, the gateway can drive a Jini printer over the local WiFi network to print out a pizza order receipt.

- The UPnP service (service.upnp) allows an OSGi-based gateway to interact with UPnP network devices.

- The HTTP service (service.http) we discussed earlier is available to any HTTP-compatible devices. For example, MIDP-based or browser-based devices on the local WiFi network can order pizza through the OSGi HTTP service on the gateway device.

- The OSGi container also provides a generic device access service (service.device) that allows developers to plug in device drivers for arbitrary devices and network protocols.

The architecture is illustrated in Figure 4.8. But still, why do we need to run gateways in OSGi containers? Wouldn't a full-blown J2EE portal server be a much more powerful option? There are two important reasons.

- Since OSGi containers run on J2ME, we can place the OSGi-based gateway in the same mobile network as the pervasive devices it serves. For example, in an in-hand network, the PDA can be the gateway; in an in-home network, the TV-set top box is the gateway; in an in-car network, the entertainment console could be the gateway. Since the local wireless network is much faster, cheaper, and easier to maintain compared with national cellular networks, the local gateways are crucial to enable high-availability mobile applications.

- The OSGi specification supports dynamic service provisioning and deployment through bundles. This is a very important feature when you have thousands of mobile gateways around in your company.

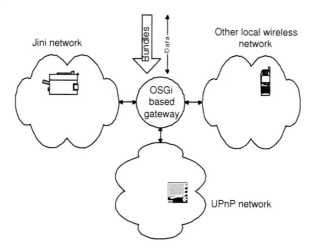

Figure 4.8. The OSGi-based local gateway architecture.

4.6 Summary

In this chapter, we discussed the benefits and architecture of managed smart clients. We introduced the OSGi specification and IBM's implementation: the SMF. Through a simple echo example, we demonstrated how to build the bundles, implement required life-cycle methods, import and export packages, expose and consume bundle services, and add UIs to a bundle application. The pizza order example shows how to reduce UI complexity and separate application layers using the available HTTP service. The pizza order application also demonstrates complex application service use and service tracking. In the last section, we briefly introduced the architectures and benefits of mobile gateways implemented over the OSGi platform.

Resources

[1] The Open Services Gateway initiative (OSGi). http://www.osgi.org/

[2] IBM WebSphere Studio Device Developer IDE (free evaluation). The page also contains a link to download the latest IBM Service Management Framework (SMF) software for free evaluation. http://www.ibm.com/embedded/

[3] The Espial DeviceTop is a clientside OSGi container with GUI support. http://www.espial.com/index.php?page=sol_devices_suite_over

Chapter 5

Mobile Design Patterns: The Smart Ticket Blueprint

CHAPTER OVERVIEW

- Java Technology Blueprints

- Smart Ticket in Action

- Patterns and Techniques

- The Model-View-Controller Pattern

- The Remote Facade Pattern

- Chained Data Handlers

- Binary Remote Procedure Call Over HTTP

- Advanced Threading Model

Sun's Java Blueprints is a program to promote good design practices among Java developers. The blueprints cover a wide range of Java technology application areas, including J2EE, Web Services, security, and mobility. The Wireless Blueprints contain a sample application and a design guidelines white paper for end-to-end mobile commerce solutions. The wireless blueprints' Java Smart Ticket sample application is a mobile movie ticket-ordering system with a J2ME/MIDP wireless front end and a J2EE application server back end. It showcases a number of important design patterns and best practices for end-to-end mobile applications. Using the Smart Ticket sample, we study the mobile design patterns in this chapter.

We start with a quickstart guide on how to install and run the sample application. Then, using the source code, we analyze the key architectural patterns and their benefits. In the last section of this chapter, we review important behavioral patterns and coding techniques used in the implementation.

5.1 Getting Started

The Smart Ticket application is available from Sun Microsystems' blueprints Web site (see "Resources"). The zip package contains source code; ANT build scripts; and prebuilt, deployable application binaries.

A Brief History of the Smart Ticket Blueprint

The Smart Ticket blueprint v1.0 was officially released in early 2002. It featured simple and straightforward designs that did the job but had limited educational value. The first mature implementation is v1.1.1, which was released in both English and Japanese languages.

Smart Ticket v1.2, released in March 2003, features a major architectural revision, which provides excellent examples of several important end-to-end design patterns. The code version covered in this chapter is v2.0 Early Access (EA), which was released on April 15, 2003. The v2.0 EA has the same architecture as the v1.2. The only change is that the v2.0 EA has an enhanced implementation of the presentation layer, which takes advantage of the new MIDP v2.0 UI capabilities.

When you read this book, a newer version of the Smart Ticket application is likely to be out already. But you can still download the exact v1.2 final release and v2.0 EA code referenced in this chapter from this book's Web site.

The Smart Ticket sample contains a J2EE component for the enterprise back end and a J2ME component for the mobile front end. Running the application requires a J2EE application server and a MIDP v2.0-compatible device (or emulator) with Internet connectivity. For learning and testing purposes, we can run both the J2EE server and MIDP emulator on the same computer as follows.

1. Set up the following environment variables:

   - JAVA_HOME: The JDK installation directory (JDK v1.4.1 and above required)
   - J2EE_HOME: The J2EE reference implementation (RI) installation directory (J2EE v1.3.1 and above required)
   - J2MEWTK_HOME: The J2ME Wireless ToolKit installation directory (J2ME WTK v2.0 and above required)

2. Start the J2EE server using the following two commands:

```
J2EE_HOME\bin\cloudscape -start
J2EE_HOME\bin\j2ee -verbose
```

3. Deploy the J2EE application using the following script. The setup script in turn invokes the corresponding ANT task in setup.xml:

```
setup deploy
```

4. Point your browser to http://localhost:8000/smartticket and click on the *populate database* link to import the mock theater and movie data to the Smart Ticket database. This could be a very slow process on older computers, so be patient! The mock data set contains theater information in two zip code areas: 95054 and 95130.

5. Start the J2ME WTK v2.0 and run MIDlet smart_ticket-client.jad.

Now, you are ready to order some movie tickets from the phone emulator!

Note

If you want to run the MIDP client on an actual smart phone device, the J2EE server must run on an Internet-accessible computer and you must configure the MIDP client for the correct server IP address.

5.2   Smart Ticket in Action

The Smart Ticket client allows the user to manage user preferences, browse movie schedules, order tickets, rate watched movies, and pre-download the schedule. We discuss those features one by one in this section.

Note

> The Smart Ticket blueprint is designed for educational purposes. It demonstrates the use of design patterns. As developers, we should judicially use patterns learned from the Smart Ticket. The overuse of design patterns results in unnecessary abstraction layers and produces slow and large applications.

5.2.1   Manage User Preferences

When the user starts the MIDP client for the first time, she will be asked to create a profile. The profile includes two types of information:

- *Account credentials*: The username, password, and optional credit card numbers.

- *User preferences*: The theater search zip codes, favorite day of the week, and preferred seating. Figure 5.1 shows how to manage user preferences.

Figure 5.1. Manage user preferences.

After the user submits the profile, a corresponding user account is created on the J2EE server. The preference information is cached on the device. The user could configure the MIDP client to cache the account credentials so that she does not need to manually sign in every time she wants to purchase tickets or submit movie ratings. User preferences can be modified at any time through the MIDP UI.

Note

The Smart Ticket client does not encrypt the account and preference information stored on the device. That could create problems if the device is lost. To secure on-device data, please refer to discussions in Chapters 19 and 20.

5.2.2   Search and Purchase Tickets

Once logged in, the user can browse theaters, movies, and show times in her zip code areas. This process involves a series of real-time queries to the J2EE server. Once she selects a show, she will be asked to select currently available seats from an interactive seating map to make reservations. The reservation is persisted to the server database. Figure 5.2 illustrates the browsing and reserving process from the user's perspective.

Note

The interactive seating map allows the user to move a flashing cursor using the phone's navigation pad. The currently reserved and available seats are differentiated by colors. It demonstrates the rich UI capabilities of the MIDP.

5.2.3   Rate Movies

The user can rate movies she has seen (Figure 5.3). The ratings are not immediately submitted to the server. They are cached on device and can be synchronized to the server upon the user request. That allows the user to rate movies even when the phone is out of network range (for example, in a shielded cinema building!). The synchronization agent is smart: When the same user rates the same movie multiple times, it resolves the issue by keeping only the most recent rating in the backend database.

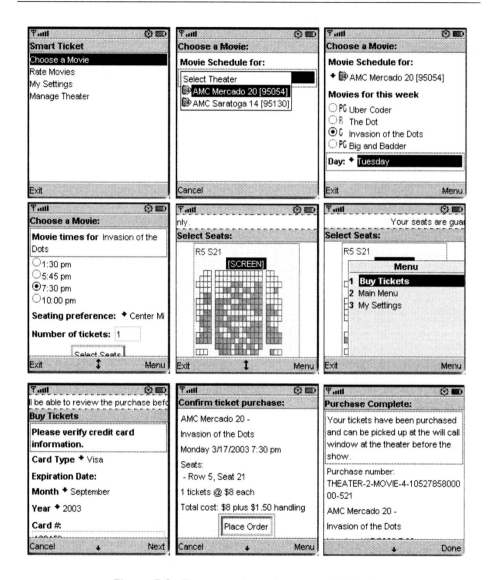

Figure 5.2. Browse and purchase movie tickets.

Note

The user can only rate movies for which she has purchased tickets via the Smart Ticket system. This is necessary to ensure the integrity of the rating system. It also simplifies the UI design.

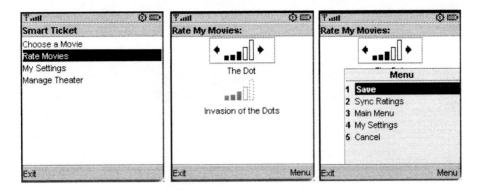

Figure 5.3. Rate watched movies.

5.2.4 Cache Theater Schedules

Smart Ticket allows the user to download a theater's schedule to the mobile client. The cached schedule enables offline browsing and improves the performance by reducing network round trips. The user can delete or re-download the schedule as needed (Figure 5.4).

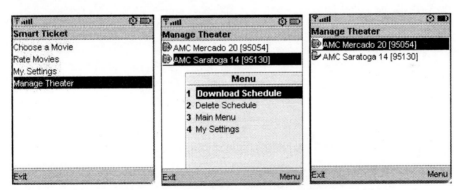

Notice the change of icon

Figure 5.4. Download movie schedules into the on-device cache.

Note

Notice that the theaters with cached schedules have a different icon. That helps the user to avoid downloading the same schedule multiple times. It also helps the user to make quick choices of theaters in the browsing mode (Figure 5.2).

Now, let's examine how those features are implemented in the Smart Ticket application.

5.3 Important Architectural Patterns

Smart Ticket utilizes several architectural design patterns, which are commonly used by enterprise architects. It is important for enterprise mobile developers to understand those patterns.

5.3.1 The Overall MVC Pattern

The overall architecture of the Smart Ticket application follows the Model-View-Controller pattern. According to Martin Fowler in his *Patterns of Enterprise Application Architecture*, the MVC pattern "splits user interface interaction into three distinct roles." In an MVC application, the view and controller components work together as the UI, which primarily concerns how to present the information to the user through a series of displays and interactions. The model component represents the domain model. The model's primary concern is business logic and machine-to-machine interactions (e.g., database access). The use of the MVC patterns brings some important benefits:

- Since the presentation and the underlying data model are separated, we can employ different experts to work on different parts of the code. For example, a UI expert can design the views while a database expert optimizes the database connections at the same time.

- MVC allows us to develop multiple views for the same model. For example, the Smart Ticket v2.0 EA and v1.2 applications have the exact same model layer. The MVC pattern allows Sun developers to rewrite the UI for MIDP v2.0 in a short period of time.

- Nonvisual objects in the model layer are easier to test using automatic tools than are the UI components.

In the Smart Ticket application, the MVC pattern is implemented as follows:

- *Model*: Classes in the model layer contain all the business logic. In fact, the entire J2EE server component, on-device caches, and communication classes all belong to the model layer. The most notable design pattern in the model layer is the facades, which we discuss in the next sections.

- *View*: Each interactive screen is represented by a view class. There are 17 view classes in the Smart Ticket v2.0 EA client. Once the user generates a UI event (e.g., by pressing a button or selecting an item from a list), the view class's event handler captures the event and passes it to the controller class. Listing 5.1 demonstrates the UI classes for the screen to confirm ticket purchase.

- *Controller*: The controller class knows all the possible interactions between the user and the program. In the Smart Ticket application, the controller is the **UIController** class (Listing 5.2). It has one method for each possible action (e.g., **purchaseRequested()**). The action method often starts two new threads: one to perform the action in the background and the other to display a progress bar for the user. The background action thread is represented by the **EventDispatcher** class. The **EventDispatcher**.run() method contains a long list of **switch** statements that invoke the corresponding methods in the model layer to perform the action. When the model method returns, the controller displays the next UI screen using the appropriate view class.

Listing 5.1. The ConfirmTicketUI class represents the screen for confirming the ticket purchase

---

```
package com.sun.j2me.blueprints.smartticket.client.midp.ui
public class ConfirmTicketUI extends Form
          implements CommandListener, ItemCommandListener {

    private UIController uiController;
    private Command cancelCommand;
    private Command confirmCommand;
    private StringItem theater, movie, showTimeStr, seatsStr;
    private StringItem cost, totalCost, placeOrderBtn;
```

```
public ConfirmTicketUI(UIController uiController) {
  super(uiController.getString(UIConstants.CONFIRM_TITLE));

  this.uiController = uiController;

  createItems();
  append(theater); append(movie); append(showTimeStr);
  append(seatsStr); append(cost); append(totalCost);
  append(placeOrderBtn);

  confirmCommand =
     new Command(uiController.getString(UIConstants.CONFIRM),
                 Command.OK, 5);
  cancelCommand =
      new Command(uiController.getString(UIConstants.CANCEL),
                 Command.EXIT, 5);
  addCommand(confirmCommand);
  addCommand(cancelCommand);
  setCommandListener(this);
  placeOrderBtn.setDefaultCommand(confirmCommand);
  placeOrderBtn.setItemCommandListener(this);
}

public void init(String theaterName, String movieName,
                           int[] showTime, Seat[] seats) {
  // Set the display strings to the correct values
}

// Command callback for UI events for text button "placeOrderBtn"
public void commandAction(Command command, Item item) {
  if (command == confirmCommand) {
    uiController.purchaseRequested();
  }
}

// Command callback for UI events on the command buttons
public void commandAction(Command command, Displayable displayable) {
  if (command == cancelCommand) {
     uiController.mainMenuRequested();
  } else if (command == confirmCommand) {
     uiController.purchaseRequested();
  }
}
}
```

Listing 5.2. Process the purchaseTickets action in the UIController class in the controller layer

---

```
package com.sun.j2me.blueprints.smartticket.client.midp.ui;
public class UIController {

  // references to all UI classes
  // ... ...

  public UIController(MIDlet midlet, ModelFacade model) {
    this.display = Display.getDisplay(midlet);
    this.model = model;
  }

  // ... ...

    public void purchaseRequested() {
    runWithProgress(
       new EventDispatcher(EventIds.EVENT_ID_PURCHASEREQUESTED,
                           mainMenuUI),
       getString(UIConstants.PROCESSING), false);
  }

  class EventDispatcher extends Thread {
    private int taskId;
    private Displayable fallbackUI;

    EventDispatcher(int taskId, Displayable fallbackUI) {
      this.taskId = taskId;
      this.fallbackUI = fallbackUI;
      return;
    }

    public void run() {
      try {
        switch (taskId) {

          // cases ... ...

          case EventIds.EVENT_ID_PURCHASEREQUESTED: {
            model.purchaseTickets(reservation);
            purchaseCompleteUI.init(reservation.getId(),
                               selectedTheater.getName(),
                               selectedMovie.getTitle(),
```

```
                              selectedShowTime);
        display.setCurrent(purchaseCompleteUI);

        break;
      }

      // Other cases ... ...

    }
  } catch (Exception exception) {
    // handle exceptions
  }
  } // end of run() method
} // end of the EventDispatcher class
}
```

The overall end-to-end architecture of the Smart Ticket application is illustrated in Figure 5.5). The model layer is by far the most sophisticated. Now, let's study how the model is assembled around a series of facades.

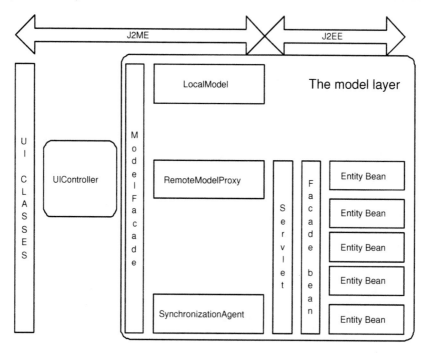

Figure 5.5. The overall architecture of the Smart Ticket application.

5.3.2   The Clientside Facade

The facade pattern is a structural pattern that provides a simple interface for complex subsystems. In the Smart Ticket application, the clientside subsystems in the model layer, such as the LocalModel, RemoteModelProxy, and SynchronizationAgent classes, are behind the facade class ModelFacade (Listing 5.3), which is the entry point from the controller to the model. The ModelFacade class contains one method for each action in the model layer. It delegates the actions to the subsystems as follows.

- The LocalModel class handles actions that access the local on-device storage. For example, the purchaseTickets() method adds the purchased movie to the on-device rating list. The addMovieRating() action method in the LocalModel class is called.

- The RemoteModelProxy class, which implements the RemoteModel interface, handles actions that require access to the remote J2EE server. For example, if the user decides to purchase tickets (reserveSeats() and purchaseTickets()), the transaction has to be done on the server side and be persisted to the database through the RemoteModelProxy. Action methods in the RemoteModelProxy class invoke remote procedure calls (RPC) to the remote facade on the server side. The details of the remote facade and the RPC format are discussed later in this chapter.

- The SynchronizationAgent class handles all synchronization actions from the local data storage to the remote server. In the case of the Smart Ticket application, it handles only the movie ratings synchronization. It has two action methods: The synchronizeMovieRatings() method synchronizes the ratings; the commitMovieRatings() method commits the resolved synchronization requests to the back end and updates the content of the local store.

The three interactions are illustrated in the following code snippet (Listing 5.3).

Listing 5.3. The ModelFacade class

```
package com.sun.j2me.blueprints.smartticket.client.midp.model;

public class ModelFacade {

  private SynchronizationAgent syncAgent;
```

```
private RemoteModelProxy remoteModel;
private LocalModel localModel;


// Action methods ... ...
public Reservation reserveSeats(String theaterKey,
     String movieKey, int[] showTime, Seat[] seats)
                    throws ApplicationException {
  try {
    return remoteModel.reserveSeats(theaterKey,
                    movieKey, showTime, seats);
  } catch (ModelException me) {
    // ... ...
  }
}


public void purchaseTickets(Reservation reservation)
                    throws ApplicationException {
  try {
    remoteModel.purchaseTickets(reservation.getId());

    // Purchased movies are eligible for rating.
    localModel.addMovieRating(
      new MovieRating(
        remoteModel.getMovie(reservation.getMovieId()),
              reservation.getShowTime()));
  } catch (ModelException me) {
    // ... ...
  }
  return;
}

public void synchronizeMovieRatings(
              int conflictResolutionStrategyId)
                    throws ApplicationException {
  try {
    syncAgent.synchronizeMovieRatings(conflictResolutionStrategyId);
    return;
  } catch (ModelException me) {
    // ... ...
  }
}
// ... ...
}
```

5.3.3   The Serverside Facade

One of the most important benefits of the facade pattern is that it reduces network round trips between remote systems. A properly designed facade allows us to use fine-grained objects in the subsystems yet still have a coarse-grained, simple network interface. It is especially important for mobile applications, since the wireless network is very slow.

When an RPC is made from the RemoteModelProxy to the server side, the HTTP servlet SmartTicketServlet (Listing 5.4) invokes the corresponding action method in Session EJB SmartTicketFacadeBean (Listing 5.6) through a business delegate object SmartTicketBD (Listing 5.5). Depending on the nature of the action, it is further delegated to either TicketingBean or SynchronizingBean, both of which are session EJBs too. The application data on the server side is persisted to the relational database through an array of Container Managed Persistence (CMP) v2.0 entity EJBs.

Listing 5.4. The gateway servlet SmartTicketServlet

```
package com.sun.j2me.blueprints.smartticket.server.web.midp;

public class SmartTicketServlet extends HttpServlet {

  public static final String SESSION_ATTRIBUTE_SMART_TICKET_BD =
   "com.sun.j2me.blueprints.smartticket.server.web.midp.SmartTicketBD";

  protected void doPost(HttpServletRequest request,
                        HttpServletResponse response)
                        throws ServletException, IOException {
    HttpSession session = request.getSession(true);
        SmartTicketBD smartTicketBD =
(SmartTicketBD) session.getAttribute(SESSION_ATTRIBUTE_SMART_TICKET_BD);

    // Calls handleCall() method and encode the URL for
    // session tracking
  }

  public int handleCall(SmartTicketBD smartTicketBD, InputStream in,
                        OutputStream out) throws IOException,
                        ApplicationException {
    // Identifies the requested action method

    // Execute the method through a list of switch -- case statements
    switch (method) {
```

```
    // ... ...

    case MessageConstants.OPERATION_GET_MOVIE:
        getMovie(smartTicketBD, call, successfulResult);
    break;

    // ... ...

    }
  }
}
```

Listing 5.5. The business delegate class SmartTicketBD

```
package com.sun.j2me.blueprints.smartticket.server.web.midp;

public class SmartTicketBD implements RemoteModel {
  public static final String EJB_REF_FACADE = "ejb/SmartTicketFacade";
  private SmartTicketFacadeLocal facade;
  private ServletContext servletContext = null;

  public SmartTicketBD(ServletContext servletContext)
        throws ApplicationException {
    this.servletContext = servletContext;

    try {
      Context context =
          (Context) new InitialContext().lookup("java:comp/env");
      facade =
 ((SmartTicketFacadeLocalHome)context.lookup(EJB_REF_FACADE)).create();

      return;
    } catch (Exception e) {
      throw new ApplicationException(e);
    }
  }

  public Movie getMovie(String movieKey)
          throws ModelException, ApplicationException {
    try {
      MovieLocal movieLocal = facade.getMovie(movieKey);
      Movie movie = new Movie(movieLocal.getId(),
```

```
                                        movieLocal.getTitle(),
                                        movieLocal.getSummary(),
                                        movieLocal.getRating());

      return movie;
    } catch (SmartTicketFacadeException stfe) {
      throw new ModelException(ModelException.CAUSE_MOVIE_NOT_FOUND);
    } catch (Exception e) {
      throw new ApplicationException(e);
    }
  }


  // Other action methods in RemoteModel interface


}
```

Listing 5.6. The facade session bean SmartTicketFacadeBean

```
package com.sun.j2me.blueprints.smartticket.server.ejb;

public class SmartTicketFacadeBean implements SessionBean {

  // ... ...

  public void ejbCreate() throws CreateException {
    // ... ...
    Context context =
        (Context) new InitialContext().lookup("java:comp/env");
    ticketingHome =
        (TicketingLocalHome) context.lookup(EJB_REF_TICKETING);
    synchronizingHome =
      (SynchronizingLocalHome) context.lookup(EJB_REF_SYNCHRONIZING);
    // ... ...
  }

  public MovieLocal getMovie(String movieId)
          throws SmartTicketFacadeException {
    try {
      return movieHome.findByPrimaryKey(movieId);
    } catch (FinderException fe) {
      throw new SmartTicketFacadeException("No matching movie.");
    }
  }
}
```

```
public void purchaseTickets(String reservationId)
        throws SmartTicketFacadeException {
  if (ticketing != null) {
    ticketing.purchaseTickets(reservationId);
    return;
  }
  throw new SmartTicketFacadeException("User not logged in.");
}

public MovieRatingData[] synchronizeMovieRatings(
                  MovieRatingData[] movieRatings,
                  int conflictResolutionStrategyId)
                    throws SmartTicketFacadeException {
  if (synchronizing != null) {
    return synchronizing.synchronizeMovieRatings(movieRatings,
            conflictResolutionStrategyId);
  }
  throw new SmartTicketFacadeException("User not logged in.");
}

// ... ...
}
```

5.4   Implementation Techniques

The MVC and facade patterns define the overall architecture of the application. In addition, Smart Ticket showcases some important behavioral patterns and implementation techniques that could greatly improve developer productivity.

5.4.1   Chain of Handlers

On the J2ME device side, the RemoteModelProxy class (see Listing 5.3) further delegates the action to a chain of handler classes that transparently work out the dirty plumbing of the RMS and HTTP serialization. The chained handlers are based on the RequestHandler interface and the RemoteModelRequestHandler abstract class (Listing 5.7), which implements the former:

Listing 5.7. The RemoteModelRequestHandler class

```
public interface RequestHandler {
```

```
    RequestHandler getNextHandler();
    void init() throws ApplicationException;
    void destroy() throws ApplicationException;
}

abstract public class RemoteModelRequestHandler
           implements RequestHandler, RemoteModel {

  private RemoteModelRequestHandler nextHandler;
  private Preferences preferences;
  protected static ProgressObserver progressObserver;

  public RemoteModelRequestHandler(
      RemoteModelRequestHandler nextHandler) {
    this.nextHandler = nextHandler;
  }

  public RequestHandler getNextHandler() {
    return nextHandler;
  }

  public void init() throws ApplicationException {
    if (nextHandler != null) {
      nextHandler.init();
    }
    return;
  }

  public void destroy() throws ApplicationException {
    if (nextHandler != null) {
      nextHandler.destroy();
    }
    return;
  }

  public void login(String userName, String password)
           throws ModelException, ApplicationException {
    getRemoteModelRequestHandler().login(userName, password);
    return;
  }

  public void createAccount(AccountInfo accountInfo)
           throws ModelException, ApplicationException {
    getRemoteModelRequestHandler().createAccount(accountInfo);
    return;
```

```
}

    // Other action methods declared in RemoteModel
    // ... ...
}
```

Concrete handler classes extend the RemoteModelRequestHandler class. A chain of handlers is established through nested constructors. Two handler classes are available in the Smart Ticket application: the RMSCacheHandler and HTTPCommunicationHandler classes. Listing 5.8 illustrates how the chain is assembled and used (e.g., getMovie()) in the RemoteModelProxy class.

Listing 5.8. Assemble the handler chain in class RemoteModelProxy

```
public class RemoteModelProxy extends ModelObjectLoader
                            implements RemoteModel {

    private RemoteModelRequestHandler requestHandlerChain;
    private Preferences preferences = null;
    private Hashtable movies = new Hashtable();

    public RemoteModelProxy(String serviceURL)
                throws ApplicationException {
        requestHandlerChain =
            new RMSCacheHandler(
                new HTTPCommunicationHandler(null, serviceURL));
        return;
    }

    // ... ...

    // get a movie from the chain of handlers
    public Movie getMovie(String movieKey)
                throws ModelException, ApplicationException {
        Movie movie = (Movie) movies.get(movieKey);

        if (movie == null) {
            movie = requestHandlerChain.getMovie(movieKey);
            movies.put(movieKey, movie);
        }
        return movie;
    }
```

```
// Other action methods etc.


}
```

A handler can selectively implement any action methods in the Remote-
Model interface. There are two possibilities:

- If a RemoteModelProxy class calls an action method not implemented
  by the first handler class in the chain, the default implementation in the
  base class RemoteModelRequestHandler ensures that the call is passed
  to the next handler in the chain.

- If a handler in a chain decides that it has finished processing an action,
  it returns directly. Otherwise, it can invoke the same action method
  in the base class to pass it to the next handler in the chain.

The following code snippets (Listing 5.9 and 5.10) illustrate how to implement the getMovie() method in the two handlers. The RMSCacheHandler
looks up the on-device cache for the requested movie. If the requested movie
is not cached, RMSCacheHandler calls its base class's getMovie() method,
which passes the control to the next handler in the chain: the HTTPCommunicationHandler class. The getMovie() method in HTTPCommunication-
Handler performs some network tasks to retrieve the movie object from the
J2EE back end. To understand the inner workings of the HTTPCommunicationHandler class, you need to read on to the next section.

Listing 5.9. The getMovie() method in RMSCacheHandler

```
public class RMSCacheHandler extends RemoteModelRequestHandler {

  // ... ...

  public Movie getMovie(String movieKey)
          throws ModelException, ApplicationException {
    IndexEntry indexEntry = rmsAdapter.getIndexEntry(movieKey,
            IndexEntry.TYPE_MOVIE, IndexEntry.MODE_ANY);

    if (indexEntry != null) {
      return rmsAdapter.loadMovie(indexEntry.getRecordId());
    }
    return super.getMovie(movieKey);
  }
```

```
// ... ...
}
```

Listing 5.10. The getMovie() method in HTTPCommunicationHandler

```
public class HTTPCommunicationHandler
           extends RemoteModelRequestHandler {
  // ... ...

  public Movie getMovie(String movieKey)
         throws ModelException, ApplicationException {
    HttpConnection connection = null;
    DataOutputStream outputStream = null;
    DataInputStream inputStream = null;

    try {
      connection = openConnection();
      updateProgress();

      outputStream = openConnectionOutputStream(connection);
      outputStream.writeByte(MessageConstants.OPERATION_GET_MOVIE);
      outputStream.writeUTF(movieKey);
      outputStream.close();
      updateProgress();

      inputStream = openConnectionInputStream(connection);
      Movie movie = Movie.deserialize(inputStream);
      updateProgress();
      return movie;
    } catch (IOException ioe) {
      throw new
          ApplicationException(ErrorMessageCodes.ERROR_CANNOT_CONNECT);
    }
    finally {
      closeConnection(connection, outputStream, inputStream);
    }
  }

  // ... ...
}
```

5.4.2   Binary RPC over HTTP

In the model layer, the HTTPCommunicationHandler class in the RemoteModelProxy class invokes remote procedures on the J2EE server side through a binary RPC protocol over the HTTP.

All RPC requests from the client to the server follow the same basic pattern: The first byte in the HTTP request data stream specifies the action method to be executed on the serverside session facade EJB. The RPC request code constants are defined in the MessageConstants class (Listing 5.11).

Listing 5.11. The RPC action codes in MessageConstants

```
package com.sun.j2me.blueprints.smartticket.shared.midp;

  public final class MessageConstants {
  public static final byte OPERATION_LOGIN_USER = 0;
  public static final byte OPERATION_CREATE_ACCOUNT = 1;
  public static final byte OPERATION_UPDATE_ACCOUNT = 2;
  public static final byte OPERATION_GET_THEATERS = 3;
  public static final byte OPERATION_GET_THEATER_SCHEDULE = 4;
  public static final byte OPERATION_GET_MOVIE = 5;
  public static final byte OPERATION_GET_MOVIE_POSTER = 6;
  public static final byte OPERATION_GET_MOVIE_SHOWTIMES = 7;
  public static final byte OPERATION_GET_SEATING_PLAN = 8;
  public static final byte OPERATION_RESERVE_SEATS = 9;
  public static final byte OPERATION_PURCHASE_TICKETS = 10;
  public static final byte OPERATION_CANCEL_SEAT_RESERVATION = 11;
  public static final byte OPERATION_GET_LOCALES = 12;
  public static final byte OPERATION_GET_RESOURCE_BUNDLE = 13;
  public static final byte OPERATION_INITIATE_SYNCHRONIZATION = 14;
  public static final byte OPERATION_SYNCHRONIZE_MOVIE_RATINGS = 15;
  public static final byte OPERATION_COMMIT_MOVIE_RATINGS = 16;
  public static final byte ERROR_NONE = 0;
  public static final byte ERROR_UNKNOWN_OPERATION = 1;
  public static final byte ERROR_SERVER_ERROR = 2;
  public static final byte ERROR_MODEL_EXCEPTION = 3;
  public static final byte ERROR_REQUEST_FORMAT = 4;

  private MessageConstants() {}
}
```

The second byte to the end of the request stream encodes a sequence of UTF strings that represent the parameters to be passed to the remote method. The response HTTP stream contains the RPC return value. The format is unique to each method, and you have to look at the source code for each method to figure out the exact format. The two code snippets below demonstrate the entire RPC round trip to get a list of theaters using a zip code. The RPC request is assembled in HTTPCommunicationHandler's action method getTheaters() (Listing 5.12), and the response array is unmarshaled by the shared model object Theater (Listing 5.13).

> **Listing 5.12.** The HTTPCommunicationHandler class generates the RPC request in the handler chain

```
package com.sun.j2me.blueprints.smartticket.client.midp.model;

public class HTTPCommunicationHandler
            extends RemoteModelRequestHandler {
  // ... ...

  public Theater[] getTheaters(String zipCode)
            throws ModelException, ApplicationException {
    HttpConnection connection = null;
    DataOutputStream outputStream = null;
    DataInputStream inputStream = null;

    try {
      connection = openConnection();
      updateProgress();
      outputStream = openConnectionOutputStream(connection);

      outputStream.writeByte(MessageConstants.OPERATION_GET_THEATERS);
      outputStream.writeUTF(zipCode);
      outputStream.close();
      updateProgress();

      inputStream = openConnectionInputStream(connection);

      // The first number in the response stream indicates
      // the number of theater objects to follow.
      Theater[] theaters = new Theater[inputStream.readInt()];

      // Iterate to unmarshal all theater objects in the response.
      for (int i = 0; i < theaters.length; i++) {
        theaters[i] = Theater.deserialize(inputStream);
      }
      updateProgress();
```

```
      return theaters;
    } catch (IOException ioe) {
      throw new
        ApplicationException(ErrorMessageCodes.ERROR_CANNOT_CONNECT);
    } finally {
        closeConnection(connection, outputStream, inputStream);
    }
  }

  // Other action methods
}
```

Listing 5.13. The Theater class in the J2ME model layer unmarshals the RPC response

---

```
package com.sun.j2me.blueprints.smartticket.shared.midp.model;

public class Theater {
  private String primaryKey;
  private String name;
  private String address;
  private String zipCode;

  // ... ...

  public static Theater deserialize(DataInputStream dataStream)
                                  throws ApplicationException {
    try {
      Theater theater = new Theater();
      theater.zipCode = dataStream.readUTF();
      theater.primaryKey = dataStream.readUTF();
      theater.name = dataStream.readUTF();
      theater.address = dataStream.readUTF();
      return theater;
    } catch (IOException ioe) {
      throw new ApplicationException(ioe);
    }
  }
  // ... ...
}
```

The SmartTicketServlet first determines the RPC action code from the first byte in the request stream. It then dispatches the RPC to the corresponding action method through the facade and passes all the RPC parameters remaining in the stream. In the Smart Ticket application, the client and server are tightly coupled. This approach can improve network efficiency, since each RPC exchange can be specially designed and optimized. However, the trade-off is development speed and robustness. If we make small changes to the server, the protocol and the parsing code on the client are likely to need to change too. We need to keep track of and update the code in multiple places, which could prove error prone. We also often need to recompile and redistribute clients.

5.4.3   The Clientside Thread Model

The Smart Ticket application uses a sophisticated threading model on the mobile client side. During a prolonged background task, another thread displays a moving gauge to the user indicating the progress (Figure 5.6). The gauge screen could also provide a button for the user to cancel the long action if she does not want to wait.

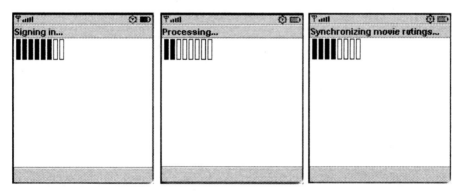

Figure 5.6. The progress gauge.

As we have seen, action methods in the UIController class are simply wrappers of the runWithProgress() method (Listing 5.14), which sets the display to ProgressObserverUI and starts the EventDispatcher thread. The ProgressObserverUI screen displays a gauge and an optional Stop button, which is monitored by the main MIDlet system UI thread. As we described in Section 5.3.1, the EventDispatcher thread eventually delegates the action to methods in the model layer. The model action method calls the ProgressObserverUI's updateProgress() method (Listing 5.15) at certain stages over the execution to update the gauge and inform the user of the progress (see Listing 5.12).

Listing 5.14. The runWithProgress() method in the UIController class

---

```
public class UIController {

  // Action methods ...

  public void chooseMovieRequested() {
    runWithProgress(
      new EventDispatcher(
        EventIds.EVENT_ID_CHOOSEMOVIEREQUESTED, mainMenuUI),
        getString(UIConstants.PROCESSING), false);
  }

  // Action methods ...

  public void runWithProgress(Thread thread, String title,
                              boolean stoppable) {
    progressObserverUI.init(title, stoppable);
    getDisplay().setCurrent(progressObserverUI);
    thread.start();
  }

  class EventDispatcher extends Thread {
    // ... ...

    public void run() {
      // Switch -- case statements to delegate
      // actions to the model layer
    }
  }
}
```

Listing 5.15. The ProgressObserverUI class

```
public class ProgressObserverUI extends Form
      implements ProgressObserver, CommandListener {
  private UIController uiController;
  private static final int GAUGE_MAX = 8;
  private static final int GAUGE_LEVELS = 4;
```

```java
int current = 0;
Gauge gauge;
Command stopCommand;
boolean stoppable;
boolean stopped;

public ProgressObserverUI(UIController uiController) {
    super("");
    gauge = new Gauge("", false, GAUGE_MAX, 0);
    stopCommand =
        new Command(uiController.getString(UIConstants.STOP),
                              Command.STOP, 10);
    append(gauge);
    setCommandListener(this);
}

public void init(String note, boolean stoppable) {
  gauge.setValue(0);
  setNote(note);
  setStoppable(stoppable);
  stopped = false;
}

public void setNote(String note) {
  setTitle(note);
}

public boolean isStoppable() {
  return stoppable;
}

public void setStoppable(boolean stoppable) {
  this.stoppable = stoppable;
  if (stoppable) {
    addCommand(stopCommand);
  } else {
    removeCommand(stopCommand);
  }
}

// Indicates whether the user has stopped the progress.
// This message should be called before calling update.
public boolean isStopped() {
  return stopped;
}
```

```
public void updateProgress() {
  current = (current + 1) % GAUGE_LEVELS;
  gauge.setValue(current * GAUGE_MAX / GAUGE_LEVELS);
}

public void commandAction(Command c, Displayable d) {
  if (c == stopCommand) {
    stopped = true;
  }
}
}
```

5.5 Summary

In this chapter, we introduced the Smart Ticket Wireless Blueprint from Sun Microsystems. The blueprint demonstrates the use of several important end-to-end application design patterns, including

- The Model-View-Controller pattern in rich client and J2EE application server settings.

- The clientside and serverside facade patterns.

- The chain of responsibility pattern for transparent network and persistence support on the client side.

- The binary RPC protocol for tight integration between the mobile client and the J2EE server.

- The worker thread pattern for non-blocking background tasks and user notification.

This chapter intends to get you started with end-to-end design patterns. I highly recommend that you explore the Smart Ticket source code and official white papers yourself to gain deeper understandings of the patterns.

Resources

[1] The Java wireless blueprint program. You can find the latest Smart Ticket code release and white papers there.
http://java.sun.com/blueprints/wireless/index.html

[2] The Smart Ticket v1.2 final release and v2.0 Early Access source code referenced in this chapter is available for download from this book's Web site. http://www.enterprisej2me.com/book/code/

[3] *Patterns of Enterprise Application Architecture.* Martin Fowler. Addison-Wesley, 2003. This is an excellent book on design patterns and architectural designs.

[4] *Applied Java Patterns.* Stephen Stelting and Olav Maassen. Sun Microsystem Press and Prentice Hall, 2002. This book gives design pattern code examples in Java.

Chapter 6

Advanced HTTP Techniques

CHAPTER OVERVIEW

- The Decorator Approach

- The Process-Chain Approach

- Session Tracking via HTTP Cookies

- HTTP Basic Authentication

- HTTP Digest Authentication

- Secure HTTP

In the previous three chapters, we used HTTP to transport text and binary data back and forth between mobile devices and backend servers. HTTP is crucial in end-to-end mobile commerce solutions, since it is ubiquitously supported by today's application servers, gateway servers, and mobile devices. Emerging integration standards such as XML Web Services are all based on HTTP. However, HTTP was originally designed to carry stateless and unencrypted HTML content to anonymous Internet surfers. J2ME, especially the MIDP, supports only the most basic HTTP features. MIDP's HTTP support is not sufficient for enterprise applications.

Fortunately, HTTP is a flexible protocol. We can use HTTP headers to pass additional information. HTTP headers are just HeaderName: Header-Value pairs that are attached to HTTP requests and responses. The use of many HTTP header fields has already been standardized. This chapter first presents two generic ways to handle HTTP headers. Code examples are then used to illustrate how to support HTTP cookies and authentication headers (both basic and digest authentication) under our framework. Finally, we discuss secure HTTP.

6.1 The Decorator Approach

One way to enhance the MIDP standard HTTP I/O is to provide a decorator class (CustomConnection) that wraps around the default MIDP HttpConnection implementation but overrides some methods to handle custom headers. Since the decorator class also implements the HttpConnection interface, it is transparent to existing MIDP applications that use HttpConnection.

6.1.1 The CustomConnector Factory Class

In order to instantiate the CustomConnection decorator, we need to write a new connection factory class CustomConnector (Listing 6.1). The custom request headers are set in the CustomConnector.open() method when a new connection is established.

Listing 6.1. The CustomConnector factory class

```
// In CustomConnector class
public static HttpConnection open(String url) throws IOException {
  HttpConnection c = (HttpConnection) Connector.open(url);
  setRequestHeaders(c);
  c.setRequestProperty("User-Agent",
    "Profile/MIDP-1.0, Configuration/CLDC-1.0");
```

```
  c.setRequestProperty("Content-Language", "en-US");
  CustomConnection sc = new CustomConnection(c);
  return sc;
}

private static void setRequestHeaders(HttpConnection c) {
  // Generate custom header for the request and
  // set the headers to the connection object.
}

private static void getResponseHeaders(HttpConnection c) {
  // Retrieve headers from the response stream
  // and process it.
}
```

6.1.2   The CustomConnection Class

Now, let's have a closer look at class **CustomConnection** (Listing 6.2). It
overrides only two methods, **openInputStream()** and **openDataInputStream()**,
which process custom headers when the response data is retrieved.

Listing 6.2. The CustomConnection class

```
class CustomConnection implements HttpConnection {
  private HttpConnection c;

  public CustomConnection(HttpConnection c) {
    this.c = c;
  }

  public String getURL() {
    return c.getURL();
  }

  public String getProtocol() {
    return c.getProtocol();
  }

  public String getHost() {
    return c.getHost();
  }

  // More HttpConnection methods
```

```
  public InputStream openInputStream() throws IOException {
    CustomConnector.getResponseHeaders(c);
    return c.openInputStream();
  }

  public DataInputStream openDataInputStream() throws IOException {
    CustomConnector.getResponseHeaders(c);
    return c.openDataInputStream();
  }
}
```

6.1.3   Decorator Pros and Cons

The decorator solution is elegant and transparent to existing applications.
However, it has several weaknesses.

- It is not scalable. For each task involving custom HTTP headers, we
  need to write a pair of decorator and connector factory classes.

- The decorator solution does not work correctly with HTTP tasks that
  require automatic header resubmission from the client side. An example of such tasks is the HTTP Digest Authentication (see Section 6.5).

For general-purpose HTTP headers handling, we need a new framework
that is more powerful than simple decorators.

6.2   The Process-Chain Approach

In this section, I present a process-chain-based HTTP transport framework
that works on all J2ME platforms. For simplicity, the new transport class
treats all requests and responses as byte arrays rather than streams. If your
application requires stream I/O (e.g., a SAX XML parser), you can easily
wrap a ByteArrayInputStream or ByteArrayOutputStream around those arrays.
The key components in the new framework are listed in Table 6.1.

6.2.1   The HttpClient Source Code

The source code of the HttpClient class is shown in Listing 6.3. Notice how
we walk through the handlers chain twice to process both the request and
response headers in the query() method. The maxIteration property is used
to prevent infinite loops in case of failed challenge-response cycles.

Table 6.1.   The HttpClient Framework

Class	Description
HttpClient	It is the main class. Developers first set the connection URL and HTTP request method using setUrl() and setRequestMethod() methods. Then, the request byte array is passed to method query(). The return value of query() is the response byte array.
Handler	Class HttpClient can have a chain of HTTP header handlers. Each handler implements the Handler interface. The Handler interface declares only two methods. The prepareHeaders() method sets headers for the request; the processHeaders() method processes headers from the response. The processHeaders() method returns a boolean value indicating whether the HttpClient object needs to resubmit its request after this round of header processing.

Listing 6.3.   The HttpClient class

```
public class HttpClient {

  private String url;
  private String requestMethod;
  private Vector handlers = new Vector ();
  // Max number of challenge/response cycles.
  private int maxIteration = 3;

  public HttpClient() {}

  public void setUrl (String url) {
    this.url = url;
  }

  public void setRequestMethod (String method) {
    this.requestMethod = method;
  }

  public void setMaxIteration (int n) {
    maxIteration = n;
  }

  public void addHandler (Handler h) throws Exception {
```

```
      handlers.addElement(h);
  }

  public void removeAllHandlers () throws Exception {
    handlers = new Vector ();
  }

  public byte [] query (byte [] req) throws Exception {
    boolean needConnect = true;
    HttpConnection c = null;
    int currentIteration = 0;
    while (needConnect) {
      currentIteration++;
      if (currentIteration > maxIteration)
        throw new Exception("Too many Iterations");
      needConnect = false;

      if ( c != null ) {
        try {
          c.close();
        } catch (Exception ignore) {
        }
      }
      c = (HttpConnection) Connector.open (url);
      c.setRequestMethod( requestMethod );
      for (int i = 0; i < handlers.size(); i++)
((Handler) handlers.elementAt(i)).prepareHeaders(c);
      c.setRequestProperty("User-Agent",
       "Profile/MIDP-1.0, Configuration/CLDC-1.0");
      c.setRequestProperty("Content-Language", "en-US");

      if ( req != null ) {
        OutputStream os = c.openOutputStream ();
        os.write(req);
        os.close();
      }
      for (int i = 0; i < handlers.size(); i++) {
        needConnect =
    ((Handler) handlers.elementAt(i)).processHeaders(c) || needConnect;
      }
    }
    InputStream is = c.openInputStream ();
    ByteArrayOutputStream bos = new ByteArrayOutputStream();
    byte[] buf = new byte[256];
    while (true) {
```

```
        int rd = is.read(buf, 0, 256);
        if (rd == -1) break;
        bos.write(buf, 0, rd);
      }
      buf = bos.toByteArray();
      is.close();
      c.close();
      return buf;
    }
}
```

Now, let's look at how to use those two frameworks to handle HTTP headers in the real world.

6.3   Session Tracking via HTTP Cookies

Cookies are pieces of **NAME=VALUE** formatted text embedded in HTTP headers. They are used to track client states. Since cookies reside in HTTP headers, they are transparent to applications and users. The server assigns new cookies to the client through the HTTP header set-cookie. The set-cookie header takes the following format:

```
set-cookie: NAME=VALUE; expires=DATE; path=PATH;
domain=DOMAIN_NAME; secure
```

The first **NAME=VALUE** is the cookie itself and is required. All the following attributes, such as expiration time, domain, and path, are optional. When the client makes subsequent requests, it sends the cookies back in the cookies header to identify itself.

```
cookie: NAME1=VALUE1; NAME1=VALUE2; ...
```

Note

The server can send out multiple cookies in one connection using multiple set-cookie headers. The client can send back multiple cookies in one header by delimiting them using semicolons.

6.3.1   Handle Cookies via Decorator Classes

Sun Microsystems' Smart Ticket blueprint v1.1 provides a class SessionConnector that utilizes the decorator pattern to add cookie support into the standard MIDP HTTP framework. The source code of this class is available from this book's Web site. The following snippet demonstrates how to use this class.

```
HttpConnection c =
  (HttpConnection) SessionConnector.open(url);
// You can use "c" as a normal HttpConnection
// but it is session aware now.
```

6.3.2 Handle Cookies via HttpClient Handlers

To support cookie headers in the HttpClient framework, we need to write the handler class. The source code of handler class (CookieHandler) is shown in Listing 6.4. Method getCookie() parses the response header and stores cookies in a static data member cookies. Method addCookie() matches stored cookies with the current request URL to determine which cookies to send out. Please refer to this book's Web site for complete source code.

Listing 6.4. The CookieHandler class

```
public class CookieHandler implements Handler {

  private static Vector cookies;
  private static Vector domains;

  public CookieHandler() {
    cookies = new Vector ();
    domains = new Vector ();
  }

  public void prepareHeaders(HttpConnection c) throws Exception {
    String url = c.getURL ();
    addCookie(c, url);
  }

  public boolean processHeaders (HttpConnection c) throws Exception {
    getCookie(c);
    return false;
  }

  // Remove all cookies.
  public void removeCookies() throws Exception {
    cookies = new Vector ();
    domains = new Vector ();
```

```
    return;
  }

  // Retrieve cookies from the connection header
  // and save them with domain information
  private void getCookie(HttpConnection c) throws Exception {
    // Parse the incoming cookies and store them in
    // cookies and domains vectors.
  }

  private void addCookie(HttpConnection c,
              String url) throws Exception {
    // Match the url domain with existing cookies
    // in the cookies vector. If a match is found,
    // set it into the connection header.
  }
}
```

The use of **CookieHandler** is illustrated in Listing 6.5.

Listing 6.5. The CookieHandler usage

```
HttpClient client = new HttpClient ();
Handler h = new CookieHandler();
client.addHandler( h );
client.setUrl( url );
client.setRequestMethod( HttpConnection.GET );
byte [] result = client.query(null);
```

6.4 HTTP Basic Authentication

Some HTTP headers can carry client credential information. Those credentials are used by servers to determine the client's identity and then grant or deny access to the requested resources. In the HTTP basic authentication scheme, the client sends its username and password in plain text with every request. The procedure is the following:

1. Use the Base64 algorithm to encode a **username** : **password** string

2. Send the encoded string and string **Basic** in the HTTP header **Authorization**

For example, if the username is *Aladdin* and password is *open sesame,* the HTTP authentication header is the following.

```
Authorization: Basic QWxhZGRpbjpvcGVuIHNlc2FtZZQ==
```

6.4.1 Code Example

To enable HTTP basic authentication in the HttpClient class, we need to plug in a handler (BasicAuthHandler). We can easily use BasicAuthHandler together with CookieHandler to make the HttpClient object keep track of a client session over an authentication connection (Listing 6.6).

Listing 6.6. Use cookies with HTTP basic authentication

```
HttpClient client = new HttpClient ();
Handler h1 = new CookieHandler();
Handler h2 = new BasicAuthHandler(user, pass);
client.addHandler( h1 );
client.addHandler( h2 );
client.setUrl( url );
client.setRequestMethod( HttpConnection.GET );
byte [] result = client.query(null);
```

Sample source code for the BasicAuthHandler class is shown in Listing 6.7.

Listing 6.7. The BasicAuthHandler class

```
public class BasicAuthHandler implements Handler {

  private String username;
  private String password;

  public BasicAuthHandler (String u, String p) {
    username = u;
    password = p;
  }

  public void prepareHeaders(HttpConnection c) throws Exception {
    String s = encode(username + ":" + password);
    c.setRequestProperty("Authorization", "Basic " + s);
  }

  public boolean processHeaders(HttpConnection c) throws Exception {
```

```
    // Do nothing.
    return false;
  }

  // Base64 encoding.
  //
  // This implementation is adopted from
  // Kenneth Ballard's HttpClient package.
  // Released under LGPL.
  private String encode(String d) {
   // Implementation details skipped
  }
}
```

6.5 HTTP Digest Authentication

Basic authentication can be used in a secure network environment. However, in an insecure network, such as the Internet, the problem for basic authentication is obvious: A cracker can easily intercept the clear text username and password, and forge the user's identity. A more secure scheme is to use one-way hashes (digests) to carry user credentials. The HTTP Digest Authentication works as follows.

1. The client contacts the server and requests a restricted resource.

2. The server sends a challenge to the client, including a randomly generated **nonce** value in predefined HTTP headers.

3. The client calculates a hash using its username, password, and the **nonce** value according to an algorithm defined in the specification.

4. The client resends its request with the new authentication header.

5. The server compares hashes with its own calculations. If the authentication is successful, the client will continue to use the same hash until the server changes the **nonce** value or the user changes its username and password.

Besides eliminating the clear text username and password, the digest authentication scheme has other important benefits. The server knows only the hash of the password but not the password itself. This prevents insider abuses. The server nonce value is embedded in the hash and therefore cannot be forged. This allows the server to have better control over the authentication process.

6.5.1   Code Example

We can use the DigestAuthHandler class to make the HttpClient object aware of digest authentication. The implementation of DigestAuthHandler is based on Kenneth Ballard's Open Source package "HttpClient." Code snippet from the DigestAuthHandler class is shown in Listing 6.8. Please note that the processHeaders() method returns false when the authentication fails, causing the HttpClient to recalculate the digest headers and resubmit its request. The digest value is generated using code adopted from the Bouncy Castle package (see Chapter 20).

Listing 6.8. The DigestAuthHandler class

```
public class DigestAuthHandler implements Handler {

  public DigestAuthHandler (String u, String p) {
    username = u;
    password = p;
  }

  public void prepareHeaders(HttpConnection c) throws Exception {
    String h = "Digest ";

    if(username != null)
      h = h + "username=\"" + username + "\", ";
    if(realm != null)
      h = h + "realm=\"" + realm + "\", ";
    if(nonce != null)
      h = h + "nonce=\"" + nonce + "\", ";
    if(uri != null)
      h = h + "uri=\"" + uri + "\", ";
    if(opaque != null)
      h = h + "opaque=\"" + opaque + "\", ";

    if(qop != null) {
      h = h + "qop=\"" + qop + "\", ";
      // cnonce is a random number generated by the
      // client. You should use your device build-in
      // random number generator to produce it.
      cnonce = "0123456789";
      h = h + "cnonce=\"" + cnonce + "\", ";
```

```
    h = h + "nc=" + count + ", ";

    // Increase counter by one. The counter will
    // be reset when a new nonce comes in.
    ncount++;
    String nc = Integer.toHexString(ncount);
    count = new String("00000000").substring(nc.length()) + nc;
  }
  h = h + "algorithm=\"MD5\", ";
  h = h + "response=\"" + getDigest() + "\"";
  c.setRequestProperty("Authorization", h);
}


public boolean processHeaders (HttpConnection c)
                                 throws Exception {
  if ( c.getResponseCode() == 401 ) {
    httpMethod = c.getRequestMethod();
    uri = c.getFile();
    parse (c.getHeaderField("WWW-Authenticate"));

    // need to re-send request
    return true;
  } else {
    return false;
  }
}

// Other utility methods
}
```

6.6   Secure HTTP

Both basic and digest HTTP authentication schemes discussed above are
weak security measures. They only authenticate users but do not protect
the communication content. They do not prevent crackers from intercepting
or even tampering with the communication data. For complete point-to-
point HTTP security, we need the HTTPS protocol that is based on secure
underlying transport protocols such as the Secure Socket Layer (SSL) and the
Transport Layer Security (TLS). Compared with thin client solutions where
security is provided by the fixed infrastructure, direct HTTPS connections
allow more flexible security schemes. For example, the communication parties can decide what to encrypt, the level of encryption and how often the

session key should be changed based on their business needs. In addition, by eliminating the middleman, HTTPS smart clients avoid the single point of failure and hence they are not affected by infrastructure level security holes. The discovery of security weaknesses in WAP gateways and WiFi access points has made this an important concern. Figure 6.1 illustrates the difference between HTTPS end-to-end solutions and WAP thin client solutions.

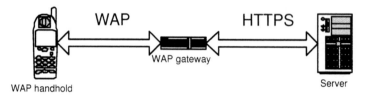

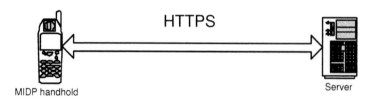

Figure 6.1. HTTPS end-to-end security versus WAP security.

6.6.1   HTTPS Support in the MIDP

Support for HTTPS is mandatory in the MIDP v2.0 but optional in the MIDP v1.0. To establish an HTTPS connection, all you need to do is pass an https://-style URL string to the Connector.open() factory method.

- On an HTTPS-enabled MIDP v1.0 device, a normal HttpConnection object will be returned. You can open input and output streams as usual. But the underlying data are properly encrypted. The entire process is transparent to developers.

- On a MIDP v2.0 device, an HttpsConnection object will be returned. Interface HttpsConnection extends HttpConnection with two more methods: getPort() and getSecurityInfo(). The getSecurityInfo() method returns a SecurityInfo object, which can be used to obtain further information on cipher and server certificate.

For mobile security schemes beyond the point-to-point connections, please refer to Part VI of this book.

6.7 Summary

Although HTTP has become the most important network protocol for end-to-end mobile applications, the high-level J2ME support for HTTP custom headers is limited. In this chapter, we introduced a framework to extend the basic HTTP support in J2ME. After reading this chapter, you can now use the HttpClient class to transparently handle HTTP sessions (using cookies), basic authentication, and digest authentication in your J2ME applications. For more advanced custom tasks, you can implement and plug in your own HTTP header Handlers. Near the end of this chapter, we also briefly discussed secure HTTP (HTTPS) and its J2ME support.

Resources

[1] The SessionConnector decorator and the HttpClient framework source code is available from this book's Web site.
http://www.enterprisej2me.com/book/code/

[2] HTTP State Management Using Cookies.
http://www.ietf.org/rfc/rfc2109.txt

[3] HTTP Authentication: Basic and Digest Access Authentication.
http://ftp.ics.uci.edu/pub/ietf/http/rfc2617.txt

[4] Kenneth Ballard's "HttpClient" package.
http://www.geocities.com/ballarke/Projects/HttpClient/

Chapter 7

End-to-End Best Practices

CHAPTER OVERVIEW

- Limited Device Hardware
- Slow, Unreliable Networks
- Pervasive Devices
- Ubiquitous Integration
- The Impatient User

J2ME allows desktop or enterprise Java developers to migrate their exist-ing skills to build smart mobile applications for enterprises and consumers. Those skills include basic concepts of the Java language, APIs, and common design patterns. However, blind "skill transfer" from the desktop, server, or thin client world could do more harm than good. For example, although most AWT-based J2SE applications run on PersonalJava and J2ME Per-sonal Profile without modification, porting them directly to mobile devices often results in unacceptable performance and very poor usability. To build successful smart mobile applications, developers must understand the special characteristics of mobile devices and networks.

As Java developers and architects, what should we know about the mobile development? How do we retrain ourselves for the new tasks? This last chapter of Part II, "End-to-End Enterprise Applications," answers those questions. We analyze challenges in mobile application development and discuss best practices to overcome them. Many of the solutions and tools we introduce in this chapter are discussed in further detail later in this book.

7.1   Limited Device Hardware

The most visible difference between the mobile and PC platforms is the difference in computing hardware. Today's PCs have much faster CPUs and far more memory and storage spaces than any mobile computing devices. Desktop and server developers can afford the luxury to write applications with bloated features (e.g., Microsoft Office); they also have access to rich productivity features provided by large, all-in-one frameworks (such as the J2SE platform itself). However, on mobile devices, it is a completely different story. With CPUs as slow as 20MHz and RAM as little as 100KB, we must carefully evaluate the features we need, thoroughly optimize our code, and live with limited framework support. In this section, we discuss how to cope with those challenges.

7.1.1   Lightweight Libraries

The most common mistake beginners make is the "golden hammer" anti-pattern: choosing the wrong technology for the task. In the Java world, software tools are often available as reusable objects in standard or third-party libraries. To choose the best libraries that support required application features at the minimum hardware cost is essential.

J2ME Foundation and Personal Profiles (as well as PersonalJava) are compatible with J2SE at the bytecode level and inherit a large subset of the J2SE core API. In theory, we can port J2SE libraries (e.g., XML processing, cryptography, messaging, and UI) directly to mobile devices. However, to do so would defeat the purpose of J2ME and result in slow and bloated applications that can be deployed only to the most expensive devices. In most cases, we should choose from lightweight library alternatives that are specifically designed for the mobile platform. Multiple vendors often compete in the same market. Each vendor offers a slightly different lightweight product with an emphasis on different features. Chapters 11 and 19 provide examples of how to compare and choose the best lightweight embedded database and cryptography toolkits for your projects.

CLDC and MIDP standard libraries are designed from the ground up as lightweight components. However, the need to select the right tools also applies to MIDP projects when it comes to third-party libraries. For a specific library, vendors often offer a version with J2SE-compatible APIs for larger MIDP devices (e.g., Symbian OS devices) and another extremely lightweight version that uses proprietary APIs. The latter often has a smaller memory footprint and better performance, but requires extra developer training and results in less portable applications. Examples of MIDP lightweight libraries include the PointBase MIDP relational database APIs (see Chapter 12, Section 12.1) and iBus//Mobile JMS client APIs (see Chapter 10, Section 10.3).

7.1.2 Reduce Application Footprint

Pervasive mobile devices have extremely limited memory and storage spaces, requiring us to minimize both the storage and runtime footprints of the application. Specific suggestions are as follows.

- *Optimize the packaging process*: Even after carefully choosing the best lightweight library, we may still find that the application utilizes only part of the library. In the packaging process, we should include only the classes we actually use. We can do this manually for smaller libraries or use automatic tools bundled with some J2ME IDEs (such as the IBM WebSphere Studio Device Developer) for large libraries. If you want to further reduce the binary application size, you can use a bytecode obfuscator to replace long variable names and class names with shorter, cryptic ones.

- *Partition the application*: Since the MIDP runtime loads classes only as needed, we can partition the application into separate parts to reduce the runtime footprint. For MIDP applications, the MIDlet suite can contain several relatively independent MIDlets.

Note

Although the standard MIDP specification does not support shared libraries, some vendor-specific implementations do. An example is the BlackBerry Java Development Environment (JDE) for BlackBerry handheld devices. A shared library further reduces the overall footprint, since the library no longer needs to be duplicated and packaged in each application.

7.1.3   Minimize the Garbage Collector

One great advantage of Java is the built-in garbage collector that automatically frees memory space used by stale objects. This allows developers to focus on the core logic rather than on mundane details of memory management. As a result, Java developers are usually unconcerned about object creation. In fact, many popular Java design patterns promote the idea of creating more objects in exchange of more maintainable code. For example, in the Sun Smart Ticket (Chapter 5) sample application, the use of the MVC and facade patterns results in many objects that simply delegate the action to the next layer. To get a feel for this problem, just look into the numerous classes that implement the **RemoteModel** interface.

But on mobile devices, due to the small amount of available memory, the garbage collector must run more often. When the garbage collector runs, its thread takes up precious CPU cycles and slows down all other application processes. For effective J2ME applications, we need to minimize object creation and quickly dispose of objects that are no longer in use. Specific suggestions are as follows:

- *Carefully examine design patterns in early stages of the development cycle.* For example, the screen flow-based approach demonstrated in the iFeedBack sample (Chapter 3) results in many fewer objects than a traditional MVC implementation.

- *Concisely reuse existing objects at the implementation level.* For example, if a same button (e.g., the **DONE** button) appears in many screens, we should create it once and reuse it.

- *Use arrays and StringBuffers.* Arrays are much faster and more memory efficient than collection objects. When we modify or concatenate strings, the immutable String objects result in a lot of intermediate objects. The StringBuffer is much more efficient.

- *Close network connections, file handlers, and Record Management System (RMS) record stores quickly after use.* We need to look over the documentation carefully to find out all the close(), destroy(), and dispose() methods and use them judiciously. It is usually considered a best practice to place those methods in the finally block to make sure that the resources are released even if runtime exceptions are thrown.

```
try {
  HttpConnection c =
    (HttpConnection) Connector.open("http://someurl");
  InputStream is = c.openInputStream ();
  // do something with the data
} catch (Exception e) {
  // handle exceptions
} finally {
  try {
    if ( c != null ) c.close();
    if ( is != null ) is.close();
  } catch (IOException ioe) { }
}
```

- *Free resources when using native libraries.* In smart mobile applications, we sometimes need to access native libraries for better performance, restricted functionalities (e.g., to make a phone call), or simply native UI look and feel (e.g., the IBM SWT library for PocketPC). Native resources are not subject to garbage collection. It is important to follow proper instructions of the native libraries (and their Java wrapper classes) to free resources after use.

7.1.4   Use Mobile Portals

Smart mobile devices are getting more powerful every day. However, in complex enterprise environments, many tasks are still too resource-intensive for most mobile devices. In this case, a commonly used approach is to set up portal servers to which the mobile devices can delegate complex tasks. Mobile middleware portals bridge mobile clients to enterprise backend servers. The smart portal is much more than a proxy or a surrogate for mobile devices. The uses of mobile portals include the following.

- *Allow mobile clients to utilize multiple communication and messaging protocols.* For example, mobile messaging servers described in Chapters 9 (Section 9.4) and 10 enable a wide range of devices over a wide range of networks to integrate into corporate messaging infrastructures.

- *Aggregate backend services and enable bundled services.* For example, the Oracle9iAS Wireless server provides J2ME SDKs for Oracle's SQL database, push-based messaging, and location-based services. The BlackBerry Enterprise Server supports unified access to Microsoft Exchange-based or IBM Lotus Domino-based corporate information systems from BlackBerry MIDP devices (see Chapter 8, Section 8.6).

- *Provide simple mobile interfaces for powerful and sophisticated backend services.* There are several notable examples:

  - The MapPoint facade described in Chapter 18, Section 18.2.2, shows how to build an easy-to-access interface for a complex backend Web service.

  - Database synchronization servers (Chapter 13) synchronize J2ME mobile databases with backend enterprise data sources using complex conflict resolution logic.

  - The Simplicity Enterprise Mobile Server supports simple, visual ways to build J2ME clients for legacy (mainframe) applications. (See Chapter 14, Section 14.3).

7.1.5   Use Design Patterns Judiciously

No design pattern is the silver bullet for every situation. For example, the powerful MVC and Facade patterns demonstrated in the Smart Ticket blueprint (Chapter 5) require several abstraction layers and are probably too heavy for simple applications. For simple applications, we can design the entire logic around screens, as we did in the iFeedBack example (Chapter 3).

7.2   Slow, Unreliable Networks

Unlike always-on broadband networks for desktop and server computers, wireless networks have proven to be very slow, unreliable, and insecure. Developers from the PC world, especially those who used to develop server-based with thin client solutions, tend to make excessive use of the network. In this section, we discuss ways to make the best use of network resources.

The Shortest Migration Path from Thin Clients to Smart Clients

In the mircobrowser-based thin client scenario, the client delegates all application logic to the portal server. The portal aggregates a variety of content sources (e.g., database, XML, RSS, SMTP) and automatically generates a view format that fits the device characteristics. For example, the portal can generate HTML for a PDA, WML for a cell phone, and even VoiceXML for a voice caller with the help of voice recognition and synthesis engines.

The shortest migration path from the thin client paradigm to smart client paradigm is through adding J2ME-specific interfaces to existing thin client portals. For starters, we can add new view adaptors to the portal. For example, the portal can generate XUL (XML UI Language) UIs for J2ME devices with XUL rendering libraries (e.g., Thinlet). This way, we can support new smart devices through the existing infrastructure while phasing out old thin client devices. The voice portal server can also be utilized to support multimodal mobile applications for even richer user experiences.

7.2.1 Support the Offline Mode

As we discussed in Chapter 3, one of the most important advantages of the smart client paradigm is the ability to support offline operations when the network connection is temporarily unavailable. The key enabling technology is on-device persistence storage (cache). Other advantages of the on-device cache include reduced network round trips and improved performance.

Offline operations require careful design of the data model. On-device cache can be used explicitly by the application developer or can be built into the framework and become transparently available to applications. Examples of both approaches are illustrated in the iFeedBack (Chapter 3) and Smart Ticket (Chapter 5 sample applications. For simple caches, the application-managed MIDP RMS stores, plain files, or XML documents are adequate. For more sophisticated data management solutions, we can use on-device relational data stores. For backend powered applications, we also need to keep the cache synchronized with backend data sources. Simple synchronization logic can be programmed into the application itself. Commercial mobile databases often come with advanced synchronization solutions.

For more discussions on the "occasionally connected" architecture and related tools, please refer to Part IV, "Mobile Databases and Synchronization Engines," of this book (Chapters 11, 12 and 13).

7.2.2 Use Remote Facades

As described in Chapter 5, Section 5.3.3, remote facade is an effective pattern to have the best of two worlds: fine-grained object model at the server side and coarse-grained access interface for improved network efficiency. Another excellent example of remote facade is the Axis-based MapPoint facade gateway described in Chapter 18, Section 18.2.3.

7.2.3 Place Portals Locally

Mobile portals are essential components in enterprise mobile architectures. However, fixed portals residing in remote data centers are often not accessible from the national mobile networks due to limited coverage and unreliable connections.

Compared with wide area networks, local wireless networks often have better coverage, lower bandwidth cost, higher speed and better security. Mobile portals that reside on the local wireless networks boost the performance and availability of the client devices. Examples of such mobile portals include OSGi service gateways (Chapter 4, Section 4.5), and IBM WebSphere MQe (Chapter 10, Section 10.4). In practice, we can build a mobile application architecture that contains a hierarchical structure of hubs and portals. Each portal handles part of the logic and delegates the rest to the next layer. That allows us to build an enterprise mobile architecture that continues to function with limited capabilities in different levels of network failures. Figure 7.1 illustrates the mobile portal network architecture discussed in this chapter.

7.2.4 Buffered I/O

Reading network data byte by byte is very slow. We should always read and write data in chunks. In Personal Profile applications, we can use the JDK's standard BufferedReader and BufferedWriter. In MIDP applications, we need to buffer the I/O ourselves (Listing 7.1).

> **Listing 7.1.** The buffered input in MIDP

```
HttpConnection conn = (HttpConnection) Connector.open(url);
conn.setRequestMethod(HttpConnection.GET);
DataInputStream din = conn.openDataInputStream();
ByteArrayOutputStream bos = new ByteArrayOutputStream();
byte[] buf = new byte[256];
while (true) {
```

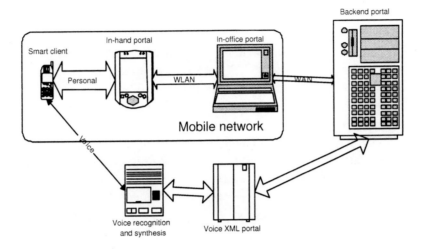

Figure 7.1. Mobile portal networks for small clients.

```
    int rd = din.read(buf, 0, 256);
    if (rd == -1) break;
    bos.write(buf, 0, rd);
}
bos.flush();
buf = bos.toByteArray();
// byte array buf now contains the downloaded data
```

7.2.5 Encrypt Your Data

Wireless networks broadcast data traffic into the air. Anyone can drop in and intercept the traffic. Built-in security for most wireless networks is not adequate for enterprise applications. The use of HTTPS (see Chapter 6, Section 6.6) for confidential communication is strongly recommended. In Chapters 19 and 20, we discuss how to implement your own security solutions. Having said that, we must also understand that cryptography tasks are often CPU-intensive. Security comes at the cost of performance. For small devices, we must carefully evaluate the security requirements and come up with balanced solutions.

7.2.6   Obtain Server Status Efficiently

Many enterprise mobile applications, such as an Instant Messaging client or a database monitoring client, need to be updated with real-time server status at all times. Since the HTTP protocol is ubiquitously supported in all J2ME devices, inexperienced developers sometimes program the device to initiate periodic HTTP connections to poll the server for its status. The polling frequency must be much faster than the expected server status-change frequency to keep the device updated. The constant polling results in a lot of redundant data. It is a waste of bandwidth, server resources, and time. There are several ways to deal with this problem:

- *Use HTTP conditional GET:* The HTTP conditional GET operation allows the server to return data only when the data source has been updated since the last query. An excellent description of the HTTP conditional GET and its usage can be found in a blog entry from Charles Miller (see the "Resources" section). This method reduces the amount of network data but does not reduce the frequency of the polling operation. In a long latency network, it could still be a performance bottleneck.

- *Use PUSH-based protocols:* To completely fix the "excessive poll" problem, let the server notify the client when the server status is updated. We cannot use the HTTP protocol for this purpose, since HTTP is designed to be a stateless request/response protocol. HTTP connections cannot be kept alive over an extended period of time. That requires us to explore other PUSH-based communication protocols on devices.

  - SMS messages can be pushed to devices and handled by the J2ME Wireless Messaging API library (see Chapter 9) or the MIDP v2 PUSH Registry.
  - SIP is a protocol specially designed for signaling in a PUSH-based network. The SIP API for J2ME has already been finalized (see Chapter 9, Section 9.6).

7.3   Pervasive Devices

Pervasive mobile devices are at the core of the mobile enterprise solution's value proposition. However, unlike PCs, which can be centrally administrated, managing a large number of small devices that people carry around all the time is an IT nightmare. Many of the device management issues are both social and technical in nature. In this section, we discuss what the problems are and the technical tools that can help IT managers and users.

Note

The successful use of the technologies described in this section rely on proper user education and corporate policies.

7.3.1   Protect On-Device Data

Small devices are very easy to lose. Stolen enterprise devices that contain sensitive business data, user credentials, or even company private keys could pose a real security risk. The only way to guard against this is to use strong encryption to protect on-device data. In Chapters 19 and 20, we compare security toolkits and provide code examples of how to protect your on-device data.

7.3.2   Synchronize Often

Today's battery technology lags far behind the device technology. A smart mobile device with a fast CPU; a large, backlit LCD; and multimedia features could drain its battery in a matter of hours. Most smart phone or high-end PDA devices require the user to recharge every day. If the user forgets, she will probably end up with drained batteries in the middle of the next day. Drained batteries could result in lost data. One way to cope with this is to synchronize the device periodically with backend data sources. Chapter 13 discusses the database synchronization options.

7.3.3   Optimize for Many Devices

Because pervasive devices are cheap and easy to carry around, there tends to be many of them in a company. Each worker could carry multiple inter-connected devices. Enterprise solutions need to support all devices in use in the company. J2ME provides a device-independent platform to develop applications. But applications still need to be optimized for the specific target UI and other device characteristics. The use of the MVC pattern could ease the pain of customizing applications: Only the view layer needs to be modified. For example, when the Sun Smart Ticket blueprint teams decide to port the application to MIDP v2.0 devices, they need to recode only the view layer in a matter of days. Another way to implement an MVC solution is to use the clientside container, as described in Chapter 4, Section 4.4.

7.3.4   Centralized Provisioning

Mobile enterprise users need to have the latest patched software and up-to-date application data. However, it just does not fit the mobile worker's busy life and work style to sit down, hook the devices to PCs, and follow detailed update instructions from the IT department every day. As a result, those instructions are often ignored. To manage and update software and data on a large number of mobile devices is a challenging task. The following are several tools that automate the device management process for both mobile users and IT administrators.

- *J2EE provisioning server*: The JSR 124 develops a specification for J2EE client provisioning servers. The server allows operators to plug in adapters for any client provision scheme. For example, the MIDP Over-the-Air (OTA) support is provided by a bundled adaptor in the reference implementation. When the device requests a client software, the provisioning server matches the device with clients in the repository and deploys the client using the appropriate adaptor. The provisioning server also provides hooks for backend billing, tracking, and CRM applications. Figure 7.2 shows the overall design of the J2EE client provisioning server.

- *OGSi bundles*: As we discussed in Chapter 4, OSGi bundles are self-contained mobile applications with managed life cycles. For devices running OSGi services, OSGi bundles could be the ideal way to deploy applications and contents.

- *Synchronization server*: Database synchronization can also be used to provision and update contents (see Chapter 13).

7.4   Ubiquitous Integration

Enterprise mobile clients need to integrate with many different back end or middleware systems. In this section, we introduce several common integration technologies and discuss how to use them judiciously. Table 7.1 is a brief layout of the pros and cons of each approach. Figure 7.3 illustrates the characteristics of each integration scheme.

7.4.1   Proprietary Binary Protocols

Since HTTP support is mandatory on all J2ME devices, it is the basis for most other approaches. HTTP can transport text as well as any arbitrary

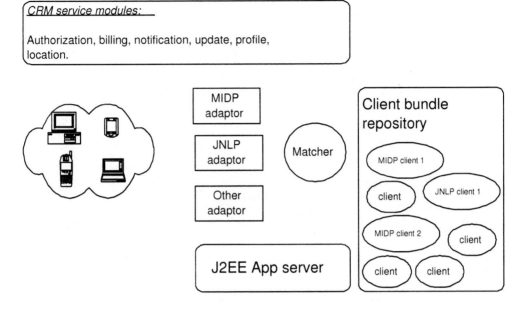

Figure 7.2. The J2EE client provisioning server.

| **Table 7.1. Integration Comparison Chart** |

Scheme	Interoperability	Coupling	Footprint
Binary over HTTP	poor	tight	light
RPC frameworks	OK	tight	light
Messaging	OK	loose	OK
XML Web Services	excellent	loose	heavy

binary content. Our examples iFeedBack (Chapter 3) and Smart Ticket (Chapter 5) both demonstrate the use of custom-designed binary protocols over HTTP. The binary protocols are designed to tailor the application needs and minimize the number of bytes needed to be sent over the network.

However, this approach results in tight coupling between the servers and clients. We have to develop both serverside and clientside components to interface with the custom protocol. If the design changes in the future, we have to change the application on both sides. If we do not have control over the server, we cannot take this approach. For applications that require frequent updates, the custom protocols are also not optimal.

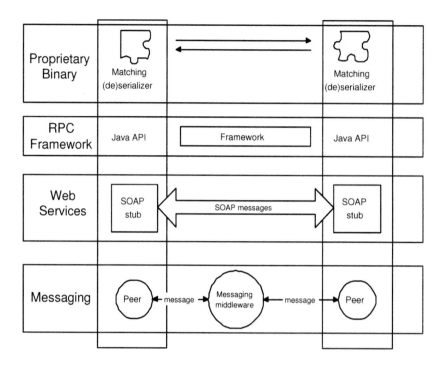

Figure 7.3. J2ME smart client and J2EE backend integration schemes.

7.4.2   Use Mobile RPC Frameworks

A more standardized integration approach is to use commercially available RPC frameworks. Such examples include the Open Source kCommand toolkit and the Simplicity transaction engine. The kCommand toolkit defines a set of open APIs that both the client and server can call to pass generic RPC parameters. Please refer to the link in the "Resources" section to find out more about its use. The Simplicity transaction engine is a proprietary solution tightly bundled with the Simplicity IDE. Using Simplicity RAD tools (Chapter 14), you can drag and drop your remote transaction components on an application composer and let the IDE generate the code for you. It is very easy to use for simple applications. However, the auto-generated source code can be hard to customize.

With the mobile RPC frameworks, we save the time to develop proprietary and hard-to-maintain interface components. But the server and client remain tightly coupled.

7.4.3 Messaging Is Our Friend

Messaging solutions, especially asynchronous messaging, decouple the client and the server through the messaging middleware. Properly designed messaging solutions could greatly improve the reliability and scalability of the system because resources can be allocated to respond to requests on a priority basis rather than a first-come-first-served basis. Chapter 10 discusses enterprise messaging based on mobile messaging-oriented middleware.

7.4.4 XML and Web Services

XML Web Services advocate platform-agnostic open interfaces. It supports both RPC style and messaging style integration. However, since XML Web Services pose large bandwidth and CPU overheads, we have to use them carefully. I suggest the use of XML Web Service only when the mobile client is interfacing external components or multiple client interoperability is required. We saw an example of Web Services integration in Chapter 3 and will see many more in Chapters 16 and 17.

7.5 The Impatient User

The "anytime, anywhere" convenience is the biggest strength of mobile applications. However, it is a major challenge to implement a truly convenient solution for human users. Users treat mobile devices as personal belongings and have high expectations for their devices.

In this section, we discuss efficient and responsive UI designs, which are crucial to the adoption of mobile applications. Another aspect of personal devices is that users would like to customize them to fit their individual style. We discuss preference management as well in this section. Most issues we discuss in this section are covered in the Smart Ticket sample application (Chapter 5).

7.5.1 Take Advantage of the Rich UI

Rich UI is one of the great appeals of smart clients. We should make judicious use of advanced UI components, such as direct draw on canvas and animation sprites. In the Smart Ticket application, the use of raw canvas to draw seating maps is an excellent example of appropriate UI usage. Advanced UI widgets are supported in the MIDP v2.0 specification. Device vendors also often provide their own UI enhancement APIs.

As described in Section 7.3.3, the MVC pattern (see Chapter 5 Section 5.3.1) is a powerful tool to support multiple optimized UIs for different devices while reusing the same business logic components.

7.5.2 Use Threads Judiciously

UI lock-up is one of the most annoying problems users can experience. On PCs, users are used to crashes in a certain popular operating system, and they can just hit the reboot button. But the user's tolerance for malfunctioning mobile devices is much lower. We expect our cell phones to work out of the box like any other electronic household appliance. The best practice to avoid hang-ups in the main UI thread is to put all lengthy or potentially blocking operations in separate threads. In fact, the MIDP specification clearly states that the UI event handler (i.e., the CommandListener. commandAction() method) must "return immediately," which implies that proper UI threading is actually mandated by the specification. Listing 7.2 shows the use of threads.

Listing 7.2. The use of threads

```
public class DemoMIDlet extends MIDlet implements CommandListener {

  // other methods

  public void commandAction(Command command, Displayable screen) {
    if (command == exit) {
      // handle exit
    } else if (command == action) {
      WorkerThread t = new WorkerThread ();
      t.start();
    }
  }

  class WorkerThread extends Thread {

    void run () {
      // Do the work
    }
  }
}
```

In the Smart Ticket sample application, the use of threads is pushed one step further: Each worker thread also has a helper thread that displays an animated gauge to indicate the progress of the worker thread. This is especially useful to keep the user informed during lengthy network operations.

7.5.3   One Screen at a Time

Mobile users have relatively short attention spans. We should break up lengthy operations into small pieces to show one screen at a time and offer users options to pause or abort in the middle of the process. Smart clients are especially well equipped to handle the screen flow process, since on-device storage could cache information between screens. A good example of screen flow is the "buy a ticket" action in the Smart Ticket application.

7.5.4   Store User Preferences

Mobile devices become more personal and hence have more value if they are customized to fit the user's personal preferences. Advanced mobile applications should store its owner's preference data on device. As we see in the Smart Ticket application, the stored preferences also allow users to have smoother workflow experiences. For example, the user does not need to stop and enter her credit card information in the middle of the purchasing flow.

7.5.5   Use Deployment Descriptors

The mobile application can also be customized at the back end before the user downloads it. For example, when a user signs up on a Web site, the site automatically customizes the download package with the profile derived from the submitted forms. We can customize the application without rebuilding it through the deployment descriptors. The MIDP specification defined the format and usage of Java Application Descriptor (JAD) files. But for other J2ME platforms, we still need to embed property files and/or other nonstandard configuration files in the custom-generated JAR package.

7.6   Summary

Despite the similarities in APIs and development tools between the J2ME and J2SE/J2EE platforms, experienced J2SE/J2EE developers do not automatically become good mobile Java developers. We need to understand the special characteristics of mobile devices, wireless networks, and mobile users. Then, we can design and optimize smart mobile clients using the best-practice guidelines laid out in this chapter. In the rest of this book, we explore J2ME tools and frameworks that help us to apply those best practices in mobile enterprise applications.

Resources

[1] *Patterns of Enterprise Application Architecture.* Martin Fowler. Addison-Wesley, 2003. This is an excellent book on design patterns and architectural designs.

[2] *Applied Java Patterns.* Stephen Stelting and Olav Maassen. Sun Microsystems Press and Prentice Hall, 2002. This book gives design pattern code examples in Java.

[3] *Wireless Java: Developing with J2ME, 2nd ed.* Jonathan Knudsen. Apress, 2003. This is an excellent MIDP v2.0 text for developers at all levels.

[4] The Sun Wireless Java Blueprint: The Smart Ticket application demonstrates many of the best practices described in this chapter. http://java.sun.com/blueprints/wireless/

[5] The Sun J2ME Wireless Toolkit is a comprehensive collection of tools for MIDP development and performance tuning. http://java.sun.com/products/j2mewtoolkit/index.html

[6] The J2EE client provisioning specification defines a flexible server architecture for smart client provisioning and user tracking/billing services. http://java.sun.com/j2ee/provisioning/

[7] The Thinlet project creates a lightweight XUL toolkit that runs on both Personal Profile and MIDP devices. http://www.thinlet.com/

[8] The kCommand toolkit is an Open Source RPC framework for J2ME clients to execute remote commands on J2EE servers. http://www.developnet.co.uk/kcommand.htm

[9] All other tools featured in this chapter are discussed in detail in other chapters throughout this book.

[10] Java blogger Charles Miller discusses HTTP conditional GET in his blog entry. http://fishbowl.pastiche.org/archives/001132.html

Part III

Mobile Messaging Applications

Chapter 8

Email and PIM

CHAPTER OVERVIEW

- Basics of Email

- Introducing Mail4ME

- Send and Receive Email from a MIDlet

- The JavaPhone API

- The PDA Optional Package

- Commercial Email and PIM Suites

- Corporate Portal Servers

Email is probably the most widely used application of the Internet. To-day's popular email suites (e.g., Microsoft Outlook) integrate email with PIM applications such as calendar, to-do list, and address book, to further boost productivity. The email and PIM combo suites are the most common tools to access corporate information such as job assignments, collaboration tasks and directories of support personnel. Mobile devices with email and PIM capabilities (e.g., Blackberry handhelds) have been greeted with huge successes in the corporate world.

Because J2ME supports advanced network and rich UI features, it is the right platform for building cross-platform mobile email and PIM solutions. In this chapter, we first explore Mail4ME: an Open Source library for J2ME email clients. Then we discuss J2ME tools for PIM solutions on the mobile client side. Finally, we look at portal solutions that allow us to extend existing corporate email and PIM solutions to mobile devices.

8.1   Basics of Email

When you send an email to a friend, it looks as though the message goes directly from your mail program to your friend's. In reality, the message is handled by many servers that reside in the Internet infrastructure. Those servers talk to each other using standard protocols defined by groups such as IETF and W3C. For users, this process is entirely transparent. But devel-opers have to understand exactly how an email message is transmitted to its destiny. In this section, we briefly go over important concepts and protocols in email.

The life cycle of an email message is as follows:

1. The sender's mail program contacts an SMTP (Simple Mail Transport Protocol) server. It tells the SMTP server the recipient and the content of the message.

2. The SMTP server finds the message recipient's mail server through an Internet registry and delivers the message to that server. The recipient server could be a POP3 (Post Office Protocol) or an IMAP (Internet Message Access Protocol) server.

3. The recipient POP3 or IMAP server stores the message. The next time the recipient logs onto that server, she will see that message.

The above process is illustrated in Figure 8.1. All data communication goes through TCP/IP sockets. SMTP, POP3, or IMAP servers are typi-cally provided by ISPs or companies that have reliable Internet connections.

As application developers, we only need to care about how the user client interacts with the mail servers (i.e., the first and third steps).

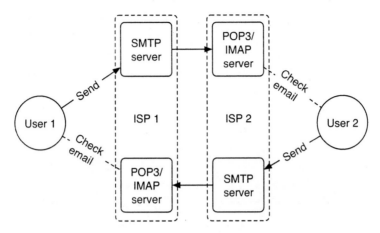

Figure 8.1. Internet mail architecture.

8.1.1   The SMTP Server

SMTP servers that do not require user authentication are called open relays. Open relays deliver all messages received. However, due to the abuse of spammers, most SMTP servers today require authentication. Your SMTP username and password are normally the same as the ones for your main ISP account.

8.1.2   The POP3/IMAP Server

A POP3 server has only one inbox for each user. You should first download all email and then organize it using your mail client program. An IMAP server can provide multiple remote folders for each user. Those remote folders act as central message repositories and simplify email management when the user uses multiple mail client programs.

8.2   Introducing Mail4ME

Mail4ME is an Open Source library that provides lightweight email APIs for all J2ME profiles. Since Mail4ME is released under the CPL (Common Public License), you are free to integrate it into your proprietary software solutions. However, I do encourage you to release your changes and enhancements back to the community. This way, your additional features can be supported in future versions of Mail4ME. This book covers the v1.0 release of Mail4ME.

For devices that support TCP/IP socket connections, Mail4ME applications connect to Internet mail servers directly. But raw socket is not mandatory in MIDP specifications. For devices or networks that support only the mandatory HTTP, Mail4ME provides a special mode that utilizes an HTTP proxy. The source code of the proxy servlet and config instructions are included in the Mail4ME download package. As we will see, the use of the HTTP proxy is largely transparent to Mail4ME client developers.

In the next two sections, I introduce a sample application, MailSample, that demonstrates how to use Mail4ME APIs. MIDlet Suite MailSample contains two MIDlets: SendDemo demonstrates how to send out email via an SMTP server; InboxDemo demonstrates how to read and manipulate email from a POP3/IMAP server. Figure 8.2 shows the application in action. Make sure that you replace the dummy server addresses and authentication information in the MailSample.jad file before you try it out.

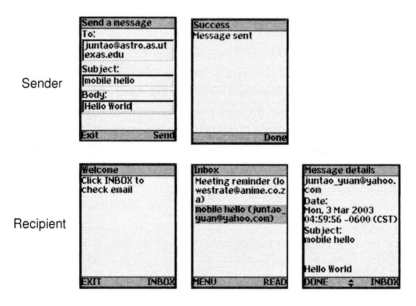

Figure 8.2. Demo: Access email from J2ME/MIDP devices.

8.2.1   Send Email

To send a text message via Mail4ME is very easy. You first need to compose a message and encapsulate it in a **Message** object. Listing 8.1 illustrates how

---

Email Attachments and MIME Types

As we know, an email message can take text or binary content as attachments. Those contents are encoded into plain text format according to rules defined in the Multipurpose Internet Messaging Extensions (MIME) specification. MIME is a standard type system defined by IETF. For example, a plain text message part has MIME type plain/text; an HTML part has MIME type text/html; a PNG image part has MIME type image/png; a JAR file has MIME type application/java-archive. The encoded parts and their MIME information are appended to the message body during transmission. The recipient decodes and displays each part according to its MIME type. Mail4ME provides limited support for MIME decoding.

---

to assemble a text message. All arguments passed to the **Message** constructor are in the **String** format.

Listing 8.1. `Assemble an outgoing message`

```
Message message = new Message(my_address, recipient_address, subject);
message.addBodyLine( body );
```

Then, you connect the SMTP server and send the message via the **Smt-pClient** object (Listing 8.2). The code comment illustrates the use of HTTP proxy. The message is successfully sent if the code does not throw an exception.

Listing 8.2. `Send a message using SmtpClient`

```
SmtpClient smtpClient = null;
// use proxy:
// smtpClient = new SmtpClient(
// new de.trantor.mail.http.ConnectionImpl(
// httpHost, 8080), hostname);
smtpClient = new SmtpClient(hostname);
smtpClient.open(smtpHost, 0, false, smtpUser, smtpPass);
smtpClient.sendMessage(message);
smtpClient.close();
```

8.2.2   Receive and Manipulate Messages

Now, let's see how we receive email via Mail4ME. First, we open a connection
to the mail server via the InboxClient object. Listing 8.3 demonstrates how
to connect to POP3/IMAP servers with or without the HTTP proxy.

Listing 8.3. Connect to a POP3 server

```
InboxClient inbox;
if (imap) {
  // If you use a proxy
  // inbox = new ImapClient(
  // new de.trantor.mail.http.ConnectionImpl(
  // httpHost, 8080));
  inbox = new ImapClient();
} else {
  // If you use a proxy
  // inbox = new Pop3Client(
  // new de.trantor.mail.http.ConnectionImpl(
  // httpHost, 8080));
  inbox = new Pop3Client();
}
inbox.open(pop3Host, 0, false, pop3User, pop3Pass);
```

Now, we can get a list of new messages and their summaries. Method
getMessageList() in Listing 8.4 returns an MIDP List object that displays a
list of new emails. Each email's sender address and subject line is displayed
as a List item. Vector msgNumbers keeps track of the index of each message
in the list. This is necessary, since if you delete messages from the list, the list
index goes out of sync with the message index on the POP3/IMAP server.

Listing 8.4. Retrieve messages from the POP3 server

```
private List getMessageList() throws MailException, IOException {
  List result = new List("Inbox", Choice.IMPLICIT);
  int count = inbox.getMessageCount();
  for (int i = 0; i < count; i++) {
    String uid = inbox.getUniqueId(i);
    int size = inbox.getSize(i);
    Message message = inbox.getHeaders(i);
    result.append(
      message.getHeaderValue("Subject", "No subject") + " ("
      + Message.getMachineAddress(
```

```
         message.getHeaderValue("From", "No sender"))
    + ")", null);
  // msgNumbers.insertElementAt(new Integer(i), 0);
  msgNumbers.addElement(new Integer(i));
 }
 return result;
}
```

Listing 8.5 deletes the selected message from the server, the message list, and the **msgNumbers** vector.

Listing 8.5. Delete messages from the POP3 server

```
int num = msgList.getSelectedIndex();
inbox.removeMessage(((Integer)msgNumbers.elementAt(num)).intValue());
msgList.delete(msgList.getSelectedIndex());
msgNumbers.removeElementAt(num);
```

8.2.3 Display Message Parts

What if we want to display the details of a message? Listing 8.6 illustrates how to display the selected message in an MIDP **Form**.

Listing 8.6. Display a message

```
int num = msgList.getSelectedIndex();
if (num == -1) return;
Message message = inbox.getMessage(
  ((Integer)msgNumbers.elementAt(num)).intValue());

Form readScreen = new Form("Message details");
readScreen.append(
  new StringItem("From:",
    Message.getMachineAddress(
      message.getHeaderValue("From",
                             "No sender"))));
readScreen.append(
  new StringItem("Date:",
    message.getHeaderValue("Date", "No date")));
readScreen.append(
  new StringItem("Subject:",
```

```
    message.getHeaderValue("Subject",
      "No subject")));

MimeDecoder mime = new MimeDecoder(message);
addPartToScreen(mime, readScreen);
```

The method addPartToScreen() actually displays the content of the message based on the MIME types of its parts. For more information on MIME attachments, see the sidebar "Email Attachments and MIME Types." Mail4ME supports the decoding of two MIME types: the text/plain type and image/png type. A simple text message contains only a text/plain part. Method addPartToScreen() goes through message parts recursively, as shown in Listing 8.7.

Listing 8.7. Display a multi-body message

```
private void addPartToScreen(MimeDecoder mime, Form screen) {
  if (mime.getPartCount() == 0) {
    if ("image/png".equals(mime.getType())) {
      byte[] bytes = mime.getBodyBytes();
      screen.append(Image.createImage(bytes, 0, bytes.length));
    } else if ((mime.getType() == null) ||
        ("text/plain".equals(mime.getType()))) {
      String s = "";
      for (int i = 0; i < mime.getBodyLineCount(); i++) {
        s = s + "\n" + mime.getBodyLine(i);
      }
      screen.append(s);
    } else {
      screen.append("\n[Unable to display \"" +
                mime.getType() + "\" part.]");
    }
  } else {
    for (int p = 0; p < mime.getPartCount(); p++) {
      addPartToScreen(mime.getPart(p), screen);
    }
  }
}
```

Now, we have seen the entire process of sending, receiving, displaying, and deleting email messages using the Mail4ME package. In recap, Figure 8.3 shows the classes in the Mail4ME package and illustrates their relationships.

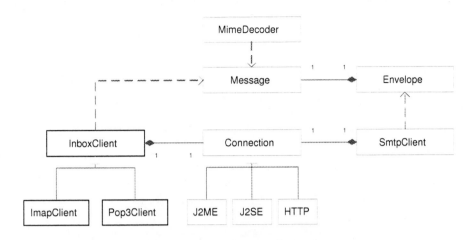

Figure 8.3. Mail4ME class diagram.

In the rest of this chapter, we go beyond simple email and look at PIM APIs for J2ME.

8.3   The JavaPhone API

The JavaPhone API v1.0 is an optional extension to PersonalJava. Designed for smart phone devices, the JavaPhone API supports telephony functionalities (e.g., call control), network datagram access, power management, and PIM access. You can download detailed JavaPhone specification, API documentation, and code examples from its Web site (see "Resources"). In this section, I give only a brief overview of the PIM package in Table 8.1.

8.4   The PDA Optional Package

The Java Specification Request 75 (JSR 75) was originally proposed to create a new CLDC-based J2ME profile (the PDA Profile) for low-end PDA devices (e.g., Palm PDAs). The PDA Profile was thought to be parallel to the MIDP. However, the progress of the JSR 75 has been very slow since August 2000. In the past three years, the MIDP has archived great success and is now a widely adopted industry standard. There is little need for another CLDC profile to compete with the MIDP now. In 2002, the JSR 75 expert group decided to reorganize and rename the JSR to the J2ME PDA Optional Package (PDA OP). This section is based on the proposed final draft of the PDA OP specification. The PDA OP runs on top the MIDP and provides two new packages to support PDA-specific features:

Table 8.1. The JavaPhone PIM API in the javax.pim Package

Package	Description
addressbook	This package allows you to store and look up contact cards (phone number, address, etc.) in address book databases. It supports multiple address books and addresses groups. The schema string used in contact entries conforms to the vCard personal data interchange format (an Internet Mail Consortium standard).
calendar	This package provides ways to store and look up schedule and to-do information in a calendar database. The schema string for calendar entries conforms to the vCalendar interchange format (an Internet Mail Consortium standard).
userprofile	This package defines objects that manipulate current user information. It uses the same format as the address book entry. On a mobile phone, this package might allow you to read and write the SIM card.

- The javax.microedition.io.file package supports access to local file systems through the J2ME Generic Connection Framework. We can open a connection to a file by passing the file://-style URL to the J2ME GCF abstract connection factory class (Connector). The package also includes support for dynamically mounted file systems (removable memory cards) through the FileSystemRegistry class and the FileSystemListener callback interface.

- The javax.microedition.pim package supports address books (ContactList and Contact), calendars (EventList and Event), and to-do lists (ToDoList and ToDo). The abstract factory class PIM provides methods to discover and retrieve those lists. If the device has a native PIM client, PDAP must provide access to all native database fields. The PDA OP imports and exports PIM entries in vCard and vCalendar formats.

The two packages in the PDA OP are independent of each other. Device vendors can choose to implement either or both of them.

8.5   Commercial Email and PIM Suites

Commercial mobile email and PIM solutions and libraries are also available from several J2ME vendors.

File Systems on Small Devices

One of the limitations of the MIDP is that it supports only RMS stores but not hierarchical file systems for local data storage. The reason is that many phone devices simply do not have file systems. This "lowest common denominator" approach is necessary to ensure the portability of MIDP applications. However, it has frustrated developers who want more power and advanced features. The PDA OP brings file systems to supported devices.

8.5.1   The Espial Suite

Espial is an industry leader of embedded Java solutions. On the client side, it has two productivity suites.

- Espial Suite for Devices runs on the CDC or PersonalJava platform. It contains four applications and libraries: Espial Escape, a Java Internet browser; Espial Ebox, a powerful email client; Espial Espresso, a lightweight UI library; and Espial DeviceTop, a graphical OSGi (see Chapter 3) client. Escape, Ebox, and DeviceTop all expose their programming APIs in SDKs. Developers can incorporate an HTML-rendering engine, an email client, or an OSGi manager in custom applications using Espial Suite for Devices SDK.

- Espial Suite for Wireless runs on the CLDC/MIDP platform. It contains three small footprint applications: Espial Escape, an 87KB Web browser; Espial Ebox, a 19KB email client; and Espial Assistant, a 42KB contact, task, and calendar manager. Again, all three applications make their programming APIs available through SDKs.

Please visit the Espial Web site (see "Resources") for software, documentation, and sample code on how to use the SDKs.

8.5.2   The ReqWireless Suite

ReqWireless offers three J2ME/MIDP libraries: The 37KB ReqWirelessWeb library provides APIs to fetch, manipulate, and display HTML/Word/PDF Web content using the LCDUI; the 43KB ReqWirelessEmail library provides APIs to access email messages and a variety of MIME attachments (including GIF, JPEG, TIFF images, ZIP archives, Word and PDF documents); the ReqWirelessDB is an MIDP JDBC driver library. ReqWireless also has three applications: WebViewer, WebViewerLite, and EmailViewer, to showcase the capability of their libraries.

The ReqWireless libraries employ a proxy-based architecture. Each library consists of a J2ME client component and a proxy server component that runs in any Java application server. The proxy handles network protocols, conducts round trips, parses the content and then feeds the display content to the client via an optimized proprietary protocol. The proxy architecture is of great importance for mobile applications. In the next section, we will have a look at more sophisticated corporate portals for mobile email and PIM applications.

8.6 Corporate Portal Servers

Although smart clients can access email and PIM information directly, clientside solutions have their limitations. Many enterprise systems have sophisticated security policies and filters that limit the direct access or synchronization to their servers. As we had discussed in Chapter 7, Section 7.1.4, corporate portals are necessary for mobile devices to access those restricted environments. Corporate portal products for smart mobile clients, especially for J2ME clients, are still rare. In this section, we introduce the BlackBerry Enterprise Server from Research In Motion (RIM), which allows BlackBerry handheld devices to access corporate Microsoft Exchange and IBM Lotus Domino environments. The BlackBerry Enterprise Server also supports additional logic on mobile management policies and filters. However, we have to note that BlackBerry handheld devices are required to access the enterprise server. We will not discuss details of the server configuration and setup here. Instead, we focus on the BlackBerry proprietary J2ME API (v3.6) on mobile devices.

Note

> Sybase iAnywhere's *Mail Anywhere Studio* is an email and PIM portal for native mobile clients. It provides access to Microsoft Exchange and IBM Lotus Domino environments to Palm OS, PocketPC, and Symbian OS native email and PIM clients.

8.6.1 BlackBerry Email

BlackBerry devices access email through the proprietary BlackBerry Java Development Environment (JDE) MIDP extension API. The BlackBerry server pushes email messages to the device. If the message is big, the server partitions it to multiple parts, each 2KB in size, and pushes only the first part to the device. The BlackBerry MIDP API allows the device to maintain multiple email folders, listen for changes of each folder, send messages, download complete multipart messages, and handle MIME attachments. Listing 8.8 shows the basic usage of the API.

Listing 8.8. The use of the BlackBerry mail API

```
import net.rim.blackberry.api.mail.*

public class MailDemo implements FolderListener, StoreListener {

  private Folder inbox;

  public MailDemo () {
    Store store = Session.waitForDefaultSession().getStore();
    store.addStoreListener(this);

    Folder[] folders = store.list(Folder.INBOX);
    inbox = folders[0];
    inbox.addFolderListener(this);
  }


  // FolderListener: Called when a new message is pushed in
  void messagesAdded(FolderEvent e) {
    // process the added messages
  }

  // FolderListener: called when a message is removed from the folder
  void messagesRemoved(FolderEvent e) {
    // process the removed message
  }

  // StoreListener: Called when messages are added and moved
  // in batch operation (e.g. during synchronization)
  void batchOperation(StoreEvent e) {
    // Do something
  }

  // Receive message number "index" from the inbox
  public void receive (int index) throws Exception {
    Message[] msgs = inbox.getMessages();
    Message msg = msgs[index];
    Address[] recipients = msg.getRecipients(Message.RecipientType.TO);
    Date sent = msg.getSentDate();
```

```
    Address from = msg.getFrom();
    String subject = msg.getSubject();
    Object o = msg.getContent();

    if ( o instanceof String ) {
      // The message is a simple string
      String body = (String)o;
      // Do something with the message
    } else {
      // The message contains a Multipart object
      // Download other BodyParts using Transport.more()
      // Do something with the message
    }
  }

  public void send () throws Exception {
    Message msg = new Message(inbox);

    // To address
    Address toList[] = new Address[1];
    toList[0]= new Address("juntao@enterprisej2me.com", "Michael Yuan");
    msg.addRecipients(Message.RecipientType.TO, toList);

    Address from = new Address("me@enterprisej2me.com", "Myself");
    msg.setFrom(from);

    //add the subject
    msg.setSubject("Hello world");

    //add the body
    msg.setContent("This is a test.");

    //send the message
    Transport.send(msg);
  }
}
```

8.6.2 BlackBerry PIM

The BlackBerry JDE's PIM API is very similar to the J2ME PDA OP's PIM
API. It mainly consists of PIMItem and PIMList interfaces (see Table 8.2).

For more information and code examples, please refer to the BlackBerry
Web site.

Table 8.2. The BlackBerry PIM API

Interface	Description
PIMItem	It represents an abstract PIM item. Interfaces Contact, Event, and ToDo are derived from the PIMItem interface to represent specific PIM items.
PIMList	It represents a collection of PIMItems. Specific lists are represented by ContactList, EventList, and ToDoList. All of them are derived from the PIMList object.
PIMListListener	Each PIMList can have an associated PIMListListener object. The listener interface provides callback hooks for events like adding, removing, or updating items.
PIM	It is the main factory class for obtaining PIMList instances.
RepeatRule	It represents repeat rules for repeatable Events. We can use the Event.setRepeat() method to set the rules.

8.7 Summary

In this chapter, we discussed the basics of the Internet email. Using the Mail4ME project as an example, we discussed how to send, receive, and view mobile emails from J2ME devices. Of course, Mail4ME does not have all the features a desktop email client might support due to the size and resource constraints. However, being an Open Source project, it provides a framework that you can extend and to which you can add needed features for your applications. In addition to email solutions, we also introduced standard and third-party libraries for mobile PIM applications. In the last section, we discussed how to use portal servers, particularly the BlackBerry Enterprise Server, to access restricted corporate email and PIM servers.

Resources

[1] The SMTP specification. http://www.ietf.org/rfc/rfc0821.txt

[2] The POP3 specification. http://www.ietf.org/rfc/rfc1939.txt

[3] The IMAP specification. http://www.imap.org/

[4] The Mail4ME project. http://mail4me.enhydra.org/

[5] The JavaPhone API. http://java.sun.com/products/javaphone/

[6] The J2ME CLDC PDA Optional Package.
http://jcp.org/en/jsr/detail?id=075

[7] Espial applications and SDKs. http://www.espial.com/

[8] ReqWireless libraries and applications. http://www.reqwireless.com/

[9] The BlackBerry Enterprise Server.
http://www.blackberry.net/products/software/server/index.shtml

[10] The BlackBerry JDE documentation.
http://www.blackberry.net/developers/na/java/doc/index.shtml

[11] The Sybase Mail Anywhere Studio.
http://www.sybase.com/products/mobilewireless/ianywheremobilemail

Chapter 9

Converged Mobile P2P Messaging

CHAPTER OVERVIEW

- What Is SMS?

- Introducing the Wireless Messaging API

- WMA in Action

- Synchronous and Asynchronous SMS Using WMA

- WMA Reference Implementation

- SMS from the Back End

- Beyond SMS: Interoperate with General IM Systems

- Mobile Jabber Clients

- SIP-Based IM Applications

SMS-based peer-to-peer (P2P) mobile messaging is already a major revenue source for wireless carriers. It could become mobile commerce's killer application. In the past, SMS (Short Message Service) was a non-programmable device native feature. It was difficult to integrate SMS functionalities into custom mobile solutions. But with emerging tools on both the J2ME smart client side and the messaging server side, SMS is becoming increasingly available to enterprise mobile developers. This chapter focuses on the J2ME Wireless Messaging API (WMA), which standardizes SMS APIs for all J2ME platforms. We also discuss third-party tools to integrate SMS functionalities into your J2EE backend applications.

The limitation of SMS is that it works only on the wireless networks. As a result, mobile phone SMS messages cannot reach PDAs in a local WiFi network or PCs using popular Internet instant messaging (IM) systems (e.g., AOL, MSN, Yahoo! IM systems). We also discuss J2ME toolkits and clients for general IP network-based IM systems that can bridge this gap. In particular, a development library for Jabber is discussed.

9.1   Introducing the Wireless Messaging API

Mobile phone network infrastructures provide standard ways to pass text messages between phones. The best known mobile phone messaging protocols include SMS and CBS (Cell Broadcast Short Message Service), both of which work on both Global Systems for Mobile Communications (GSM) and Code Division Multiple Access (CDMA) networks. SMS has become a major source of income for wireless operators; in Europe, SMS services already account for 40 percent of mobile phone carriers' profits. However, because not all J2ME devices are SMS-compatible, the standard J2ME API does not provide a way to access an underlying device's SMS features.

The J2ME WMA specifies a standard set of APIs that J2ME applications running on SMS-enabled devices can use to communicate with network peers via the SMS and CBS protocols. The WMA can be implemented on both the CLDC platform (Connected Limited Device Configuration, for mobile phones and low-end PDAs) and the CDC platform (Connected Device Configuration, for high-end PDAs).

One very important feature of the WMA is that it allows J2ME devices to run SMS-based server applications. You would use an SMS server to automatically process and respond to incoming messages in your J2ME application. Unlike traditional HTTP servers, SMS servers do not rely on the IP network. Server addresses are identified by telephone numbers.

The WMA specification has been developed by the JCP under JSR 120. It is supported by such major phone vendors as Motorola, Siemens, and Nokia, as well as such major mobile network operators as SprintPCS, Cingular, and France Telecom. In this book, we cover WMA v1.0. The WMA v2.0 specification under development by JSR 205 will support Multimedia Messaging Services (MMS).

Since SMS is much more popular than CBS, we focus on SMS messaging here. I first introduce the general concepts of the API and its use. Then, I discuss WMA implementations, particularly the reference implementation that works on PC-based wireless device emulators. Using the reference implementation, I will show you how to implement and run a sample P2P SMS messaging application called WMATester.

9.1.1   Top-Level WMA Classes

Application developers can access WMA features through three top-level interfaces in the javax.wireless.messaging package (Listing 9.1).

Table 9.1.   Interfaces in the javax.wireless.messaging **Package**

Interface	Description
Message	This interface represents a message. The TextMessage and BinaryMessage interfaces are derived from Message and provide more specific message structures.
MessageConnection	This interface represents a network connection for messages. It defines basic methods for sending and receiving messages. For example, the MessageConnection.newMessage() method returns Message instances for outgoing messages; the MessageConnection.receive() method captures synchronously incoming messages.
MessageListener	This interface has only one method: notifyIncomingMessage(). A MessageListener instance is registered with a server MessageConnection. Its notifyIncomingMessage() method is asynchronously invoked when there is an inbound message. The specification requires that the notifyIncomingMessage() return quickly. Thus, it is recommended that you start a new thread to process the inbound message.

Figure 9.1 is a UML diagram illustrating relationships of these interfaces.

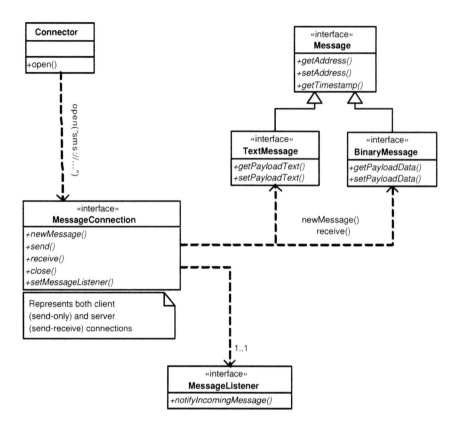

Figure 9.1. Top-level WMA interfaces in the javax.wireless.messaging package.

9.1.2   URLs and Message Connections

The GCF connector class javax.microedition.io.Connector instantiates instances
of MessageConnection. The URL that is passed to the Connector.open()
method determines the connection that will be opened. The following URL
patterns and message connection types are supported by the WMA:

- The URL sms://+18005555555 specifies a connection to send SMS messages to the phone number 1-800-555-5555. (Note that the WMA has
  no phone number format requirements; you can use any series of digits
  that your phone and network will recognize.)

- The URL sms://+18005555555:1234 specifies a connection to send
  SMS messages to port number 1234 at the phone number 1-800-555-
  5555.

- The URL sms://:1234 specifies a server connection to receive messages on port 1234. A server connection can also send messages.

- The URL cbs://:3382 specifies a connection that listens for inbound CBS messages on port 3382. Unlike an SMS server connection, this CBS connection cannot send out any message.

SMS Ports

With the WMA, you can specify a port number for each SMS message that you send. If an SMS message is sent to a phone number without a port number, it is interpreted as an inbox message and handled by the receiving phone's native inbox client. No WMA server connection should pick up such inbox messages. WMA peers communicate with each other through pre-agreed private SMS ports.

Now that we understand the basics of the WMA, let's take a look at some concrete code examples.

9.2 WMA in Action

The WMATester sample application, available from this book's Web site (see "Resources"), demonstrates the basic use of the WMA and the Sun Microsystems Reference Implementation (RI). You can use the provided ANT script to build and run the project. Commands ant run1 and ant run2 bring up two emulator windows that can send emulated SMS messages to each other (see Section 9.3.1). Peer 1 listens at SMS port 3333 and peer 2 listens at port 3334. So, if you want to send a message from peer 1 to peer 2, you can use an address like 18005555555:3334. Upon receipt of the message, peer 2 will display it. If the message comes from a server connection (using the Send2 button), peer 2 will send an acknowledgment back to peer 1. The process is illustrated in Figure 9.2.

There are two MIDlets in the WMATester suite. They have identical functionalities from the user point of view. The difference is that WMAsync uses a synchronous messaging model and WMAasync uses an asynchronous model. In the next two sections, I walk you through basic features of WMA and its RI using code snippets from the WMATester.

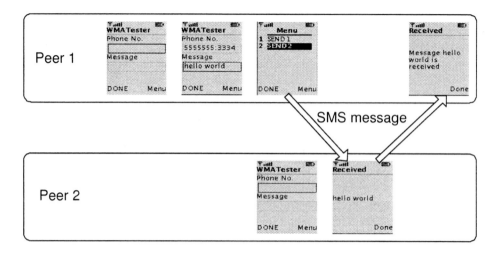

Figure 9.2. WMATester work flow.

9.2.1   Send SMS Messages

Sending messages with the WMA is very simple. You can send a message to an arbitrary phone number and/or an SMS port through a MessageConnection constructed for that destination, as shown in Listing 9.1.

Listing 9.1. Sending an SMS message

```
String addr = "sms://+123456789";
// Or: String addr = "sms://+123456789:1234";
MessageConnection conn = (MessageConnection) Connector.open(addr);
TextMessage msg = (TextMessage) conn.newMessage(
                     MessageConnection.TEXT_MESSAGE);
msg.setPayloadText( "Hello World" );
conn.send(msg);
```

You can also send out messages through a server connection, as shown in Listing 9.2.

Listing 9.2. Sending an SMS message via a server connection

```
MessageConnection sconn =
    (MessageConnection) Connector.open("sms://:3333");
TextMessage msg = (TextMessage) sconn.newMessage(
```

```
                    MessageConnection.TEXT_MESSAGE);
msg.setAddress("sms://+123456789:1234");
msg.setPayloadText( "Hello World" );
sconn.send(msg);
```

If you choose to use a server connection to send your message, you gain a number of benefits:

- The connection can be reused again and again.

- The message contains the sender's port number and phone number. Hence, it gives the recipient peer the opportunity to respond.

9.2.2   Synchronously Receive SMS Messages

To receive SMS messages in a Java application, we need to have a server MessageConnection listening at the message's target port. The MessageConnection.receive() method blocks until a message is received or the connection is closed. We can loop the receive() method to automatically handle incoming messages when they arrive. Listing 9.3 illustrates a server loop that listens, receives, and replies to incoming SMS messages.

Listing 9.3. Receive and reply to all incoming SMS messages

```
MessageConnection sconn =
    (MessageConnection) Connector.open("sms://:3333");
while (true) {
  Message msg = sconn.receive();
  if (msg instanceof TextMessage) {
    TextMessage tmsg = (TextMessage) msg;
    String msgText = tmsg.getPayloadText();

    // Construct the return message
    TextMessage rmsg = (TextMessage) sconn.newMessage(
                       MessageConnection.TEXT_MESSAGE);
    rmsg.setAddress ( tmsg.getAddress() );
    rmsg.setPayloadText( "Thanks!" );
    sconn.send(rmsg);
  } else {
    // process the non-text message
    // maybe a BinaryMessage?
  }
}
```

Note

In the real world, the server loop in Listing 9.3 must run in a separate background thread to avoid blocking the user interface. To see how that works, please refer to our sample application, WMATester.

9.2.3 Asynchronously Receive SMS Messages

The polling loop using the **receive()** method is often tedious to program with. WMA provides an event-based model for incoming message processing. The following code snippet (Listing 9.4) is adopted from the WMATester example to illustrate the asynchronous messaging technique.

Listing 9.4. Asynchronously receive messages

```
// Implements the MessageListener IF
public class WMAasync extends MIDlet
   implements CommandListener, MessageListener {

  // Init a server connection and assign
  // a listener for it.
  public void startApp() {
    try {
      displayBlankForm ();
      sconn = (MessageConnection) Connector.open("sms://:"+serverPort);
      sconn.setMessageListener(this);
    } catch (Exception e) {/* process error*/}
  }

  // ... ...

  // Implement the message handler
  // method required in the MessageListener
  // interface.
  public void notifyIncomingMessage(
                MessageConnection c) {
    // 'c' is sconn. No need to pass into
    // the handling thread
    new Thread(new SMSHandler()).start();
    return;
  }
```

```
class SMSHandler implements Runnable {
  public void run () {
    try {
      Message msg = sconn.receive();
      if (msg instanceof TextMessage) {
        TextMessage tmsg = (TextMessage) msg;
        String msgText = tmsg.getPayloadText();

        // Construct the return message
        TextMessage rmsg = (TextMessage) sconn.newMessage(
                            MessageConnection.TEXT_MESSAGE);
        rmsg.setAddress ( tmsg.getAddress() );
        rmsg.setPayloadText( "Message " +
                            msgText + " is received" );
        sconn.send(rmsg);

        // Display mesgText

      } else {/* not a text mesg */}
    } catch (Exception e) {/* handle error */}
  }
}
}
```

Please note how to put message handling in a separate thread so that we can quickly return from the notifyIncomingMessage() method, as required by the specification. The handler thread is similar to Listing 9.4 except that we do not need the loop anymore.

9.2.4   Receive SMS Message via MIDP PUSH

Through the MIDP v2.0 PUSH architecture, we can push the concept of asynchronous messaging one step further. The MIDP 2.0 AMS can listen for incoming connections. When a registered connection comes in, the AMS invokes a corresponding MIDlet to handle it. This way, the user does not even need to manually start up the server MIDlet. When the AMS picks up an SMS incoming message, it first buffers the message and then triggers the handling MIDlet. The MIDlet can read and delete the message. For more information on the PUSH architecture, please refer to the MIDP 2.0 specification and WMA documentation (see "Resources").

9.3   WMA Reference Implementation

To run the WMATester, we have to implement the WMA. An SMS wireless messaging client depends on the underlying device and mobile network infrastructure to send and receive messages. Thus, each implementation of the WMA is device- and network-dependent. Sun has come up with a WMA RI for PC emulators so that you can develop WMA applications independent of any actual phone or live network. Currently, the WMA RI works with the MIDP emulator. MIDP is a J2ME platform that targets mobile phone devices. WMA implementations for other J2ME platforms (such as PersonalJava, CDC) will come soon.

9.3.1   Runtime Properties

The RI provides a transport mechanism that emulates SMS over the host PC's TCP/IP ports. All SMS messages are routed as datagram messages to host ports specified by the RI's runtime properties. The properties can be specified in an internal config file or from the command line. Listing 9.5 illustrates the use of the command-line properties in the WMATester sample.

Listing 9.5. The reference implementation's runtime properties

---

```
emulator -classpath MyApp.jar \
-Xdescriptor:MyApp.jad \
-Dcom.sun.midp.io.enable_extra_protocols=true \
-Dcom.sun.midp.io.j2me.sms.Impl=
        com.sun.midp.io.j2me.sms.DatagramImpl \
-Dcom.sun.midp.io.j2me.sms.DatagramHost=localhost \
-Dcom.sun.midp.io.j2me.sms.DatagramPortIn=54321 \
-Dcom.sun.midp.io.j2me.sms.DatagramPortOut=12345 \
-Dcom.sun.midp.io.j2me.sms.permission.receive=true \
-Dcom.sun.midp.io.j2me.sms.permission.send=true \
-Dcom.sun.midp.io.j2me.cbs.permission.receive=true \
-Djavax.microedition.io.Connector.sms=true \
-Djavax.microedition.io.Connector.cbs=true \
-Dcom.sun.midp.io.j2me.sms.CBSPort=24680 \
-Dwireless.messaging.sms.smsc=+17815511212
```

Of course, the command in Listing 9.5 assumes that the WMA RI classes are already pre-verified and packed in MyApp.jar. Let's examine each parameter in the listing in detail:

- Property com.sun.midp.io.enable_extra_protocols enables the datagram protocol. It is needed for the MIDP 1.0 RI, which by default allows only HTTP GCF connections.

- Property com.sun.midp.io.j2me.sms.Impl designates a class that supplies the low-level network transport for SMS messages in the WMA RI.

- The com.sun.midp.io.j2me.sms.Datagram* properties specify the host and datagram ports to emulate SMS. In Listing 9.5, all outgoing SMS messages, regardless of destination phone numbers, are sent to local-host's 12345 datagram port. All messages received from port 54321 will be captured by the WMA RI as incoming SMS messages. In the WMATester sample, the input and output datagram ports of the peer 1 are mapped to the output and input ports of the peer 2 respectively. This way, each of them captures all messages sent out by the other.

- The com.sun.midp.io.j2me.sms.permission.* and javax.microedition.io. Connector.* properties specify the default permission to access SMS and CBS resources. Those properties are used by the MIDP 2.0 security manager.

- Property com.sun.midp.io.j2me.sms.CBSPort specifies the SMS port on which to receive CBS messages.

- Property wireless.messaging.sms.smsc specifies an SMS service center phone number. In the PC emulator, this property is irrelevant.

9.3.2   WMA Console in J2ME WTK v2.0

Sun's J2ME Wireless ToolKit (J2ME WTK) v2.0 provides a GUI-based console to configure WMA settings for each emulated phone (Figure 9.3).

9.3.3   Architecture

The WMA RI sports a multiple-layer architecture, illustrated in Figure 9.4. It is relatively straightforward to port the RI to use proprietary SMS stacks on real devices. The low-level transport layer is just a thin wrapper of Java native methods over device-native SMS libraries. The implementation classes layer aggregates those native methods into concrete implementation classes for WMA interfaces. For a detailed discussion on the architecture and port guide of the WMA RI, please read its accompanying documentation (see "Resources").

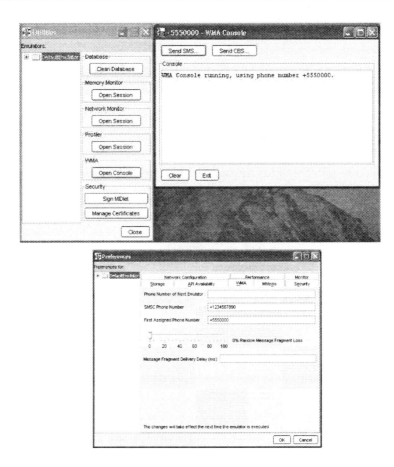

Figure 9.3. The WMA console in J2ME WTK v2.0.

9.4   SMS from the Back End

The WMA enables mobile Java peers to communicate with each other via SMS. SMS is also often used to deliver enterprise information from backend servers to mobile users. For example, a stock price monitoring server could send price alerts to mobile subscribers. In some countries (e.g., China), SMS has become a major micro-payment mechanism for mobile commerce services and small scale Web sites. SMS-based transactions can be traced to individual phones and users. The wireless carriers can act as the middleman to provide user authentication and billing services.

To handle SMS on server computers, we could develop a J2SE/J2EE WMA implementation that uses a modem or TCP/IP connection to interact

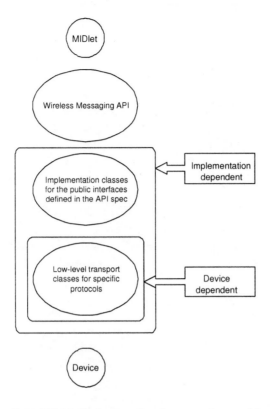

Figure 9.4. WMA Reference Implementation architecture.

with a wireless carrier's SMS Center (SMSC). In fact, the "Generic Connection Framework Optional Package for J2SE" (JSR 197) provides a GCF implementation for J2SE and hence allows the WMA to be ported to Java platforms beyond J2ME.

But such an enterprise server-compatible WMA implementation is not available today. The following sections briefly introduce you to two Java SMS tools that are already available for enterprise markets.

9.4.1   The jSMS API

Object XP's jSMS (v1.6) package provides an easy-to-use Java SMS API. It runs on a J2SE computer (a standard PC). In order for the PC to send and receive any SMS message, it has to be connected to a general mobile phone network using one of the two following techniques:

Email SMS Gateways

Some wireless carriers open email interfaces to their SMS services. Each phone number is associated with an email address. If you send a message to that address, it will be delivered to the phone as an SMS message. We can potentially use the JavaMail API to send messages programmatically from the back end. However, the email gateways do not provide a mechanism to receive SMS messages from the back end.

- The PC can connect to a GSM phone via a serial port. jSMS passes outgoing SMS messages to the phone, and the phone sends them out. When a new SMS message comes in, the phone sends a signal through the serial port, and a monitoring jSMS server thread receives the message. This mode allows you to quickly incorporate SMS functionality into backend applications.

- If you have an account with an SMSC, the jSMS application running on your PC can connect to that SMSC via a modem, an ISDN line, or a TCP/IP connection. This mode is designed to handle large numbers of messages.

Please refer to the jSMS Web site (see "Resources") for developer kit and sample code examples.

9.4.2   The Simplewire Java SMS SDK

Simplewire is a leading wireless messaging solution provider. The Simplewire Wireless Messaging Protocol Server relays messages between your server application and wireless networks. Those servers provide such enterprise features as logging, monitoring, and caching. They are also highly extendible.

You can purchase and run your own messaging protocol servers. But most users can simply use the servers from Simplewire's Wireless Messaging Network, which have access to carriers of over 300 networks in 118 countries. The Wireless Messaging Network charges a usage fee that varies based on SMS message volumes.

Simplewire's client SDK (v2.4) contains the necessary library and interfaces to interact with its messaging protocol servers. The SDK is available on multiple programming platforms, including Java. Please refer to the Simplewire Web site (see "Resources") for more information and code examples.

9.4.3   The Nokia Mobile Server Services SDK

If you are interested in sending and receiving MMS messages from the back end, the Nokia Server Services SDK (v1.2) is the perfect tool. The SDK include the following components.

- *Nokia Mobile Server Services Emulator*: This is a J2EE-based (JBoss, Tomcat and Axis) PC emulator for Nokia mobile servers for wireless carriers. The emulated services are the MMSC Server, Delivery Server, Presence Server and Terminal Management Server. The MMSC server is responsible for MMS messaging. This tool is essential for development since wireless carriers rarely open their live servers to developers.

- *Nokia Mobile Server Services API and Library*: This is a set of Java API libraries to access Nokia mobile servers. For the MMSC server library, it supports both Nokia's External Application InterFace (EAIF) and the 3GPP standard MM7 protocol. The API supports message composition, sending and receiving.

- *MMS Terminal Emulator Support*: This tool emulates MMS handsets on PCs. It allows developers to test MMS applications without the expensive live network.

- *Nokia Mobile Server Services Documentation*: It contains installation instruction, configuration guide and JavaDoc for the emulators and Java API libraries.

Listings 9.6 and 9.7 illustrate how to send and receive MMS messages from a backend Java application.

Listing 9.6. Sending an MMS message using the Nokia Java library

---

```
// Retrieve the following from the database
String qid;
String question;
String attachments[] = {
  urlPrefix + "png/" + qid + ".png",
  urlPrefix + "midi/" + qid + ".mid"
};

// creates engine for sending messages
factory = MMSDriverFactory.getInstance(args[1]);
engine = factory.createEngine();
```

```
engine.connect();

// Construct the message
toBeSendMsg = factory.createMMSMessage(attachments);
toBeSendMsg.setContentType(MimePart.CT_MULTIPART_MIXED);
//add the text
ContentPart cp = new ContentPart();
cp.setCharEncoding("UTF-8");
cp.setContent(question, "text/plain");
toBeSendMsg.getMultipart().addPart(cp);
toBeSendMsg.setTO(new MMSAddress("7650/TYPE=PLMN"));
toBeSendMsg.setFROM(new MMSAddress("1234/TYPE=PLMN"));
toBeSendMsg.setSubject("Trivia question");

// sends the message
engine.send(toBeSendMsg);
engine.disconnect ();
```

Listing 9.7. Receiving an MMS message using the Nokia Java library

---

```
// Creates engine for receiving messages
factory = MMSDriverFactory.getInstance(args[2]);
engine = factory.createEngine();
engine.connect();

System.out.println("Waiting for MMS ...");
receivedMsg = engine.receive();

// Print out or do something else with the reply message
System.out.println("FROM: " + receivedMsg.getFROM());
System.out.println("SUBJECT: " + receivedMsg.getSubject());
String submittedAnswer = (String) receivedMsg.getMultipart().
                         getBodyPart(0).getContent();
System.out.println("BODY: " + submittedAnswer);

engine.disconnect();
```

9.4.4 Standardize the Serverside Messaging API

The "Server API for Mobile Services: Messaging—SAMS: Messaging" (JSR 212) is a community effort led by Nokia to standardize serverside SMS/MMS

APIs. Its goal is to develop a high-level, protocol-independent J2SE/J2EE API for mobile messaging. Due to the abstract nature of the API, its implementation must provide a plugin framework (Service Provider Interface, SPI) that allows carriers and vendors to supply their own proprietary protocol and message handlers. The reference implementation of this specification will be provided by Nokia and licensed free of charge. The reference implementation will support common standard SMS/MMS protocols by default. This is definitely an important JSR to watch out for.

9.5   Beyond SMS: The IM Convergence

SMS by itself is a great text messaging system. However, a key problem that hinders SMS's adoption in the enterprise world is the lack of interoperability with other popular, TCP/IP-based IM systems. IM has become one of the killer applications of our age. Millions of users use IM applications from America Online, Yahoo!, and Microsoft every day, and their ISPs use the ownership of those IM networks as the basis for their premier monthly subscription fees. In the corporate world, IM applications have also become increasingly important: As of this writing, IBM and Microsoft have 230,000 and 50,000 corporate IM users respectively. Unified messaging brings obvious values to convenience-motivated mobile users. The ability to receive and process all communications in a single application on a single device is appealing. Converged messaging is the idea behind the new generation of devices like PDA phones.

However, communications providers are reluctant to work with competitors. For example, wireless carriers make a large portion of their profits from SMS usages. They are reluctant to provide interoperability with Internet IM services that could allow users to bypass expensive SMS services. It took major efforts to make U.S. wireless phone carriers make their SMS compatible with each other. Major Internet IM providers still block each other out of their networks. So, the convergence of mobile messaging is not likely to happen in the infrastructure level any time soon.

Fortunately, there are workarounds on a smaller application scale. For example, for enterprise applications that are used within controlled environments, we can actually control and converge all messaging functionalities. In the next several sections, we discuss how to do that.

9.5.1   Introducing Jabber

Before the grand-scale convergence can take place, we first have to invent a simple way to access all the incompatible Internet IMs. One way to do it is through the Open Source, standards-based Jabber Instant Messaging systems.

Jeremie Miller invented Jabber so that he could correspond with friends on different IM systems using a single GUI client. Jabber employs a really flexible and powerful set of messaging protocols. With the strong expressing power behind it, Jabber messages and administrative commands can be easily translated to interoperate with other IM systems. Jabber messaging servers are designed to be extendible. With proper plugins, they can interface with any other IM servers. Another important feature of Jabber is that it does not have a central server. Jabber servers can form P2P networks themselves. Each peer can talk with all other peers as if they were on the same network, creating a distributed but federated domain of Jabber networks. This approach has some important advantages:

- There is no single point of failure. Any server failure only affects the client it serves. Even then, the client can be free to join other Sun networks and use another server. This makes the infrastructure much more reliable and scalable.

- Identity management is conducted locally, which eliminates the feature of a controlling monopoly. An example is a closed IM system in a company: The company needs to have full control of the security yet still wants to allow its employees to access certain outside IM networks.

Today, Jabber goes far beyond its original goal of "scratching an itch." It becomes one of the most successful Open Source projects and is a widely used IM system in both consumer and enterprise sectors. The Jabber community itself has grown to more than 2 million strong. Jabber's underlying protocol, the Extensible Messaging and Presence Protocol (XMPP), has recently become an IETF standard.

Presence

A core feature of any advanced IM system is *presence*. Each user should be able to broadcast her status and availability to an authorized group of peers. Accurate and up-to-date information greatly improves the messaging efficiency. It adds value to the IM systems and opens doors to brand new applications. For example, in an IM-based customer support application, the customer can find out the currently available representatives and send requests only to them.

9.5.2 The Jabber Protocol: XMPP

XMPP describes XML streams over TCP/IP sockets. Unlike protocols such as HTTP, where there are headers, bodies, and attachments, conversations among Jabber clients and servers are completely expressed as XML documents. Key XML building blocks in the Jabber protocol include the **message** element, the **presence** element, and the **iq** (info/query) element.

- The **message** element describes the messages to be exchanged.

- The **presence** element is used to announce a peer's availability.

- The **iq** element is to allow structured conversation. It can be used to pass administrative messages such as user registration, authentication, and roster query.

A simple Jabber session might look like the following (Listing 9.8).

Listing 9.8. A simple Jabber session

```
SEND: <iq type='set'>
        <query xmlns='jabber:iq:auth'>
          <username>mjy</username>
          <password>secret</password>
          <resource>phone</resource>
        </query>
      </iq>
RECV: <iq type='result' id='sessionid' />
NOTE: Now we have the session

SEND: <presence>
        <status>Online</status>
      </presence>

NOTE: ... as time passes ...

RECV: <message id='1' to='juntao@ut/home' from='ju@ut' type='chat'>
        <thread>12345ABCDE</thread>
        <body>What's up</body>
      </message>
NOTE: send/receive more messages ...
```

Of course, the complete Jabber specification is much more than those simple elements. There are many optional attributes for each element. Complete Jabber coverage is beyond the scope of this book. Please see the "Resources" section for more information on this subject. Now, we need to check out Jabber client libraries that run on the J2ME platform.

9.5.3   The KVMJab Jabber Library

Al Sutton's KVMJab (v1.0) is a Jabber library that runs on MIDP v1.0 and above. It is an Open Source project but requires a $1,000 donation and 1 percent of after-tax profits if you include the library in a commercial product.

In the KVMJab library, the **JabberStream** class represents a permanent TCP/IP connection from device to a Jabber server. It is instantiated with a connector object.

```
JabberStream stream = new JabberStream(
  new meConnector(ServerName, ServerPort) );
```

Note

The KVMJab library also works in J2SE environments. However, since J2SE does not support the J2ME GCF, a new connector object is required. You can just replace the meConnector class to seConnector.

The stream object can be used to send messages or presence documents. Examples are illustrated below.

```
// How to compose and send a presence
Presence presence = new Presence();
JabberDataBlock bloc = new JabberDataBlock("status", null, null);
bloc.addText("available");
presence.addChild(bloc);
stream.send(presence);

// How to compose and send a message
Message mesg = new Message("juntao@ut/home", "hello");
stream.send(mesg);
```

Since a Jabber client reacts to incoming messages, it makes sense that the stream uses a listener object to handle event-triggered callback functions. Any listener object must implement the **JabberListener** interface and register itself with the stream object using the **setJabberListener()** method. The **JabberListener** interface declares three methods.

- The beginConversation() method describes what to do when the stream first connects. It often performs login.

```
public void beginConversation() {
  try {
    Login login = new Login("user name", "password", "resource");
    stream.send(login);
  } catch (Exception e) {
    // handles exception
  }
}
```

- The connectionTerminated() method describes what to do when a connection is dropped.

- The blockArrived() method holds the core business logic. The stream caller passes the incoming XML document as a JabberDataBlock object to this method. It needs to figure the nature of the document (is it an Iq or a Message document?) and send responses through the stream object.

Please refer to the examples in the KVMJab library for more advanced features.

9.5.4   Other Commercial Jabber Clients

In addition to Al Sutton's KVMJab, there are a number of commercial J2ME Jabber libraries or clients. Most of them use proprietary protocols, and some of them require proprietary mobile messaging servers. None of them makes the source available to the public.

- The Antepo J2ME Jabber library connects directly to Jabber servers. Source code SDK license is available, but only binary redistribution is allowed.

- The TipicME wireless proxy supports its proprietary J2ME-based Jabber clients. Source code SDKs are not yet commercially available.

- The uppli J2ME Jabber client is available for co-branding with other vendors. The SDK is not available to developers.

- Streampath provides a J2ME Jabber client, but no SDK is available.

What about the JXTA Network?

The JXTA project develops a generic P2P system that goes beyond simple messaging. JXTA peers can advertise themselves, discover others, and provide services to each other. The JXME project develops J2ME clients in the general JXTA networks through special proxy peers. For more information about the JXME architecture and APIs, please refer to its Web site (see "Resources").

9.6   SIP-Based IM Applications

The current breed of J2ME Jabber clients connect to servers via permanent socket connections or through HTTP proxy servers. That is not particularly efficient for IM applications in which messages are mostly pushed to devices. In socket-based IM applications, reconnecting dropped connections is also a big problem, especially in the unreliable wireless networks. A promising new technology for mobile IM is the Session Initiation Protocol (SIP). SIP is a high-level protocol over TCP/IP. It is a signaling protocol widely used in Voice over IP (VoIP) systems.

The JSRs 164 (JAIN SIMPLE Presence) and 165 (JAIN SIMPLE Instant Messaging) are community efforts to standardize SIP-based IM and presence APIs. The SIP Lite API planned by those specifications is specially designed for J2ME devices.

9.6.1   The SIP API for J2ME

At the time of this writing, neither JSR 164 nor 165 are available to the general public. However, the SIP API for J2ME (JSR 180) is already in the public review stage. JSR 180 is the basis for JSRs 164/165.

In the SIP API for J2ME specification, the SIP connections are defined within the J2ME Generic Connection Framework.

1. A SipClientConnection object is created when we pass a sip:username@host.domain:port URL to the Connector.open() method. It is used to send outgoing SIP messages.

2. A SipConnectionNotifier object is created when we pass a sip:port URL to the Connector.open() method. It listens at the specified port number for incoming SIP connections.

3. When a new session connection comes in, the SipConnectionNotifier object creates a new SipServerConnection to respond to the request.

4. For each session, the corresponding connection objects and other context information are persisted in the SipDialog object.

As a session-oriented protocol, SIP makes it very easy to signal presence and push instant messages as needed.

9.7 Summary

Although the SMS/MMS systems on mobile devices and the IM systems on desktop computers are largely incompatible today, new smart clients and open messaging servers have made it possible for the two worlds to converge and create a vast IM network accessible to any device and computer. In this chapter, we first introduced the J2ME Wireless Messaging API, which allows smart clients to access SMS/MMS messages. Then, we discussed how to extend Jabber-based desktop presence/IM systems to smart mobile devices. In both cases, we also discussed mobile messaging servers that enable desktop users to send and receive SMS/MMS or IM messages to and from mobile clients. We also introduced SIP-based mobile presence and IM systems, which are being standardized in the JCP.

Resources

[1] The J2ME Wireless Messaging API, reference implementation and documentation. http://java.sun.com/products/wma/

[2] The WMATester sample code.
    http://www.enterprisej2me.com/book/code/

[3] JSR 205 develops WMA v2.0 specification, which includes support for MMS. http://www.jcp.org/en/jsr/detail?id=205

[4] The MIDP specification, including documentation of the PUSH architecture for MIDP v2.0. http://java.sun.com/products/midp/

[5] JSR 197: Generic Connection Framework Optional Package for J2SE.
    http://www.jcp.org/en/jsr/detail?id=197

[6] Object XP's jSMS package. http://www.objectxp.com/products/jSMS/

[7] Simplewire's Java SMS SDK.
    http://www.simplewire.com/developers/sdk/java/

[8] The Nokia Mobile Server Services SDK.
http://www.forum.nokia.com/nokia_mobile_server

[9] The Server API for Mobile Services: Messaging—SAMS: Messaging.
http://www.jcp.org/en/jsr/detail?id=212

[10] All about Jabber. http://www.jabber.org/

[11] XMPP IETF drafts. http://www.jabber.org/ietf/

[12] Al Sutton's KVMJab library.
http://www.alsutton.com/software/kvmjab/index.html

[13] Antepo PresenceWare and Jabber SDK. http://www.antepo.com/

[14] TipicME wireless proxy. http://www.tipic.com/index.php

[15] Uppli J2ME Jabber clients. http://www.uppli.com/

[16] Streampath SIM J2ME Jabber client. http://www.streampath.com/

[17] An introduction to SIP. http://www.cs.columbia.edu/sip/

[18] JSR 164: JAIN SIMPLE Presence.
http://www.jcp.org/en/jsr/detail?id=164

[19] JSR 165: JAIN SIMPLE Instant Messaging.
http://www.jcp.org/en/jsr/detail?id=165

[20] JSR 180: The SIP API for J2ME.
http://www.jcp.org/en/jsr/detail?id=180

[21] The JXTA project. http://www.jxta.org/

[22] The JXME project. http://jxme.jxta.org/

Chapter 10

Enterprise Messaging

CHAPTER OVERVIEW

- The Case for MOM

- Introducing the JMS

- Mobile JMS from iBus//Mobile

- The IBM WebSphere MQ Everyplace

Mobile messaging applications have proven extremely successful in the consumer world to support flexible person-to-person communications. However, messaging is much more than interperson communications. The wide use of messaging-oriented middleware (MOM), such as the Java Messaging Service (JMS), has made messaging one of the most important person-to-machine or machine-to-machine integration schemes in modern enterprise applications. Compared with tightly integrated applications, messaging-based solutions are more reliable, flexible, and scalable. Those are critical advantages in the mobile enterprise world. Using iBus//Mobile and IBM WebSphere MQ Everyplace as examples, we discuss design principles of mobile MOM applications. We also walk through sample code for simple applications using both systems.

10.1 Mobile Enterprise Messaging

In Chapters 3 and 5, we explored ways to integrate smart clients with back-end servers using RPC. More examples on the RPC scheme can be found in Chapters 16 and 17. Although RPC style integration is simple and does not require any middleware, it is sometimes not optimal in the occasionally connected, unreliable, and heterogeneous mobile environments. Error handling and quality-of-service (QoS)-level guarantees are difficult to implement in RPC environments. The messaging scheme, however, offers great advantages in some key enterprise areas. The benefits of enterprise messaging are as follows.

- *Universal integration:* In the messaging scheme, the message sender and receiver are completely decoupled. They interact only with standard interfaces defined by the messaging protocol and do not need to know the status or availability of the other party. This allows automatic and seamless integration between enterprise components. For mobile applications that run on many different devices and use different network transport protocols, messaging-based integration is crucial.

- *Reliability:* Due to the intermittent nature of wireless networks, communication reliability is a big concern for mission-critical mobile applications. In a messaging application, we can guarantee message delivery or at least notify the sender when the delivery is failed or not completed after a certain amount of time.

- *Scalability:* In an asynchronous messaging solution, the server resource is not tied up by idle connections. Therefore, more concurrent users can be supported. Compared with the one-user-one-PC scenario in the wired world, each mobile worker might have several pervasive devices. Asynchronous messaging solutions allow us to build an infrastructure that accommodates those extra connection points.

- *Quality-of-service:* Another advantage of asynchronous messaging is that it provides ways to differentiate service levels. During network "rush hours," the messaging system can prioritize messages and deliver the urgent and important ones first. For mobile applications, it is a smart use of precious bandwidth.

In real-world enterprise applications, we probably need a hybrid of RPC and messaging schemes.

10.1.1 Mobile MOM

The key infrastructure component in any messaging solution is messaging middleware servers. The middleware servers route, filter, hold, and deliver the messages when the client becomes available. Examples of such servers include email servers (e.g., SMTP, POP3 and IMAP), SMS Service Centers, and instant messaging servers (e.g., Jabber, AIM, MSN and Yahoo!). Those servers are available as part of the worldwide data communication infrastructure.

However, for enterprise applications, companies want to have fine control over their own messaging servers. The key technology behind enterprise solutions is MOM products. Mobile MOM solutions should support the following features.

- Handle multiple client protocols.

- Manage one-to-one or publish-subscribe message queues.

- Store and forward messages.

- Confirm message delivery.

- Provide interfaces for popular backend messaging systems.

- Provide interfaces for J2ME, native or even thin client devices.

The JMS specification defines MOM servers with the above features. In the next several sections, we discuss the JMS and then go through two mobile MOM products.

10.2   Introducing the JMS

The JMS is a formal J2EE specification for enterprise messaging servers. JMS defines Java interfaces for both clients and servers. JMS vendors supply implementations of those interfaces. Mobile MOM servers that implement JMS are guaranteed to work with all J2EE application servers. In addition, using JMS in mobile MOM solutions allows existing enterprise Java developers to leverage their skills. Now, let's have a look at the overall JMS architecture from its public interfaces.

10.2.1   Top-Level Interfaces

Table 10.1 lists the top-level interfaces in the javax.jms package. Built on top of those general-purpose interfaces, JMS provides subinterfaces to support two important messaging models.

10.2.2   Publish-and-Subscribe Model

In the publish-and-subscribe model, the message Destinations are Topics. Messages sent to a topic are duplicated and distributed to all the subscribers of that topic (see Figure 10.1). If a subscriber is temporarily unavailable, the server will hold the message and try later.

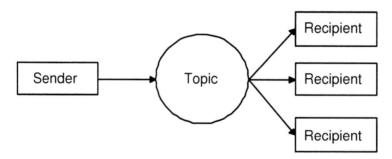

Figure 10.1. The publish-subscribe messaging model.

A client can start a new topic or send messages to an existing topic. Listing 10.1 illustrates how a publisher client works.

Listing 10.1. A JMS publisher in action

```
// The startup process is a tedious bootstrap
// process until we get the TopicPublisher object
```

Table 10.1.   Interfaces in the javax.jms Package

Interface	Description
Message	Represents a message to be exchanged. It supports both text and binary messages as well as message headers.
Destination	Represents a delivery destination maintained by the JMS server. The JMS server forwards messages to their destination clients, stores messages for unavailable clients, and handles delivery failures and acknowledgments.
MessageConsumer	Represents a client that receives messages. It has to be associated with a Destination. To receive messages synchronously, we can use the receive() method. It blocks the I/O until a new message arrives.
MessageListener	This is a callback interface for a MessageConsumer to receive messages asynchronously. Once the listener object is registered with a MessageConsumer, the listener's onMessage() method is called when a new message arrives.
MessageProducer	Represents a client that sends out messages. A MessageProducer sends messages to a Destination.
Connection	Represents a data channel between the JMS client and server. JMS implementations can support connections via many protocols besides the TCP/IP. Connection objects are usually obtained through a factory method, which is in turn configured in the JNDI directory.
Session	Represents a persistent connection where the client state information is maintained. The Session interface declares factory methods for the client to create message, publisher, and consumer objects.

```
Properties env = new Properties();
InitialContext jndi = new InitialContext(env);
TopicConnectionFactory factory =
  (TopicConnectionFactory) jndi.lookup("MyBroker");
TopicConnection conn =
  factory.createTopicConnection(username, password);
TopicSession pubSess =
  conn.createTopicSession(false, Session.AUTO_ACKNOWLEDGE);
Topic topub = (Topic)jndi.lookup("My topic");
```

```
TopicPublisher publisher = pubSess.createPublisher(topub);
conn.start();

// Now, let's send a message!

StreamMessage mesg = pubSess.createStreamMessage();
mesg.writeString("something important");
mesg.writeFloat( 123.45 );
// complete writing your message content
// mesg.setJMSReplyTo( replyTopic );
publisher.publish(mesg, DeliveryMode.PERSISTENT,
                  Message.DEFAULT_PRIORITY, 18000);
```

Once a topic is created, any authorized client can subscribe to it and start to receive messages. Listing 10.2 illustrates how to receive messages from a topic asynchronously through the MessageListener.

Listing 10.2. A JMS subscriber in action

```
// Provide an implementation of the listener

public class MyListener implements MessageListener {
  public MyListener () { }

  // This is the only method we need to implement
  public void onMessage (Message mesg) {
    TextMessage tmesg = (TextMessage) mesg;
    String text = tmesg.getText();
    // do something ...
  }
}

// The startup process is a tedious bootstrap
// process until we get the TopicSubscriber object.
// Then we set the listener as an instance of the
// MyListener class

Properties env = new Properties();
InitialContext jndi = new InitialContext(env);
TopicConnectionFactory factory =
  (TopicConnectionFactory) jndi.lookup("MyBroker");
TopicConnection conn =
  factory.createTopicConnection(username, password);
TopicSession subSess =
```

```
conn.createTopicSession(false, Session.AUTO_ACKNOWLEDGE);
Topic tosub = (Topic)jndi.lookup("Interesting topic");
TopicSubscriber subscriber = subSess.createSubscriber(tosub);
subscriber.setMessageListener(new MyListener());
conn.start();
```

10.2.3   Point-to-Point Model

In the point-to-point model, the message Destinations are Queues. Multiple senders and receivers can connect to a queue. But each message in the queue is consumed only once. Once a message is delivered to a receiver, it is removed from the queue (see Figure 10.2).

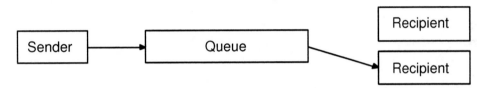

Figure 10.2. The point-to-point messaging model.

Code snippets in Listings 10.3 and 10.4 illustrate how to work with point-to point-message queues. Notice how strikingly similar they are compared with listings 10.1 and 10.2.

Listing 10.3. A JMS queue sender in action

```
// The startup process is a tedious bootstrap
// process until we get the QueueSender object

Properties env = new Properties();
InitialContext jndi = new InitialContext(env);
QueueConnectionFactory factory =
  (QueueConnectionFactory) jndi.lookup("MyBroker");
QueueConnection conn =
  factory.createQueueConnection(username, password);
QueueSession sendSess =
  conn.createQueueSession(false, Session.AUTO_ACKNOWLEDGE);
Queue toque = (Queue)jndi.lookup("My queue");
QueueSender sender = sendSess.createSender(toque);
conn.start();
```

```
// Now, let's send a message!

StreamMessage mesg = sendSess.createStreamMessage();
mesg.writeString("something important");
mesg.writeFloat( 123.45 );
// complete writing your message content
// mesg.setJMSReplyTo( replyTopic );
sender.send(mesg, DeliveryMode.PERSISTENT,
                  Message.DEFAULT_PRIORITY, 18000);
```

Listing 10.4. A JMS queue receiver in action

```
// Provide an implementation of the listener
public class MyListener implements MessageListener {
  public MyListener () { }

  // This is the only method we need to implement
  public void onMessage (Message mesg) {
    TextMessage tmesg = (TextMessage) mesg;
    String text = tmesg.getText();
    // do something ...
  }
}

// The startup process is a tedious bootstrap
// process until we get the QueueReceiver object.
// Then we set the listener as an instance of the
// MyListener class

Properties env = new Properties();
InitialContext jndi = new InitialContext(env);
QueueConnectionFactory factory =
  (QueueConnectionFactory) jndi.lookup("MyBroker");
QueueConnection conn =
  factory.createQueueConnection(username, password);
QueueSession recSess =
  conn.createQueueSession(false, Session.AUTO_ACKNOWLEDGE);
Queue recque = (Queue)jndi.lookup("Interesting topic");
QueueReceiver receiver = recSess.createReceiver(recque);
receiver.setMessageListener(new MyListener());
conn.start();
```

10.2.4   Combine the Two Messaging Models

The publish-subscribe and point-to-point messaging models often work together. For example, in a marketplace application, sellers send out multicast messages to buyers who subscribe to certain topics. Interested buyers can get back to the seller via the specified queues.

Although JMS is a powerful and standard tool for enterprise messaging, it is designed for the J2EE platform. Most JMS providers are hence too heavy for mobile applications. The next two sections introduce two mobile JMS or JMS-like solution providers: iBus//Mobile from Softwired and WebSphere MQ Everyplace from IBM.

10.3   Mobile JMS from iBus//Mobile

iBus//Mobile (v3.0) is a JMS-based mobile MOM solution. It contains a standalone JMS server that runs on gateway computers (PCs). The real value of iBus//Mobile is its extensive clientside library that runs on mobile devices and supports all popular mobile network protocols.

iBus//Mobile provides lightweight JMS client libraries for all J2ME platforms and a special JMS-like lightweight client for the MIDP. Nonprogrammable devices with native SMS, email, or WAP clients are also supported.

The iBus//Mobile server manages message queues and topics. It can also serve as a gateway to fully JMS-compatible J2EE application servers. Now, let's look at iBus//Mobile's extensive client library.

10.3.1   J2ME JMS Clients

iBus//Mobile provides JMS client libraries for all J2ME platforms, including CDC, PersonalJava, and MIDP. Since the javax.jms package is supported, any existing JMS application can be ported to mobile devices with minimum effort. However, since the iBus//Mobile client does not run in the J2EE environment, it does not have access to JNDI services. Hence, any JNDI-dependent initialization code must be changed to conform to the iBus//Mobile API.

Listing 10.5 demonstrates how to initialize a JMS connection from the client side. The ProtocolStackRegistry class specifies the protocol-dependent message transport, iBus//Mobile gateway URL, and QoS settings. The code snippet is based on the MIDP Queue Producer sample distributed with iBus//Mobile download.

Listing 10.5. iBus//Mobile JMS connection initialization

```
private QueueConnectionFactory qcf_;
private QueueConnection connection_;
private QueueSession session_;
private Queue queue_;
private QueueSender sender_;
public TextMessage msg_;
public String url_ = "socket://gatewayIP:8738";

public void initJms() {
  try {
    ProtocolStackRegistry.registerQos(
         "qos-tcp",
         url_,
         new Hashtable(),
         "mySessionId"
    );
    Hashtable jndiEnv = new Hashtable();
    jndiEnv.put(Context.INITIAL_CONTEXT_FACTORY,
"ch.softwired.mobileibus.jndi.InitialContextFactory"
    );
    jndiEnv.put(
  ch.softwired.mobileibus.jndi.Context.QOS_NAME,
      "qos-tcp");
    Context ctx = new InitialContext(jndiEnv);

    QueueConnectionFactory qcf_ =
      (QueueConnectionFactory)ctx.lookup(
          "QueueConnectionFactory");
    connection_ = qcf_.createQueueConnection();
    connection_.setClientID("myClientId");
    session_ =
      connection_.createQueueSession(false,
            QueueSession.AUTO_ACKNOWLEDGE);
    queue_ = (Queue)ctx.lookup("queue");
    sender_ = session_.createSender(queue_);
    connection_.start();
  } catch (Exception e) {
    System.out.println("Error: " + e.toString());
  }
}
```

10.3.2   The Lightweight Client for MIDP

Although iBus//Mobile's J2ME JMS client libraries run on MIDP, it is still
too big for some low-end devices. For those devices, iBus//Mobile provides
a lightweight JMS-like API called JmsLc. JmsLc also works on the MIDP
platform. The use of JmsLc is very simple if you are familiar with basic
concepts of JMS. Code Listings 10.6, 10.7, and 10.8 demonstrate how to
initialize a new connection and send and receive messages using JmsLc. All
code examples are based on the JmsLc tutorial sample application bundled
in the iBus//Mobile download.

Listing 10.6. Initialize a JMS connection using JmsLc

```
public void initJms() {
  try {
    jmsLcConnector_ =
      new JmsLcConnector(url_, debugMode_);

  } catch (JmsLcException ex) {
    // Handle the error
  }
}
```

Listing 10.7. Send a message to the queue using JmsLc

```
public void sendToQueue() {
  JmsLcTextMessage aTextMessage = null;

  try {
    aTextMessage = jmsLcConnector_.createTextMessage();
    aTextMessage.setText(MESSAGE_TEXT_ + msgNumber_);
    jmsLcConnector_.sendToQueue(DESTINATION_NAME_,
                      aTextMessage, new Hashtable());
    msgNumber_++;
    displayMessageTextBox("Send message:", aTextMessage.getText());
  } catch (JmsLcException ex) {
    // Handle error
  }
}
```

Listing 10.8. Receive a message from the queue using JmsLc

```
public void receiveFromQueue() {
  try {
    IJmsLcMessage receivedMessage =
      jmsLcConnector_.receiveFromQueue(
        DESTINATION_NAME_, 10000, new Hashtable());

    if (receivedMessage != null) {
      if ( receivedMessage instanceof JmsLcTextMessage) {
        JmsLcTextMessage aTextMessage =
                (JmsLcTextMessage)receivedMessage;
        displayMessageTextBox("Rec. message:", aTextMessage.getText());
    } else {
      // Handle non-text message
    }
  } catch (JmsLcException ex) {
      // Handle error
  }
}
```

10.3.3 Non-Programmable Clients

In addition to smart J2ME devices, iBus//Mobile middleware server also
supports non-programmable devices. Since there is no way to make API
calls, those devices use code words buried inside the message content to
trigger appropriate delivery actions on the server side. We can define special
mappings between message prefixes and message queues in the iBus//Mobile
serverside configure file. For example, we can associate the SX prefix to a
queue that is connected to a stock quote producer. In this case, if a user
sends "SX IBM" in an SMS message, he will receive a return SMS message
of the current IBM stock quote. iBus//Mobile server supports the following
native messaging clients.

- *SMS:* The iBus//Mobile server connects to an SMS service center op-
  erated by the wireless carrier or an SMS-enabled smart phone via a
  cable.

- *Email:* The iBus//Mobile server connects to SMTP, POP3, and IMAP
  mail servers.

- *WAP:* Through a WAP servlet residing on a WML server, iBus//Mobile receives messages from WML form submissions and sends messages as WML responses to WAP clients.

For more information on iBus//Mobile's native device/protocol support, please refer to its documentation.

10.4   The IBM WebSphere MQ Everyplace

The IBM WebSphere MQ Everyplace (or, MQseries Everyplace: WMQe) is another mobile MOM server. The version of WMQe covered in this book is v2.0. It provides a set of JMS-like APIs in the com.ibm.mqe package. The WMQe API supports features beyond the JMS specification, such as message compression and built-in encryption. In addition, it supports a rich set of server administration APIs. For example, it allows the developer to manage queues and server settings programmatically. WMQe supports JMS through an optional adapter JAR file.

10.4.1   A Truly Mobile MOM Solution

WMQe runs on Windows, Linux, and many flavors of UNIX OSs. But like the IBM SMF (see Chapter 4) and DB2e (DB2 Everyplace; see Chapter 11), its most distinguished feature is that the WMQe server also runs on mobile devices! This allows the ultimate mobility for the middleware server and the mobile network it serves. WMQe runs natively on major mobile platforms, including PocketPC, Symbian OS, Palm OS, Embedded Linux, and QNX. It also runs on any device that supports PersonalJava or IBM's WebSphere Micro Environment. One of those Java environments is required for the Java API to work.

The portable WMQe server allows a TV settop box or a PDA to be the messaging gateway for other pervasive devices in the in-home or in-hand network. WMQe can be integrated with SMF and DB2e to build sophisticated mobile enterprise applications. As we discussed in section 4.5, locally placed mobile middleware can drastically improve overall system performance, availability, and reliability.

Now, let's have a look at the HelloWorld example bundled in the WMQe distribution. It covers some simple administration APIs of WMQe and highlights the differences between WMQe and JMS.

WMQe on Mobile Phones

Fully featured WMQe server runs on PersonalJava and CDC/FP devices, but
not on CLDC/MIDP devices. On those low-end devices, we can only run
WMQe client with a limited number of compressors and encryptors.

10.4.2   HelloWorld Code Walk Through

The HelloWorld example demonstrates how to use a queue manager to send
and receive simple messages. The underlying persistence mechanism for messages is the local file system. The queue manager and its queues (message,
system, and administration) are all stored in a directory. First, we have to
configure the queue manager. Listing 10.9 illustrates how to set up and initialize the appropriate file system directory and files for the queue manager.

Listing 10.9. Configure the queue manager

```
String queueManagerName = "HelloWorldQM";
String baseDirectoryName = "./QueueManagers/" + queueManagerName;

// Create all the configuration information needed
// to construct the queue manager in memory.
MQeFields config = new MQeFields();

// Construct the queue manager section parameters.
MQeFields queueManagerSection = new MQeFields();

queueManagerSection.putAscii(MQeQueueManager.Name,
                             queueManagerName);
config.putFields(MQeQueueManager.QueueManager,
            queueManagerSection);

// Construct the registry section parameters.
// In this example, we use a public registry.
MQeFields registrySection = new MQeFields();

registrySection.putAscii(MQeRegistry.Adapter,
       "com.ibm.mqe.adapters.MQeDiskFieldsAdapter");
registrySection.putAscii(MQeRegistry.DirName,
       baseDirectoryName + "/Registry");

config.putFields("Registry", registrySection);
```

```
// Construct a queue manager configuration
// utility object.
MQeQueueManagerConfigure configurator =
  new MQeQueueManagerConfigure(config,
    "com.ibm.mqe.adapters.MQeDiskFieldsAdapter" +
    ":" + baseDirectoryName + "/Queues");

// Define a queue manager.
configurator.defineQueueManager();

// Define some queues on the queue manager.
configurator.defineDefaultAdminQueue();
configurator.defineDefaultAdminReplyQueue();
configurator.defineDefaultDeadLetterQueue();
configurator.defineDefaultSystemQueue();

// Close the queue manager configuration utility.
configurator.close();
```

After the underlying disk files are properly initiated and configured, we can start the queue manager (Listing 10.10). We have to pass the configured directory to the **MQeQueueManager** object.

Listing 10.10. Start the queue manager

```
String queueManagerName = "HelloWorldQM";
String baseDirectoryName = "./QueueManagers/" + queueManagerName;

// Create all the configuration information
// needed to construct the queue manager in memory.
MQeFields config = new MQeFields();

// Construct the queue manager section parameters.
MQeFields queueManagerSection = new MQeFields();

queueManagerSection.putAscii(MQeQueueManager.Name,
                             queueManagerName);
config.putFields(MQeQueueManager.QueueManager,
                 queueManagerSection);

// Construct the registry section parameters.
// In this example, we use a public registry.
MQeFields registrySection = new MQeFields();
```

```
registrySection.putAscii(MQeRegistry.Adapter,
    "com.ibm.mqe.adapters.MQeDiskFieldsAdapter");
registrySection.putAscii(MQeRegistry.DirName,
        baseDirectoryName + "/Registry");

config.putFields("Registry", registrySection);

myQueueManager = new MQeQueueManager();
myQueueManager.activate(config);
```

Now, using the **MQeQueueManager** instance, the client application can create queues and send out messages. Listing 10.11 demonstrates both sending and receiving messages via the system default queue.

Listing 10.11. Send and receive a message via the default queue

```
public void put() throws Exception {

  MQeMsgObject msg = new MQeMsgObject();

  // Add my hello world text to the message.
  msg.putUnicode("myFieldName", "Hello World!");

  myQueueManager.putMessage(queueManagerName,
    MQe.System_Default_Queue_Name, msg, null, 0L);
}

public void get() throws Exception {

  MQeMsgObject msg = myQueueManager.getMessage(queueManagerName,
                                MQe.System_Default_Queue_Name,
                                             null, null, 0L);

  if (msg != null) {
    if (msg.contains("myFieldName")) {
      String textGot = msg.getUnicode("myFieldName");
      System.out.println(
        "Message contained the text '" + textGot + "'");
    }
  }
}
```

The shutdown process involves closing the queue manager object and removing the underlying files (Listing 10.12).

Listing 10.12. Shutdown the queue manager and delete underlying files

---

```
// Close the queue manager
myQueueManager.closeQuiesce(QUIESCE_TIME);
myQueueManager = null;

// Delete the configured directory.
String queueManagerName = "HelloWorldQM";
String baseDirectoryName = "./QueueManagers/" + queueManagerName;

// Create all the configuration information needed
// to construct the queue manager in memory.
MQeFields config = new MQeFields();
// Construct the queue manager section parameters.
MQeFields queueManagerSection = new MQeFields();

queueManagerSection.putAscii(MQeQueueManager.Name,
                             queueManagerName);
config.putFields(MQeQueueManager.QueueManager,
                queueManagerSection);

// Construct the registry section parameters.
// In this example, we use a public registry.
MQeFields registrySection = new MQeFields();

registrySection.putAscii(MQeRegistry.Adapter,
      "com.ibm.mqe.adapters.MQeDiskFieldsAdapter");
registrySection.putAscii(MQeRegistry.DirName,
      baseDirectoryName + "/Registry");

config.putFields("Registry", registrySection);

System.out.println("Queue manager " +
    queueManagerName + " will now be deleted.");

MQeQueueManagerConfigure configurator =
    new MQeQueueManagerConfigure();

configurator.activate(config,
      "com.ibm.mqe.adapters.MQeDiskFieldsAdapter"
      + ":" + baseDirectoryName + "/Queues");
```

```
// Remove the configured entries for the queues
// we defined.
configurator.deleteSystemQueueDefinition();
configurator.deleteDeadLetterQueueDefinition();
configurator.deleteAdminReplyQueueDefinition();
configurator.deleteAdminQueueDefinition();
// Remove the queue manager itself.
configurator.deleteQueueManagerDefinition();
configurator.close();
```

10.4.3   Storage Adapters

Adapters map WMQe's high-level messaging concepts to underlying, concrete implementations. In the above example, we used the MQeDiskFieldsAdapter class to persist message queues to disk files. A disk file system is not available on all J2ME devices. Even for devices that support disk files, they might not be the most efficient persistence storage. Other persistence mechanisms must be supported if WMQe is to run efficiently on a large variety of devices. All storage adapters inherit from the MQeAdapter class. Table 10.2 lists the methods the storage adapters could override.

| Table 10.2. Methods in the MQeAdapter Class |

Method	Description
activate	Initiates and activates an adapter. It is used only once in the life cycle.
open	Opens an adapter for use.
control	Defines the behaviors of the adapter.
close	Closes an adapter.

WMQe bundles the following standard storage adapters (Table 10.3). Custom storage adapters can be developed by directly subclassing the MQeAdapter class.

10.4.4   The Administration Queue

Any queue manager can be configured at runtime through a special administration queue. Basically, the user or developer can send specially format-

---
Table 10.3. Standard Storage Adapters

Adaptor	Description
MQeDiskFieldsAdapter	Persists messages to disk files.
MQeMappingAdapter	Enables the use of long file names but maps those long file names to shorter formats (e.g., 8.3 format).
MQeMemoryFieldsAdapter	Persists data to memory.
MQeMidpFieldsAdapter	Persists data to MIDP RMS record stores.

---

ted messages to the administration queue and the queue manager will act accordingly.

For example, in the Hello World sample, we only demonstrated how to pass messages through a local queue. Through the administration queue, we can configure the queue manager to manipulate a remote queue or listen for incoming messages at a specified server port (Listing 10.13). We can see that WMQe provides convenient ways to encrypt and compress remote messages for the best security and performance.

Listing 10.13. Administration messages for remote queues and message
                 listeners

```
// Create a connection from this queue manager
// to a remote queue manager
public void createConnection (String onQMgr,
          String name, String parms,
          String options) throws Exception {

  // TCP/IP adapter
  String adapter = "com.ibm.mqe.adapters.MQeTcpipHistoryAdapter";
  // Or MIDP HTTP adapter for MIDP clients
  // String adapter = "com.ibm.mqe.adapters.MQeMidpHttpAdapter";

  MQeConnectionAdminMsg msg = new MQeConnectionAdminMsg();
  MQeFields msgTest = primeAdminMsg(onQMgr, msg);
  msg.setName(name);

  // Set the admin action to create a new queue
  msg.create(adapter, parms, options,
      "DefaultChannel", "Route to: " + name);
```

```java
  MQeAdminMsg respMsg = processAdminMsg(onQMgr, msg);
  checkAdminReply(respMsg);
}

// Create a remote listener for the queue manager
public void createListener (String listenerName) throws Exception {
  // Part 1 - Create the listener

  MQeCommunicationsListenerAdminMsg msg =
    new MQeCommunicationsListenerAdminMsg();
  MQeFields msgTest =
    primeAdminMsg(queueManager.getName(), msg);

  String listenAdapter =
    "com.ibm.mqe.adapters.MQeTcpipHistoryAdapter";
  int listenPort = 8092;

  msg.setName(listenerName);
  msg.create(listenAdapter, listenPort);

  // Send the admin message, wait for a reply
  // and check for success.
  MQeAdminMsg respMsg = processAdminMsg(queueManager.getName(), msg);
  checkAdminReply(respMsg);

  // Part 2 - Start the listener

  msg = new MQeCommunicationsListenerAdminMsg();
  MQeFields msgTest2 = primeAdminMsg(queueManager.getName(), msg);

  msg.setName(listenerName);
  msg.start();

  respMsg =
    processAdminMsg(queueManager.getName(), msg);
  checkAdminReply(respMsg);
}

// Create a remote queue
public void createRemoteQueue( String onQMgr,
        String qm, String q, boolean sync,
        String compressor, String cryptor)
                          throws Exception {

  MQeRemoteQueueAdminMsg msg = new MQeRemoteQueueAdminMsg();
```

```
  primeAdminMsg(onQMgr, msg);
  msg.setName(qm, q);

  // Define the parameters of the new queue using
  // an MQeFields object
  MQeFields parms = new MQeFields();

  parms.putUnicode(MQeQueueAdminMsg.Queue_Description,
    "Remote Queue " + q + " on qm " + onQMgr);

  // Add cryptor and/or compressor if required
  if (compressor != null) {
    parms.putAscii(MQeQueueAdminMsg.Queue_Compressor, compressor);
  }

  if (cryptor != null) {
    parms.putAscii(MQeQueueAdminMsg.Queue_Cryptor, cryptor);
  }

  // Set queue as being accessed synchronously
  // or asynchronously
  if (sync) {
    parms.putByte(MQeQueueAdminMsg.Queue_Mode,
        MQeQueueAdminMsg.Queue_Synchronous);
  } else {
    parms.putByte(MQeQueueAdminMsg.Queue_Mode,
        MQeQueueAdminMsg.Queue_Asynchronous);
  }

  // Set the admin action to create a new queue
  // with these parameters and send it
  msg.create(parms);
  MQeAdminMsg respMsg = processAdminMsg(onQMgr, msg);
  checkAdminReply(respMsg);
}

// Two utility methods for sending the receiving
// administration messages

// Give the message a unique identifier
public MQeFields primeAdminMsg(String onQMgr,
            MQeAdminMsg msg) throws Exception {
  // Set the target queue manager that will process
  // this message, who to reply to and the 'style'
```

```
// of the message to be a request
msg.setTargetQMgr(onQMgr);
msg.putInt(MQe.Msg_Style, MQe.Msg_Style_Request);
msg.putAscii(MQe.Msg_ReplyToQ, MQe.Admin_Reply_Queue_Name);
msg.putAscii(MQe.Msg_ReplyToQMgr, onQMgr);

// Setup the correl id so we can match the
// reply to the request
msg.putArrayOfByte(MQe.Msg_CorrelID,
    Long.toString(MQe.uniqueValue(), 16).getBytes());

// Ensure matching response message is retrieved
MQeFields msgTest = new MQeFields();

msgTest.putArrayOfByte(MQe.Msg_CorrelID,
    msg.getArrayOfByte(MQe.Msg_CorrelID));

// Return the unique filter for this message
return msgTest;
}


// Process the message
public MQeAdminMsg processAdminMsg(String onQMgr,
              MQeAdminMsg msg) throws Exception {
  // Setup the match field to check for a matching
  // reply message. The correl id is used as the
  // match parameter.
  MQeFields msgTest = new MQeFields();

  msgTest.putArrayOfByte(MQe.Msg_CorrelID,
      msg.getArrayOfByte(MQe.Msg_CorrelID));

  // Put the admin message to the admin queue and
  // return the reply
  queueManager.putMessage(onQMgr,
      MQe.Admin_Queue_Name, msg, null, 0);
  MQeAdminMsg respMsg =
      (MQeAdminMsg) waitForReply(onQMgr,
        MQe.Admin_Reply_Queue_Name, msgTest);

  return respMsg;
}
```

10.4.5   Communications Adapters

In Listing 10.13, we use communication adapters, such as the MQeTcpipHistoryAdapter, to handle underlying message transport over the network. WMQe supports common mobile network communication protocols as message transports. Abstract class MQeCommunicationsAdapter defines a common interface for all communication adapters. Abstract methods in MQeCommunicationsAdapter are listed in Table 10.4. The standard WMQe distribution supplies implementations for several communication adapters support HTTP, TCP/IP, and UDP protocols (Table 10.5).

Table 10.4. Abstract Methods in MQeCommunicationsAdapter	

Method	Description
activate	Initiates and activates an adapter. It is used only once in the life cycle.
open	Opens an adapter for use.
waitForContact	Waits for incoming data.
read	Reads data from the adapter stream.
writeData	Writes a request to the adapter stream.
writeResponse	Writes response information to the adapter stream.
temporaryClose	Closes a nonpersistent adapter. That is, the adapter has to open a new connection every time the open method is called.
close	Closes an adapter.

In theory, WMQe runs on MIDP devices with limited options. But in reality, few MIDP devices have the required memory space and CPU power to support WMQe queue managers. Also, as we have discussed, MIDP queue managers cannot receive messages. A much better approach is to have the pervasive device send and receive messages through its native messaging programs such as the SMS and IM clients. They can then utilize WMQe queue managers running on more capable devices in the local network. WMQe does not provide standard adapters to handle native message transports. If you need to handle SMS/IM messages in your queue managers, you need to write a custom communication adapter, possibly using the J2ME Wireless Messaging API.

Table 10.5. Standard Communication Adapters

Adapter	Description
MQeMidpHttpAdapter	Supports HTTP on MIDP devices. Due to the limitations of MIDP devices, it only supports sending not receiving messages (client only).
MQeTcpipHistoryAdapter	Supports cached TCP/IP connection. It has the best performance and is recommended by IBM.
MQeTcpipLengthAdapter	Supports direct access to TCP/IP streams.
MQeTcpipHttpAdapter	Supports HTTP over TCP/IP connections. It also supports HTTP proxy servers.
MQeWESAuthenticationAdapter	Provides support for passing HTTP requests through WebSphere MQ Everyplace authentication proxy servers.
MQeUdpipBasicAdapter	Supports the UDP protocol.

Detailed discussion of the WMQe API is beyond the scope of this book. Interested readers should download their software (see "Resources") and study the bundled documentation and tutorial examples.

10.5 Summary

In this section, we discussed why messaging, especially asynchronous messaging, is essential for reliable and scalable enterprise mobile applications. Enterprise Java developers can quickly migrate their skills to the mobile space with the help of JMS-based mobile messaging middleware. After a brief review of the JMS API, we covered the basic API uses of two leading mobile messaging middleware: iBus//Mobile and IBM WebSphere MQ Everyplace (WMQe). Both of them run on server computers and support mobile clients. WMQe also runs on J2ME mobile devices and enables local messaging gateways.

Resources

[1] The JMS home page. http://java.sun.com/products/jms/

[2] The iBus//Mobile wireless JMS solution.
http://www.softwired-inc.com/products/mobile/mobile.html

[3] IBM WebSphere MQ Everyplace (WMQe).
http://www-3.ibm.com/software/integration/appconn/wmqe/

[4] The open source JMS project JORAM (Java Open Reliable
Asynchronous Messaging) introduced J2ME support in its v3.6 release
in August 2003. http://joram.objectweb.org/index.html

Part IV

Mobile Databases and Synchronization Engines

Chapter 11

Mobile Database for CDC Devices

CHAPTER OVERVIEW

- Database on the Go

- Introducing JDBC

- Portable and Efficient Code Using PreparedStatement

- Access Stored Procedures Using CallableStatement

- The JDBC Optional Package for the CDC

- HSQL Database Engine

- iAnywhere Solutions SQL Anywhere Studio

- IBM DB2 Everyplace

- Oracle9i Lite

- PointBase Micro Edition

- Example Application: Contact Manager

Data management is central to enterprise applications. Most industry leaders agree that mobile relational databases are essential tools in enterprise mobile solutions. This chapter first explains why on-device mobile databases are so important. Then, it briefly introduces you to JDBC, which standardizes database access from Java applications. A rich subset of the JDBC API is supported on high-end mobile Java devices through the J2ME JDBC Optional Package (CDC only) or PersonalJava. Vendor-specific mobile database solutions are discussed. At the end, we go through an example application utilizing mobile JDBC databases to illustrate the key concepts covered in this chapter.

11.1   Database on the Go

One of the biggest obstacles of WAP-based mobile commerce is the requirement of uninterrupted wireless network coverage. Today's unreliable and incomplete wireless network infrastructure leaves the anywhere, anytime promise of mobile commerce unfulfilled. Fortunately, the widespread adoption of the smart mobile client technology will change this picture and enable new generations of mobile applications.

A key benefit of smart clients is that they can function in the offline mode when the wireless network connection is temporarily unavailable. The offline mode drastically improves the application availability. In fact, most of today's mobile applications primarily work in the offline mode. Users carry their PDAs or barcode scanners all day. They synchronize data with desktop computers only once or twice a day. The disconnected mobile application architecture is a proven success.

To support offline operations, the mobile client must store application data locally. There are great needs for first-class data management tools on mobile devices. Lightweight relational databases are just the tools we are looking for. Compared with linear data storage facilities (e.g., plain file or the MIDP RMS) that come with J2ME standard profiles, relational databases are much more efficient for complex data. Besides supporting highly available offline applications, mobile databases offer the following benefits.

- They can be used to manage user preferences. Extreme personalization is touted as another major benefit of mobile commerce.

- They can provide performance cache to reduce network round trips. This could drastically improve application performance on slow and long latency wireless networks.

The standard API to access relational databases on the J2SE and J2EE platforms is the Java DataBase Connectivity (JDBC) API. To leverage existing developer skills, most mobile database vendors choose to support subsets of JDBC or JDBC-like APIs on J2ME platforms. For the impatient readers, a sample mobile JDBC application is given in Section 11.11 later this chapter. Now, let's have a look at the JDBC API first.

11.2 Introducing JDBC

The JDBC specification defines a set of standard interfaces. Each database vendor is responsible for supplying implementation classes that know how to talk with their proprietary databases. Those vendor-specific classes are called JDBC drivers and they are transparent to developers. Using JDBC to access a database involves several steps:

1. Obtain a **Connection** object to the specific database.

2. Build a **Statement** object from the **Connection** object.

3. Execute a SQL statement through the **Statement** object.

4. A **ResultSet** is returned from the execution.

5. Navigate and retrieve data from the **ResultSet** object.

6. Close the **Statement** and the **Connection** objects.

In Table 11.1, we list JDBC interfaces commonly supported by mobile databases.

11.2.1 A JDBC Example

Now, let's look at the use of the JDBC API through an example. For the sake of simplicity, let's assume that the database table we are dealing with has the following schema (Listing 11.1).

Listing 11.1. Example database table schema

```
CREATE TABLE PersonRecords(
  USERID INTEGER PRIMARY KEY,
  NAME VARCHAR(254),
  ENTRYTIME TIMESTAMP,
  PICTURE BLOB
};
```

Table 11.1. Commonly Used JDBC Interfaces

JDBC interface	Description
DriverManager	Manages the JDBC drivers in older versions of JDBC. It is used to obtain Connection objects.
DataSource	Factory class for Connection objects in newer JDBC versions.
Connection	Represents a connection to a database.
Statement	The interface that wraps around any SQL statement. A Statement instance is produced by the Connection object.
PreparedStatement	The interface that provides backend-independent and parameterized SQL statements. We should always use PreparedStatement instead of Statement when possible.
CallableStatement	Calls stored procedures. It is supported only in high-end databases.
ResultSet	Results table from a SQL query statement. It provides a cursor to access returned rows and fields.
ResultSetMetaData	The schema and other meta information of the result table.
DatabaseMetaData	The schema and other meta information of the database.

11.2.2 Obtain a Connection Object

The code for obtaining a Connection object is slightly database-dependent because we have to load the vendor-specific JDBC driver. Using JDBC v3.0 (or the CDC JDBC Optional Package; see Section 11.5), we can use the following code.

```
VendorDataSource ds = new VendorDataSource();
ds.setServerName("dbserver");
ds.setPortNumber(9980);
Connection conn = ds.getConnection("username", "passwd");
```

The port number, username, and password are specific to the database setup. Most on-device embedded databases are for single user only. If you use PersonalJava, the driver initialization code is slightly different because it conforms to the JDBC v1.2 specification. The database URL string (DBURI) in the code below is database-specific.

```
Class.forName("vendor.specific.DriverManager");
Connection conn=DriverManager.getConnection("DBURI",
                            "username","password");
```

11.2.3   Execute a SQL Statement

Next, we assemble a SQL string and execute it through a **Statement** object.

```
String SQLStr = "SELECT * FROM PersonRecords";
Statement stat= conn.createStatement();
ResultSet rs = stat.executeQuery(SQLStr);
```

If the SQL command is an **Update** instead of a **Select**, we should call the **Statement.update()** method. Method **update()** returns an integer number that indicates the number of rows that have been updated.

11.2.4   Extract Search Results

We can extract data columns from the **ResultSet** object returned from the **Select** query. We can use either the column index or the column name to retrieve data.

```
// Loop through all returned rows
while (rs.next()) {

  int userID = rs.getInt(1);
  // int userID = rs.getInt("USERID");

  String name = rs.getString(2);
  // String name = rs.getInt("NAME");

  Timestamp entryTime = rs.getTimestamp(3);
  // Timestamp entryTime =
  // rs.getTimestamp("ENTRYTIME");

  InputStream is = rs.getBinaryStream(4);
  // InputStream is = rs.getBinaryStream("PICTURE");
}
```

11.3   Portable and Efficient Code Using PreparedStatement

Although easy to use, the **Statement** object is not suited for large volume queries and updates over several different databases.

11.3.1   Problems with the Statement Interface

Using the Statement interface, developers have to hardcode all SQL statements. There are several serious disadvantages to this approach.

1. We have to manually escape all special characters and null values. String presentations of data types like DateTime and TimeStamp are difficult to remember. Also, it is very difficult to hardcode binary content, such as a picture in a blob field, into a SQL text string.

2. Since different databases have slightly different escaping and formatting schemes, those hardcoded SQL strings are not portable.

3. Every time we pass the SQL string to the Statement object, it has to be parsed to an internal data format. It is inefficient if the same statement is reused many times.

The PreparedStatement interface is designed to solve the above problems.

11.3.2   Use of the PreparedStatement Interface

A PreparedStatement object is instantiated with a parameterized SQL template.

```
String SQLTemplate =
  "INSERT INTO PersonRecords " +
  "(USERID, NAME, ENTRYTIME, PICTURE) " +
  "VALUES (?, ?, ?, ?)";
PreparedStatement pstmt = conn.prepareStatement(SQLTemplate);
```

The template is parsed only once and can be efficiently reused. Those ? marks are template parameters that can be specified dynamically at runtime. We use methods setXXXX, where the XXXX indicates supported JDBC types, to assign values to those parameters. For example, we can do

```
int userID;
String name;
Timestamp entryTime;
byte [] picture;

// For every userID, populate the name, entryTime and picture variables

  pstmt.setInt(1, userID);
  pstmt.setString(2, name);
```

```
pstmt.setTimestamp(3, entryTime);
pstmt.set(4, picture);
pstmt.executeUpdate();
```

// End

All the database-specific formatting and escaping will be automatically taken care of by the JDBC driver. We should almost always use the **PreparedStatement** class instead of the **Statement** class unless doing a simple statement only once.

11.4 Access Stored Procedures Using **CallableStatement**

Due to the device and network constrains, mobile database applications need to minimize the operational overhead and fully leverage the database's native optimization. The database stored procedures and the JDBC **CallableStatement** interface are very handy tools.

11.4.1 What Is a Stored Procedure?

A stored procedure is a named group of SQL statements and flow control logic that have been previously created and stored in the database. Stored procedures accept input parameters (IN parameters) just like any other types of remote procedure calls. Stored procedures can also return results by updating the values of some parameters that have been passed to it (OUT parameters). Of course, stored procedures containing query statements also return normal row sets. Stored procedures have the following advantages:

- *More robust*: Stored procedures modularize database access functionalities, which promotes code reuse and reduces the chance for human errors.

- *Bandwidth friendly*: Calling the stored procedure by its name certainly uses less bandwidth than passing the entire sequence of SQL statements.

- *More secure*: A database can be configured to prohibit generic SQL operations but allow only certain stored procedure calls from certain users. This allows fine-tuned access control and helps to ensure data integrity.

- *High performance*: Since a group of SQL statements and their controlling logic are stored together, the database can optimize the execution flow globally. However, most mobile databases on devices do not have this level of sophistication.

11.4.2   Use of the CallableStatement Interface

Using JDBC, we can access stored procedures using the CallableStatement interface, which extends the PreparedStatement interface. We have to first define stored procedures in the database through a database-specific step. The following SQL script defines a stored procedure, addPerson, in an Oracle database. The procedure takes in four parameters: pUSERID, pNAME, pENTRYTIME, and pPICTURE. It adds a new row to the PersonRecords table and returns the total number of rows in the OUT parameter pTOTAL.

```
CREATE PROCEDURE addPerson (
  pUSERID IN INTEGER,
  pNAME IN VARCHAR(254),
  pENTRYTIME IN TIMESTAMP,
  pPICTURE IN BLOB,
  pTOTAL OUT INTEGER
)
AS
BEGIN
  INSERT INTO PersonRecords
  (USERID, NAME, ENTRYTIME, PICTURE)
  VALUES (pUSERID, pNAME, pENTRYTIME, pPICTURE);

  SELECT COUNT(*) FROM PersonRecords;

  COMMIT;
END
```

Then, we use a parameterized procedure call template to instantiate a CallableStatement instance. The ? marks indicate parameters. An IN parameter is set by the setXXXX method inherited from the PreparedStatement interface. An OUT parameter must be registered so that we can retrieve its value after the call. Any parameter can be both IN and OUT. Finally, the procedure call is executed via the CallableStatement.executeUpdate() method.

```
int userID;
String name;
Timestamp entryTime;
byte [] picture;

// Init the CallableStatement
```

```
CallableStatement cstmt =
    conn.prepareCall("{call addPerson(?, ?, ?, ?, ?)}");

// Set IN parameters
cstmt.setInt(1, userID);
cstmt.setString(2, name);
cstmt.setTimestamp(3, entryTime);
cstmt.set(4, picture);
// Register the OUT parameter
cstmt.registerOutParameter(5, java.sql.Types.INTEGER);

// Execute the procedure call
cstmt.executeUpdate();

// If the procedure call returns a ResultSet,
// you can process it here

// Get the OUT parameter
int totalcount = cstmt.getInt(5);
```

Note

Stored procedures are considered to be expensive on the database server side. They are rarely available on mobile databases. But keep in mind that JDBC also allows us to access stored procedures in fully featured backend databases.

11.5   The JDBC Optional Package for the CDC

Due to the resource limits of mobile devices, we can support only part of the JDBC API on J2ME. The CDC JDBC optional package is a rich subset of JDBC v3.0. In particular, the following standard JDBC features are *not* supported.

- Connection pools.

- The ParameterMetaData interface.

- Setting parameters by name in the CallableStatement interface.

- SQL 99 types (the Struct, Array, Ref, SQLData, SQLInput, and SQLOutput interfaces).

- Custom type mapping (the setTypeMap() and getTypeMap() methods).

The J2ME subset of JDBC is supported by most mobile database vendors. In addition to the standard interfaces, vendors provide performance and productivity features to distinguish themselves from competitors. In the next several sections, we look at mobile database solutions from leading vendors.

11.6 HSQL Database Engine

The Open Source HSQL Database Engine project is based on Thomas Mueller's Hypersonic SQL database project. It is completely written in Java and is one of the most widely used Open Source embedded databases. It is included in many J2EE application servers. On mobile devices, HSQL runs on the PersonalJava and CDC/FP platforms.

HSQL (v1.7) provides a JDBC driver that supports 95 percent of the JDBC interface and all JDBC 1 data types. It supports transactions, foreign keys, and even Java stored procedures. Tables in HSQL can reside in-memory or be persisted to disk files. HSQL does all of this with a memory footprint of less than 160KB. HSQL also distributes a database management console for PersonalJava devices (tested on Sharp Zaurus; see Figure 11.1).

Note

For HSQL databases, Java stored procedures are just Java methods (in the database's classpath) that can be called from SQL statements. For Oracle databases, a developer can actually define stored procedures using Java syntax inside the database.

As an Open Source project, HSQL is free for all. You can freely distribute it with your application—this is very handy for mobile applications. Unlike many other Open Source projects, the documentation for HSQL is remarkably good. Commercial support, however, is not available.

HSQL does have shortcomings too. It does not support the entire SQL or JDBC specification; it does not provide database encryption; most important of all, it does not come with a synchronization engine. Database synchronization is essential for enterprise applications (see Chapter 13), and all other commercial mobile databases discussed in this chapter support backend synchronization.

11.7 iAnywhere Solutions SQL Anywhere Studio

The iAnywhere Solutions is a subsidiary of Sybase. According to a 2002 Gartner Group survey, iAnywhere Solutions has a market share of 73 per-

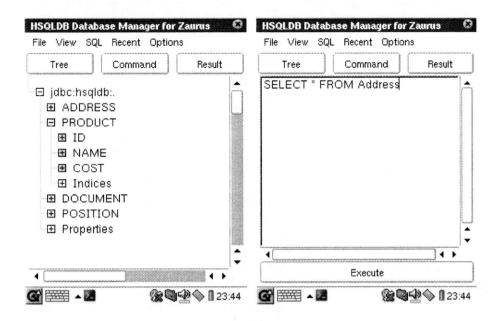

Figure 11.1. HSQL DB's PersonalJava control panel.

cent in the mobile database sector. Much of the market share comes from databases that run on laptop computers. But iAnywhere Solutions also has a formidable presence in the emerging market of databases for devices. The iAnywhere Adaptive Server Anywhere (ASA, v8.0) is a fully featured database product. ASA runs on Windows CE devices all the way up to multiple CPU boxes with 64 GB memory. It supports advanced features such as Java stored procedures, transactions, multiple indices, and encryption. However, the ASA database requires at least 3MB of memory footprint. That is too heavy for many mobile devices.

In reality, almost no mobile client requires all the advanced features provided by the ASA. Each application uses a small but different set of features. The ASA is a *generic* database that tries to satisfy all users. The iAnywhere UltraLite Deployment Option is a highly innovative solution to compromise between features and footprint. The core idea behind the UltraLite option is to generate a custom database for each application. The custom database contains only the exact features the application requires. The UltraLite deployment option has a footprint ranging from 200KB to 500KB depending on the selected features. iAnywhere SQL Anywhere Studio provides excellent tools (Sybase Central administration panel) for custom database generation.

The following brief tutorial is based on the JavaTutorial sample that comes with the SQL Anywhere Studio software. The overall process is illustrated in Figure 11.2.

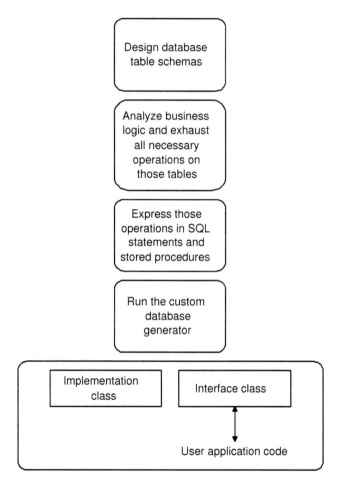

Figure 11.2. Deploy iAnywhere UltraLite databases.

11.7.1   Use an UltraLite Custom Database

The following step-by-step instructions illustrate how to build and use an UltraLite custom database for our mobile applications.

1. Build a reference database (from a SQL script or through the administration panel GUI) on the server side. This database has the same schema as our mobile deployment database.

2. Add all required SQL statements into the reference database through the GUI. Those SQL statements should cover all the database operations that we use in the application. We should also assign each of those statements a name. For example, we can assign a name INSERT_PRODUCT to the following statement.

```
INSERT INTO Product (prod_id, price, prod_name) VALUES (?, ?, ?)
```

3. Run the UltraLite Analyzer command-line tool to generate the custom database in a supported implementation platform. We can generate C/C++ native implementations for Palm OS, Windows CE, Symbian OS, and VxWorks devices. Or, we can generate a crossplatform Java implementation (PersonalJava). In this chapter, we focus on Java databases.

4. The UltraLite Analyzer generates two Java source code files. One file (SampleDB.java) contains the custom database implementation. The other file (ISampleSQL.java) contains interfaces to the predefined SQL statements in step 2.

5. We can obtain a JDBC connection to this custom database using the following code snippet. By default, an iAnywhere UltraLite database is transient: it is erased when the application closes it. The top two lines of code specify that the SampleDB database needs to persist as a file.

```
java.util.Properties p = new java.util.Properties();
p.put("persist", "file");
SampleDB db = new SampleDB(p);
Connection conn = db.connect();
```

6. We use common JDBC APIs to access the database. We should only use SQL commands predefined in the interface file (ISampleSQL.java) to ensure that the application does not reach any functionalities that are not built into this custom database. For example, the following code snippet can be used to add a product entry.

```
PreparedStatement pstmt = conn.prepareStatement (INSERT_PRODUCT);
pstmt.setInt(1, 1);
pstmt.setInt(2, 400);
pstmt.setString(3, "Drywall");
```

11.8 IBM DB2 Everyplace

DB2e is the lightweight device version of the popular DB2 database. In this book, we cover DB2e v8.1. It runs natively on many platforms, including the Palm OS, Symbian OS, PocketPC, QNX, and embedded Linux. DB2e comes with a tool called Mobile Application Builder that allows developers to visually build DB2e applications.

Note

> The Palm OS is not CDC-compatible and does not have standard JDBC support. But the IBM WebSphere Micro Environment (formerly known as J9) for Palm OS provides a JDBC extension. DB2e's JDBC driver works only on IBM's Palm OS Java runtime.

DB2e does not support stored procedures on devices. Its JDBC driver does not support the **CallableStatement** interface. DB2e supports only a subset of SQL types: **INT, VARCHAR, BLOB, DECIMAL, CHAR, SMALLINT, DATE, TIME,** and **TIMESTAMP**. The SQL statements supported by DB2e are listed in Table 11.2. It does not support advanced SQL features such as table JOINs. DB2e supports encrypted data fields and table storage optimization features. We can use the following code snippet to connect a local DB2e database.

```
Class.forName("com.ibm.db2e.jdbc.DB2eDriver");
Connection conn = DriverManager.getConnection("jdbc:db2e:mydb");

// SQL queries and updates etc.
// ... ...
```

In addition to the JDBC interface, DB2e also supports C/C++ native interfaces through the Call-Level Interface (CLI). DB2e is part of IBM's mobile strategy, and it plays well with other IBM mobile middleware tools such as the MQe, SMF, and WebSphere Studio Device Developer (see "Resources").

11.9 Oracle9i Lite

The Oracle9i Lite is Oracle's mobile database product. It runs on Palm OS, PocketPC, Symbian OS, and Win32 platforms. The Win32 edition is intended to run on laptop computers and supports JDBC, multiuser mode, and Java stored procedures. The PocketPC and Symbian OS editions of 9i Lite support JDBC. The Palm OS edition supports only Oracle's proprietary native OKAPI and ODBC.

SQL statement	Function
Table 11.2. SQL Statements Supported by DB2e	
CALL	Calls a remote stored procedure via the synchronization engine.
CREATE INDEX	Creates an index.
CREATE TABLE	Creates a table in a database.
DELETE	Deletes specified rows in a table.
DROP	Deletes a table or an index.
EXPLAIN	Obtains access path information.
GRANT	Grants encryption privilege to a user.
INSERT	Inserts rows into a table.
REORG TABLE	Reorganizes a table to defragment storage usage and so on.
REVOKE	Revokes a user's encryption privilege.
SELECT	Queries the database for a result table.
UPDATE	Updates the table contents.

The Oracle9i Lite suite includes a Mobile Development kit that automatically generates and packages mobile database applications from user custom requirements. Currently, it generates only native client applications.

11.10   PointBase Micro Edition

PointBase (v4.6) is a pure Java embedded database product. It runs on any mobile device that supports J2ME (see Chapter 12 for PointBase Micro's MIDP support). On CDC and PersonalJava platforms, PointBase Micro is just a JAR file that the user application can link to. It is very easy to deploy—you can simply embed it in your application. The footprint of PointBase Micro for the CDC and PersonalJava is 91 KB. The PointBase Micro database does not support stored procedures or the **CallableStatement** interface. In the next section, we look at an example application supplied by PointBase.

11.11   Example Application: Contact Manager

The example is an advanced mobile contact manager application provided by PointBase. The application itself is very simple: It mainly duplicates features commonly found in advanced address books. For example, it allows the user to store contact name, address, and phone numbers with pictures; provides intuitive browsing and searching interfaces; and synchronizes with backend database servers. Figure 11.3 demonstrates the application in action on a PocketPC device running Insignia's Jeode PersonalJava VM.

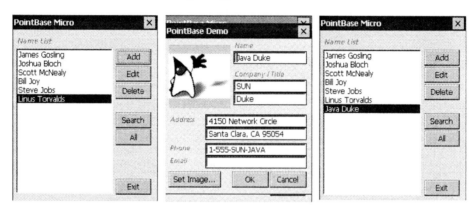

Figure 11.3. Contact Manager application in action.

The clientside application contains a set of AWT UI classes that conforms to the PersonalJava specification. Behind those UI drivers, there is a database access layer and a generic on-device JDBC database layer. Now, we focus on the code in the data access layer, which is contained in a single class: DBManager.

Class DBManager is a singleton class that provides a single point of entry to the database from the application. The singleton pattern avoids threading complexities involved with embedded databases. The code snippet below is the constructor and initialization method of DBManager. It makes a connection to the database, loads the table schema, populates the table with sample data, and creates SQL statement templates (PreparedStatement) for later use. As we can see, everything here is standard JDBC stuff. For enterprise Java developers, the DBManager class (Listing 11.2) should be easy to understand.

> **Listing 11.2.** The DBManager class (Part 1) in Contact Manager

```
class DBManager {
  // DBManager is a Singleton class
  private static DBManager instance;
  private String driver;
  private String url;
  private String user;
  private String password;
  private boolean delay;
  private Connection connection;
  private Statement statement;
  private PreparedStatement insert;
  private PreparedStatement find;
  private PreparedStatement delete;
  private PreparedStatement update;
  private PreparedStatement all;

  static DBManager getInstance() {
    if (instance == null) {
      instance = new DBManager();
    }
    return instance;
  }

  private DBManager() {
    // get parameters from runtime properties
    // This allows us to switch to different JDBC
    // DBs without changing the application code.
    Properties properties = ContactManager.getProperties();
    driver =
      properties.getProperty("driver",
          "com.pointbase.me.jdbc.jdbcDriver");
    url =
      properties.getProperty("url",
          "jdbc:pointbase:micro:pbdemo");
    user =
      properties.getProperty("user", "PBPUBLIC");
    password =
      properties.getProperty("password", "PBPUBLIC");
    delay =
      properties.getProperty("delayread","true").equals("true");
    connect();
  }
```

```
private void connect() {
  try {
    // Load the driver class
    Class.forName(driver);

    // If the database doesn't exist,
    // create a new database.
    connection = DriverManager.getConnection(url, user, password);

    // Create template statement objects
    statement = connection.createStatement();
    createStatement();

    // If the database is newly created,
    // load the schema
    boolean newdb=initDatabase();
    // Load sample data for the new tables
    if(newdb) {
        SampleDataCreator.insert(connection);
    }

  } catch (Exception e) {
    e.printStackTrace();
    System.exit(1);
  }
}

void disconnect() {
  try {
    connection.commit();
    statement.close();
    insert.close();
    find.close();
    delete.close();
    update.close();
    all.close();
    connection.close();
    System.exit(0);
  } catch (Exception e) {
    e.printStackTrace();
    System.exit(1);
  }
}
```

```java
// Create the table and load the schema
private boolean initDatabase() {
  try {
    String sql = "CREATE TABLE NameCard " +
        "(ID INT PRIMARY KEY, Name VARCHAR(254), " +
        "Company VARCHAR(254), Title VARCHAR(254), " +
        "Address1 VARCHAR(254), Address2 VARCHAR(254), " +
        "Phone VARCHAR(254), Email VARCHAR(254), "+
        "Picture Binary(1000000))";
    // if the table already exists,
    // this will throw an exception
    statement.executeUpdate(sql);
    // this means the database already exists
    return true;
  } catch (SQLException e) {
    // ignore the error - the table already
    // exists, which is good
    // so we don't need to add demo data later on
    return false;
  }
}

// create statement templates
private void createStatement() {
  try {
    insert = connection.prepareStatement(
      "INSERT INTO NameCard (ID, Name, Company, Title, " +
      "Address1, Address2, Phone, Email, Picture) " +
      "VALUES (?, ?, ?, ?, ?, ?, ?, ?, ?)");
    find = connection.prepareStatement(
      "SELECT * FROM NameCard WHERE (Name LIKE ?) "+
      "AND (Company LIKE ?) AND (Title LIKE ?) "+
      "AND ((Address1 LIKE ?) OR (Address2 LIKE ?)) "+
      "AND (Phone LIKE ?) AND (Email LIKE ?)");
    delete = connection.prepareStatement(
      "DELETE FROM NameCard WHERE ID = ?");
    update = connection.prepareStatement(
      "UPDATE NameCard SET ID=?, Name=?, Company=?, " +
      "Title=?, Address1=?, Address2=?, Phone=?, " +
      "Email=?, Picture=? WHERE ID = ?");
    all = connection.prepareStatement(
      "SELECT ID, Name, Company, Title, Address1, " +
      "Address2, Phone, Email FROM NameCard");
  } catch (SQLException e) {
    e.printStackTrace();
```

```
    }
  }

  // Other methods
}
```

Other methods in the **DBManager** provide access to the database via simple JDBC API calls. The following code snippet (Listing 11.3) demonstrates methods to search and manipulate name card records. These methods make heavy use of the SQL templates we defined earlier.

Listing 11.3. The DBManager class (Part 2) in Contact Manager

---

```
Vector findNameCardsByKeyword(String name,
        String company, String title,
        String address1, String address2,
        String phone, String email) {
  Vector NameCards = new Vector();
  String[] keywords = {name, company, title,
                        address1, address2,
                        phone, email};
  try {
    for (int i = 0; i < keywords.length; i++) {
      String criteria = (keywords[i].equals("")) ?
          "%" : "%" + keywords[i] + "%";
      find.setString(i + 1, criteria);
    }
    ResultSet resultSet = find.executeQuery();
    while (resultSet.next()) {
      NameCard nameCard = new NameCard(resultSet.getInt(1),
  resultSet.getString(2), resultSet.getString(3),
  resultSet.getString(4), resultSet.getString(5),
  resultSet.getString(6), resultSet.getString(7),
  resultSet.getString(8));
      if (!delay)
        loadPicture(nameCard);
      NameCards.addElement(nameCard);
    }
  } catch (SQLException e) {
    e.printStackTrace();
  }
  return NameCards;
}
```

```
void addNameCard(NameCard nameCard) {
  nameCard.setID(getNewID());
  try {
    insert.setInt(1, nameCard.getID());
    insert.setString(2, nameCard.getName());
    insert.setString(3, nameCard.getCompany());
    insert.setString(4, nameCard.getTitle());
    insert.setString(5, nameCard.getAddress1());
    insert.setString(6, nameCard.getAddress2());
    insert.setString(7, nameCard.getPhone());
    insert.setString(8, nameCard.getEmail());
    insert.setBytes(9, nameCard.getPicture().getBytes());
    insert.executeUpdate();
  } catch (SQLException e) {
    e.printStackTrace();
  }
}

void updateNameCard(NameCard nameCard) {
  try {
    update.setInt(1, nameCard.getID());
    update.setString(2, nameCard.getName());
    update.setString(3, nameCard.getCompany());
    update.setString(4, nameCard.getTitle());
    update.setString(5, nameCard.getAddress1());
    update.setString(6, nameCard.getAddress2());
    update.setString(7, nameCard.getPhone());
    update.setString(8, nameCard.getEmail());
    update.setBytes(9, nameCard.getPicture().getBytes());
    update.setInt(10, nameCard.getID());
    update.executeUpdate();
  } catch (SQLException e) {
    e.printStackTrace();
  }
}

void deleteNameCard(NameCard nameCard) {
  try {
    delete.setInt(1, nameCard.getID());
    delete.executeUpdate();
  } catch (SQLException e) {
    e.printStackTrace();
  }
}
```

```
void loadPicture(NameCard nameCard) {
  try {
    ResultSet resultSet = statement.executeQuery(
      "SELECT Picture FROM NameCard WHERE ID = " +
            nameCard.getID());
    resultSet.next();
    Picture picture = new Picture();
    picture.setBytes(resultSet.getBytes(1));
    nameCard.setPicture(picture);
  } catch (SQLException e) {
    e.printStackTrace();
  }
}

private int getNewID() {
  try {
    ResultSet resultSet = statement.executeQuery(
        "SELECT MAX(ID)+1 FROM NameCard");
    if (resultSet.next()) {
      return resultSet.getInt(1);
    } else {
      return 0;
    }
  } catch (Exception e) {
    e.printStackTrace();
  }
  return 0;
}
```

11.12 Summary

In this chapter, we discussed the need for mobile databases for smart mobile
enterprise applications. Those databases are embedded in powerful mobile
devices or gateway servers. Most databases are accessible from J2ME applications via subsets of the common JDBC interface. The use of JDBC enables
enterprise Java developers to migrate their skills to the mobile space and allows us to switch database providers without changing the applications.

    Since JDBC eliminates proprietary interface-based vendor lock-in,
database vendors have to compete and differentiate their products in terms
of footprint, performance, crossplatform compatibility, and extra features.
Some vendors (e.g., Sybase iAnywhere) provide complete development environments that enable developers to build custom databases for each specific

application. In this chapter, we reviewed the solutions from leading vendors. You should choose a vendor based on your specific application requirements.

Resources

[1] The JDBC specification. http://java.sun.com/products/jdbc/

[2] The CDC JDBC optional package.
http://java.sun.com/products/jdbc/download.html#cdcfp

[3] PersonalJava: Find the supported JDBC API in JDK v1.1 and v1.2 in the documentation. http://java.sun.com/products/personaljava/

[4] The HSQL DB project (check out their Sharp Zaurus page!).
http://hsqldb.sourceforge.net/

[5] The Sybase SQL Anywhere Studio (including Adaptive Server Anywhere and UltraLite Deployment Option).
http://www.ianywhere.com/products/sql_anywhere.html

[6] IBM DB2 Everyplace.
http://www-3.ibm.com/software/data/db2/everyplace/

[7] Oracle9i Lite database. http://otn.oracle.com/products/lite/content.html

[8] PointBase Micro database. http://www.pointbase.com/home.shtml

Chapter 12

Mobile Databases for MIDP Devices

CHAPTER OVERVIEW

- PointBase Micro Edition

- The Oracle J2ME SODA SDK

- The IBM DB2e FastRecordStore

On MIDP devices, full relational databases prove to be too expensive. The standard MIDP does not even support basic SQL types such as the Float type. On the other hand, the standard persistent storage facility (i.e., the RMS) on the MIDP is terribly inadequate for enterprise applications. RMS stores are very slow. They are neither indexable nor searchable. RMS's linear structure makes it a pain to handle relational or object data.

To address this problem, database vendors have developed simple database solutions on top of the RMS. Since those databases are extremely lightweight, full support for the JDBC API is not necessary. Each vendor provides its lightweight proprietary access APIs. In this chapter, we discuss those solutions and APIs.

Note

Database applications on the MIDP are in demand. After all, most corporate PDAs today run the Palm OS, which only officially supports the MIDP as of this writing. In the future, Palm OS devices will run the combination of the MIDP and the PDA optional package, which supports file system operations.

12.1   PointBase Micro Edition

Among all mobile databases, PointBase Micro (v4.5) has the best CLDC/MIDP support. It actually produces a SQL database on the MIDP platform. Point-Base provides a set of proprietary Lite APIs under the com.pointbase.me package to access its MIDP database. The PointBase Lite API is very similar to JDBC. The only thing a JDBC developer needs to know to get started is the URL to obtain a Connection object (Listing 12.1).

Listing 12.1. Connect to a PointBase Micro MIDP database

```
public void connect() {
  try {
    Connection c = DriverManager.getConnection(
              "jdbc:pointbase:micro:" +
              m_dbname, "PBPUBLIC", "PBPUBLIC");
    Statement s = c.createStatement();
  } catch (Exception ex) {
    // Handle the error
  }
}
```

The PointBase Micro Lite database has a footprint of 47 KB. In the Lite API's PreparedStatement and ResultSet classes, the setter and getter methods support only the following types: Int, String, Decimal, Date, and Bytes. The setBytes() and getBytes() methods allow us to manipulate binary database fields (i.e., Blob fields). You can use your camera phone to take pictures and store them in your on-device PointBase MIDP database! For more details, please refer to PointBase Micro documentation and sample applications (see "Resources").

PointBase also provides a utility MIDlet, com.pointbase.me.tools. MicroConsoleMIDP. It allows developers to quickly peek into a database without writing a single line of access and UI code. The console has a simple UI to browse the content and schema of currently available tables. This console MIDlet is especially useful during the testing and debugging stages of application development. We can bundle it into our testing MIDlet Suite to view the database content at real time for diagnostic purposes. Screen shots of the MIDP Micro Console in action are shown in Figure 12.1.

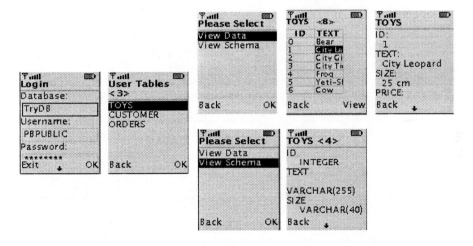

Figure 12.1. The PointBase Micro MIDP Console.

12.2   The Oracle J2ME SODA SDK

The Oracle9i Lite database does not run on the MIDP platform. Instead, Oracle provides a Java object database for MIDP devices. The Oracle J2ME SDK (beta) supports the Oracle Simple Object Database Access (SODA) data store. Built on top of the standard RMS, SODA allows us to store, search, and retrieve Java data objects directly. The oracle.wireless.me.soda package contains six classes (see descriptions in Table 12.1).

Table 12.1. Oracle Simple Object Database Access (SODA) API

Java class	Description
DBSession	It manages the databases and transactions. When you instantiate it, you can specify the maximum number of underlying RMS record stores it uses.
DBClass	It is analogous to a SQL Table in the relational world. It has a name and multiple data fields. DBClass objects can be created using the DBSession.createClass() factory method.
DBAttr	Each data field in the DBClass is represented by a DBAttr object. A DBAttr has a name and a type. The type could be one of the SQL types (e.g., INT, BOOLEAN, STRING) or an array type or a DBObject for a nested Java data object.
DBObject	It is analogous to a row of data in a table in the relational world. The DBObject class defines JDBC style getter and setter methods (e.g., getBoolean(), setString(), etc.) to access its data columns (i.e., DBAttr objects).
DBLoader	It is a helper class that loads data from a text file into DBObjects in a DBClass in a batch.
DBCursor	We can search a DBObject (row) in a DBClass (table) using the DBClass.match() method. Or, we can use the DBClass.createCursor() method to get a set of DBObjects linked to a DBCursor object. We can then navigate through those DBObjects by using methods such as DBCursor.next() and DBCursor.prior().

Listing 12.2 demonstrates the use of the SODA. The code is based on the example included in Oracle J2ME SDK.

Listing 12.2. The SODA demo

```
DBSession sess = new DBSession();

// Create a new DBClass with an INT field
// and a String field.
// The name of this DBClass is "dept". You can
// get it by its name using findClass() method
```

```
// in the sess object.
DBClass dept = sess.createClass(
    "dept",
    new DBAttr[] {
      new DBAttr("id", DBAttr.C_INT),
      new DBAttr("name", DBAttr.C_STRING)
    }
);

// Load a comma delimited database file.
// It will create a number of DBObjects
// under the "dept" DBClass.
DBLoader.loadCSV(dept, new InputStreamReader(in), dept.allAttr());

// Now, get all DBObjects (null match condition)
// in dept class in a DBCursor
DBCursor c = dept.createCursor(null, null);

// Iterate and get all field attributes
// in the DBClass.
DBAttr[] a = dept.getAttrs();
for (int i = 0; i < a.length; i++)
  System.out.print(a[i].name+", ");
  System.out.println();
  DBObject o;
  // Iterate through the cursor and get
  // data in each column (field).
  while ((o = c.next()) != null) {
    for (int i = 0; i < a.length; i++)
      System.out.print(o.getString(i)+",");
      System.out.println();
    }
    c.close();
}

// Remember to release resources.
sess.close();
```

12.3   The IBM DB2e FastRecordStore

IBM DB2e (v8.1) provides a FastRecordStore class over the MIDP standard
RMS record store. FastRecordStore packs several database rows into one
RMS record and supports indexes for fast lookup. This results in much
improved performance over the linear RMS record store.

To create a database table in a **FastRecordStore**, we have to first create the table in a DB2e backend database. Then, we synchronize the table to the MIDP device using IBM DB2e Sync. After the synchronization, a **FastRecordStore** with the same name as the backend table is created. We can now read or update data in the **FastRecordStore** via the **TableMetaData** class. All the changes we make on the MIDP client will be sent back to the backend table upon the next synchronization operation. For more information about database synchronization and the IBM Sync, please refer to Chapter 13, Section 13.3.2.

Note

We cannot start with record stores on the MIDP client first, as they will be deleted on the first synchronization.

In the **FastRecordStore**, each table row is packed into a byte array. Developers are required to manipulate those raw arrays manually. All rows start with a dirty byte and are followed by data in each column according to the following rules.

- If the column is not nullable, the data for the column is present.

- If the column is nullable there is a 1-byte boolean null indicator. If the indicator is **true**, no data follows. Otherwise, the column data follows.

To illustrate the above points, the SQL **INSERT** statement in Listing 12.3 can be interpreted as the Java code in Listing 12.4.

Listing 12.3. SQL script for a sample table

```
create table MyTable (a int, b int not null, c varchar(20),
                      id bigint not null primary key);
insert into MyTable values (null, 10, 'Have fun', 99);
```

Listing 12.4. Java code for the INSERT statement in Listing 12.3

```
DataOutputStream dout = new DataOutputStream(byteArrayOutStrm);
// The dirty byte
dout.writeByte(0);

// 'a' is null, no data follows
```

```
dout.writeBoolean(true);

// 'b', not nullable
// So there is no null indicator
dout.writeInt(10);

// 'c' is nullable, but not null
dout.writeBoolean(false);
dout.writeUTF("Have fun");

// 'id' not nullable
dout.writeLong(99);
```

The following code (Listing 12.5) demonstrates how to iterate through rows, delete a row, and read out data in a FastRecordStore.

Listing 12.5. Browse the FastRecordStore

```
TableMetaData rs = ((MIDPISync)isync).getTableMetaDataByName(sName);
int numCols = rs.getNumCols();
FastRecordStore rms = FastRecordStore.openRecordStore(sName, false);
Index index = new Index(rms, rs);
FastRecordEnumeration enum = rms.enumerateRecords(null, null, false);

// Iterate through rows
while (enum.hasNextElement()) {
  int id = enum.nextRecordId();
  int recSize = rms.getRecordSize(id);
  byte data = new byte[recSize];
  recSize = rms.getRecord(id, data, 0);

  // Example: delete a row
  if (id == rowToDelete) {
    data[0] = ISync.ROW_DELETED;
    index.updateRecord(id, data, recSize);
    continue;
  }

  // Read out each field for each row
  ByteArrayInputStream bin = new ByteArrayInputStream(data);
  DataInputStream din = new DataInputStream(bin);
  din.readByte(); // dirty byte

  for (int c = 0; c < numCols; c++) {
```

```
    int type = rs.getType(c);
    boolean isNullable = rs.isNullable(c);
    boolean ind = false;
    if (isNullable) ind = din.readBoolean();
    if (ind) continue;
    switch (type) {
      case VARCHAR:
        strval = din.readUTF();
break;
      case INTEGER:
        intval = din.readInt();
break;
      // more ...
    }
  }
}
```

12.4 Summary

Data management on small MIDP devices is largely a design issue. For most simple MIDlets, it is probably best to have developers come up with their own data storage and management schemes using standard RMS record stores. That is both cheap and fast for small projects. However, for many complex enterprise applications, using existing toolkits could help increase developer productivity in the long run. In this chapter, we went through MIDP data management toolkits provided by three leading vendors and learned about their use. The notable features of each solution are as follows.

- *The PointBase Micro Edition* provides a set of JDBC-like and easy-to-learn APIs. However, it is relatively large and is slow on the smallest phone devices.

- *The Oracle SODA* is a Java-centric solution and integrates well with Java applications. However, the API is proprietary. Multiple abstractions could make it slow when there is a large amount of data.

- *The IBM DB2e* FastRecordStore is a thin wrapper over RMS record store. It has very good performance and flexibility. FastRecordStore also synchronizes with IBM backend databases, a huge plus. However, the low-level API is difficult to use.

Now you can design the best mobile data management strategy based on the solutions given in this chapter.

Resources

[1] The PointBase Micro MIDP edition and the Lite API.
http://www.pointbase.com/home.shtml

[2] SODA is included in the Oracle J2ME SDK. Download the SDK and
documentation from the following Web site.
http://studio.oraclemobile.com/studio/sites/otn/j2me.html

[3] The IBM FastRecordStore is part of DB2 Everyplace.
http://www-3.ibm.com/software/data/db2/everyplace/

Chapter 13

Database Synchronization

CHAPTER OVERVIEW

- The Synchronized Application Architecture

- PointBase UniSync

- The Hub-and-Spoke Synchronization Architecture

- IBM DB2e Everyplace

- iAnywhere Solutions MobiLink

- Oracle9i Mobile Server

- The Synchronized Contact Manager

Information aggregation is one of the core functionalities of enterprise information systems. Disconnected mobile databases by themselves are not of much use. On one hand, field data from mobile users must be aggregated and incorporated into the enterprise system; on the other hand, mobile users must rely on the backend to keep up with latest updates. The best way to keep database contents up to date is through synchronization. Mobile database vendors offer proprietary synchronization solutions for their databases. This chapter explains the "disconnected but synchronized" mobile application architecture and discusses innovations from different vendors.

13.1   Synchronization and Mobility

Isolated mobile databases are just discrete islands of data packets. Backend databases play an essential role to glue mobile databases together to form a complete IT network.

- Most business processes require field data to be aggregated at the back end for centralized decision making and access control.

- Mobile users need to get periodic data updates from the enterprise back end. For example, a sales representative needs to update his inventory database with new data from the warehouse server several times a day.

- The backend database is a content provisioning hub for mobile databases. This reduces the complexity of distributed data management.

- The backend database is also a backup repository for mobile databases. This reduces the chance of data loss from dead batteries or lost devices.

13.1.1   The Disconnected but Synchronized Architecture

As we discussed in Chapter 11, the need for the backend database does not always justify always-on connectivity. For most applications, the changes on both ends are not time critical and several-times-a-day updates are more than enough. That allows us to design disconnected but synchronized mobile applications. Under that architecture, the backend databases do not need to synchronize every little change at real time. It is a scalable and reliable solution (see Figure 13.1).

The technical challenge for the synchronized mobile database architecture is to develop efficient, secure, and reliable two-way communication channels between mobile databases and back ends. This is where mobile database vendors sell their value-added proprietary synchronization solutions.

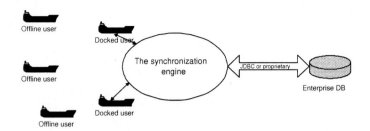

Figure 13.1. The disconnected but synchronized mobile application architecture.

13.1.2   Mobile Database Synchronization

Mobile database vendors offer synchronization engines that synchronize their mobile databases to either their own or third-party backend databases. A typical synchronization engine works as the following. The process is also illustrated in Figure 13.2.

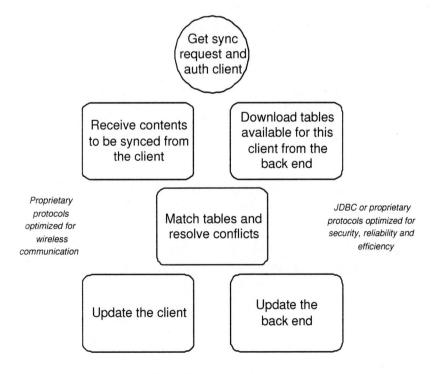

Figure 13.2. The synchronization process.

- The synchronization engine (a.k.a. server) is part of the mobile middleware. It connects to both backend databases and the mobile devices it serves.

- We can configure the synchronization server and specify which backend tables are available (publication) to which users. Filters and custom conflict resolution logics can also be programmed into the synchronization server.

- The synchronization server connects to backend databases using open protocols like JDBC or database-specific protocols. Proprietary protocols allow the synchronization engine to take advantage of database-specific features and optimization.

- Mobile databases connect to the synchronization servers via proprietary protocols. Those protocols take advantage of vendor-specific optimization to reduce bandwidth usage, minimize workload on the device side, and enhance security.

What about SyncML?

Mobile devices often come pre-installed with different sets of native smart applications. Examples are calendars, address books, and contact lists (PIM applications) on smart phones or PDA devices. Those applications often synchronize data with desktop PCs or other central data repositories through proprietary protocols supported by vendor supplied driver software. The incompatible protocols have created a lot of problems for users. For example, it is difficult to synchronize a PocketPC device with a Mac or Linux desktop; if a person owns multiple mobile devices, he must install drivers that could potentially conflict. Users demand a standard synchronization protocol that allows any device to synchronize with any backend application without proprietary driver applications.

SyncML is a standard XML data format that defines the syntax to describe simple PIM data, such as vCard and vCalendar. SyncML has been widely used in enterprise applications. For example, IBM WebSphere Everyplace Access provides SyncML clients to access backend systems such as Lotus Notes and Microsoft Exchange. Important enterprise databases, such as IBM DB2 and Oracle9i, have built-in SyncML support. However, although SyncML is great for PIM type applications, it is not powerful enough to synchronize generic relational databases. SyncML is not the focus of this chapter. But, the standardization process SyncML went through provides much insight into what will happen next in today's proprietary database synchronization solution market.

Since database synchronization is highly vendor dependent, we discuss solutions from different vendors in the next several sections. Detailed discussions on vendor-specific tools and APIs are beyond the scope of this book. Interested readers should refer to vendor documentation and technical support. The source code examples listed in this chapter are only for illustration purposes.

13.2   PointBase UniSync

PointBase provides a pure Java-based, platform-independent synchronization engine called UniSync. UniSync (v4.5) can synchronize enterprise databases (Oracle, DB2, Sybase, and MS SQL Server) and workgroup databases (PointBase Embedded) with PointBase Micro mobile databases. The key concepts in UniSync are hubs and spokes. The synchronization process is as follows:

1. Create corresponding databases and tables on both the backend server and mobile devices.

2. Create a hub on the synchronization server. The hub contains publications that specify the backend tables (or partial tables) available for synchronization (publish).

3. Use the hub object to create spokes. Spokes are objects on the synchronization server representing mobile devices. Each spoke has an ID. It can subscribe to the publications in the same hub through subscription objects. Using a spoke ID, the mobile device connects to the matching spoke and synchronizes to the subscribed backend tables.

4. Start the synchronization server. This basically involves executing the main() method of class com.pointbase.me.sync.Server. The server class is available in PointBase distribution package. There are several ways to run the server in different environments. Please refer to PointBase documentation for more details and example scripts. By default, the server listens at port 8124.

5. Initiate the synchronization process using a spoke ID and spoke stub classes residing on the mobile devices.

Figure 13.3 illustrates the architectural concepts of hubs and spokes.

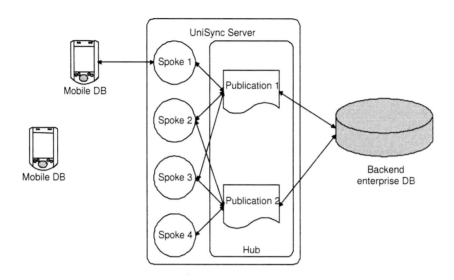

Figure 13.3. Hub and spokes in PointBase UniSync.

13.2.1   Serverside Code Walk Through

Listing 13.1 uses example code from UniSync's basicMicro_to_Oracle sample application to illustrate the synchronization process between a PointBase Micro database and an Oracle backend database. On the synchronization server side, we first create a hub and a publication to expose the tables to be synchronized. Then, we create a spoke that subscribes to that publication. Finally, we run the server at a specific port.

Listing 13.1. PointBase UniSync server application

```
import com.pointbase.unisync.api.*;

// A PB Embedded DB is used by the sync
// engine to store metadata.
String PB_DRIVER = "com.pointbase.jdbc.jdbcUniversalDriver";
String PB_EMBEDDED_URL = "jdbc:pointbase:embedded:HUBDB,new";
String PB_USER = "PBPUBLIC";
String PB_PASSWORD = "PBPUBLIC";

// Parameters to access the Oracle back end
String DB_DRIVER = "oracle.jdbc.driver.OracleDriver";
String DB_URL = "jdbc:oracle:<database>";
String DB_USER = "PBPUBLIC";
```

```
String DB_PASSWORD = "PBPUBLIC";

// Those point to the same Oracle database
String UNISYNC_URL = "jdbc:pointbase:oracle:<database>";
String UNISYNC_DRIVER =
    "com.pointbase.driver.jdbc.oracle.OracleDriver";

// Configuration constants
String DATA_SOURCE = "Data";
String HUB_NAME        = "Hub1";
String PUB             = "Pub1";
String SUB             = "Sub1";
String SPOKE_NAME      = "Spoke1";
String SPOKE_PASSWORD  = "password";

// Tables to be synchronized
String[] tableNames = new String[] {DB_USER + ".NAMECARD"};

// The Sync manager uses a PB Embedded DB for metadata
SyncManager manager = SyncManager.getInstance(PB_EMBEDDED_URL,
                              PB_DRIVER, PB_USER, PB_PASSWORD);

// Get or create a hub
Hub hub=manager.getHub(HUB_NAME);
if (hub == null)
  hub = manager.createHub(HUB_NAME);

// Get or create a backend data source
SyncDataSource dataSource = manager.getSyncDataSource(DATA_SOURCE);
if (dataSource == null)
  dataSource =  manager.createSyncDataSource(DATA_SOURCE,
             UNISYNC_URL, UNISYNC_DRIVER, DB_USER, DB_PASSWORD);

// Get or create a publication of
// the specified tables
Publication pub = hub.getPublication(PUB);
if (pub == null) {
  pub = hub.newPublication(PUB, DATA_SOURCE, tableNames);
  // Make the Publication available to Spokes
  hub.publish(pub);
}

// Get or create a spoke that
// subscribes to the publication
SpokeConfig spoke = hub.getSpokeConfig(SPOKE_NAME);
```

```
if (spoke == null) {
  spoke = hub.createSpokeConfig(SPOKE_NAME);
  spoke.savePassword(SPOKE_PASSWORD);
  // Subscribe to the Publication
  Subscription sub = spoke.newSubscription(SUB,
                    SyncDataSource.DEFAULT,PUB);
  spoke.subscribe(sub);
}

// Start the server at the default port 8124
// or the port specified by command line parameter
// -Dtcp.listenerPort = <Numeric Value>
hub.startServer();
```

13.2.2   Clientside Code Walk Through

On the client side, a mobile device contacts the server to obtain a spoke and synchronizes tables that are subscribed to that spoke (Listing 13.2). The client API works on both the CDC and CLDC.

> **Listing 13.2.** PointBase UniSync client side application

```
import com.pointbase.me.jdbc.*;

// User database parameters
String PB_MICRO_URL = "jdbc:pointbase:micro:SPOKEDB";
String PB_DRIVER = "com.pointbase.me.jdbc.jdbcDriver";
String PB_USER = "PBPUBLIC";
String PB_PASSWORD = "PBPUBLIC";

// How to connect the sync server
HUB_URL = "http://sync.server:8124";

// Constants to define the Spoke name
// and the password
String SPOKE_NAME     = "Spoke1";
String SPOKE_PASSWORD = "password";

// First establish a DB connection to PB_MICRO_URL
Class.forName(PB_DRIVER);
Connection conn = DriverManager.getConnection(PB_MICRO_URL,
                      PB_USER, PB_PASSWORD);
// SyncManager stores temp info in local DB
```

```
SyncManager manager=SyncManager.getInstance(conn);

// Get or create a spoke
Spoke spoke = manager.getSpoke(SPOKE_NAME);
if (spoke == null) {
  spoke=manager.createSpoke(SPOKE_NAME);

  // Save the URL of the Hub, so that the
  // Spoke can communicate with the Hub
  spoke.saveHubURL(HUB_URL);

  // Save the Spoke's password. This should be
  //  same as the one provided in the Hub side.
  spoke.savePassword(SPOKE_PASSWORD);

  // Load the configuration from the Hub
  // This will also create the NameCard table
  spoke.loadConfig();

  // This creates the NameCard table on the device
  spoke.getSnapshot();
}

// Call sync to synchronize the databases
spoke.sync();
```

13.3   IBM DB2 Everyplace

DB2e databases and IBM FastRecordStores (see Section 12.3) synchronize with backend DB2 Universal databases or any other JDBC data sources through the DB2e Sync server. In DB2e v8.1, multiple combinations of synchronization clients, transport mechanisms and backend data sources are supported through the adaptor architecture (Figure 13.4).

- The synchronization client on the mobile device can handle DB2e databases, native PIM lists and files.

- The clientside synchronization engine communicates with the synchronization server via HTTP, WAP or Bluetooth. Both proprietary binary protocols and SyncML are supported.

- The synchronization server supports the DB2 Universal Database, any JDBC database as well as Domino and Exchange servers.

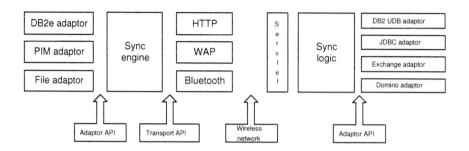

Figure 13.4. The adaptor architecture in DB2 synchronization engine.

We can start the Sync server from the Mobile Devices Administration Center in DB2e's server console. Using the administration center UI, we can create users and subscription sets, associate users with subscription sets, specify encryption levels, and define conflict resolution logic. On the client side, DB2e Sync runs natively on three mobile platforms: Palm OS, Windows CE, and Symbian OS. Using device-native GUIs, a mobile user can login to the Sync server, download the subscription sets, manage subscription sets, and synchronize mobile databases. For more information on how to configure and run the DB2e Sync server and client, please refer to DB2e documentation (see "Resources").

13.3.1 Access DB2e Sync Programmatically

The above synchronization process requires human interaction with a standalone client program. That is not always convenient. DB2e provides a set of J2ME APIs that allow users to access the DB2e Sync server programmatically. Those Java APIs are just JNI wrappers over DB2e's native Sync methods. Listing 13.3 illustrates the use of such APIs.

Listing 13.3. DB2e Sync client application

```
import com.ibm.mobileservices.isync.*;
import com.ibm.mobileservices.isync.db2e.jni.*;

// Get a synchronization provider
ISyncProvider provider = DB2eISyncProvider.getInstance();

// Connect to an IBM Sync server
// "host, port, userID, passwrd"
// specify parameters of
```

```
// the remote IBM Sync server.
ISyncService service = provider.createSyncService(host, port,
                            userID, passwrd);

// Specify a directory to sync into
ISyncConfigStore config = service.getConfigStore("path");

// Manage available subscription sets from
// the client
ISyncSubscriptionSet [] subsets = config.getSubscriptionSets();
for ( int i; i < subsets.length; i++ ) {
  ISyncSubscriptionSet subset = subsets[i];
  // Enable synchronization of all tables
  subset.enable();
}

ISyncDriver syncer = config.getSyncDriver();

// Synchronize. There could be three return values
//
// ISync.RTN_SUCCEEDED: synchronization succeeded
// ISync.RTN_CANCELED: synchronization canceled
// ISync.RTN_FAILED: synchronization failed
int rc = syncer.sync();

// Detailed results for each subscription set
//
// ssArr[i].getStatus() returns:
// ISync.STATUS_READY, ISync.STATUS_COMPLETED,
// STATUS_CANCELED or ISync.STATUS_FAILED
ISyncSubscriptionSet ssArr[] = config.getSubscriptionSets();
for (int i=0; i < ssArr.length; i++ ) {
  System.out.print ("Subscription Set: " + ssArr[i].getName() +
                    " Status: " + ssArr[i].getStatus());

// Close resources
syncer.close();
config.close();
service.close();
```

13.3.2   Sync with MIDP FastRecordStore

As we had discussed in Chapter 12, Section 12.3, DB2e supports a mechanism to synchronize backend databases with its proprietary FastRecordStores on MIDP devices. The following code snippet (Listing 13.4) illustrates the synchronization process. If this is the first time we synchronize, a new FastRecordStore with the same table name will be created and populated with data rows from the table.

Listing 13.4. Using DB2e Sync to synchronize MIDP FastRecordStore

```
import com.ibm.mobileservices.isync.*;
import com.ibm.mobileservices.isync.midp.*;

ISyncProvider provider = MIDPISyncProvider.getInstance();
ISyncService service = provider.createSyncService(host, port,
                                    user, password);
ISyncConfigStore config = service.getConfigStore(null);
ISyncDriver syncer = config.getSyncDriver();

int rc = syncer.sync();

syncer.close();
config.close();
service.close();
```

13.4 iAnywhere Solutions MobiLink

MobiLink is the synchronization engine in iAnywhere Solutions' SQL Anywhere Studio (v8.0, see Chapter 11, Section 11.7). It synchronizes iAnywhere Adaptive Server Anywhere and UltraLite mobile databases with enterprise databases, including Oracle, IBM DB2, Microsoft SQL, and Sybase Adaptive Server Enterprise. Important features of MobiLink are the following:

- Flexible synchronization logic through user-defined sync scripts.

- The synchronization script is written for and stored in the enterprise database, which allows developers to use SQL dialects that they are already familiar with.

- Multiple communication protocols are supported for synchronization streams. Those protocols include TCP/IP, HTTP, and direct serial line.

- Each synchronization operation is a transaction with guaranteed integrity.

- Adjustable parameters (such as cache size, maximum number of threads) for performance tuning.

- Strong security through user authentication and 128-bit encrypted synchronization data streams.

13.4.1 MobiLink via Standalone Native Clients

MobiLink can be manually invoked by native clients on devices. We go through the following steps to complete a synchronization cycle.

1. Create a synchronization username and password through the Sybase Central administration panel.

2. In the Sybase Central administration panel's MobiLink plug-in, select tables that are available for synchronization from backend databases.

3. Write SQL scripts for each sync event. For example, an upload_insert event might trigger a simple SQL INSERT statement, while a download_cursor event might trigger an SQL SELECT statement. We can skip this step and use the default scripts if there is no custom synchronization logic.

4. On the remote (mobile) database, create a publication containing tables to synchronize using the statement CREATE PUBLICATION.

5. On the remote database, create a user and associate a publication with the user through a subscription. Related statements are CREATE SYNCHRONIZATION USER and CREATE SYNCHRONIZATION SUBSCRIPTION. The subscription also contains the synchronization server address and the data communication protocol (e.g., TCP/IP, HTTP, or serial link).

6. Run the remote sync client.

Note

The concepts of publication and subscription in Sybase MobiLink is different from other synchronization engines.

13.4.2 Access MobiLink Programmatically

The MobiLink synchronization client can be invoked as a command-line utility. But for autogenerated UltraLite databases, the MobiLink API is already built in. The following code snippet (Listing 13.5) demonstrates how to synchronize the entire clientside Java UltraLite database.

Listing 13.5. Using MobiLink

```
UlSynchOptions synch_opts = new UlSynchOptions();
synch_opts.setUserName( "userid" );
synch_opts.setPassword( "passwd" );
synch_opts.setScriptVersion( "default" );
// We use TCP/IP socket as the sync transport.
synch_opts.setStream( new UlSocketStream() );
synch_opts.setStreamParms( "host=192.128.10.1" );
((JdbcConnection) conn).synchronize( synch_opts );
```

If you have a homogeneous environment containing only iAnywhere databases, Sybase has another synchronization product called SQL Remote. SQL Remote supports message-based asynchronous operation and is therefore scalable. Interested readers should refer to iAnywhere documentation for that technology.

13.5 Oracle9i Mobile Server

The Oracle9i Mobile Server is part of Oracle9i Application Server (AS). It works with native synchronization clients distributed with Oracle9i Lite databases. The 9i synchronization engine has the following features.

- If our application was created using the Oracle9i Lite Mobile Development Kit, the Mobile Server could automatically generate synchronization logic for the application.

- Oracle9i Lite supports synchronization over any TCP/IP-based network, including HTTP, CDPD, and 802.11b Wireless LAN. We may also add new transports by using the Mobile Server Open Transport APIs.

- The synchronization server provides rich controls over conflict resolution, data subsetting, and security settings.

- The Mobile Server supports asynchronous synchronization. During "rush hours," each device just submits the synchronization content in a queue and leaves. The server processes the queue when it is not busy. The client later retrieves updates from the server from another queue. This allows it to support a large number of mobile devices at a time.

The Oracle Mobile Server synchronization engine is also available programmatically through administration and clientside APIs. However, those APIs are available only in C/C++, not in Java yet.

13.6   The Synchronized Contact Manager

Now, we revisit the PointBase Contact Manager application discussed in Section 11.11. We can use PointBase's UniSync engine to simplify both the data backup and database provisioning processes. Figure 13.5 demonstrates the synchronized Contact Manager application in action.

Using techniques and APIs we learned in Section 13.2, we use class ResetServer to set up the hub, publications, and spokes on the UniSync server. Listing 13.6 shows the relevant code snippets from class ResetServer.

Listing 13.6. Snippet from the ResetServer class to setup the UniSync server

---

```
// Connects to the backend server
manager = SyncManager.getInstance(caturl,catdriver, catuser,catpassword);
String dsname;
dsname=SyncDataSource.DEFAULT;

String hubname="Hub";
Hub hub=manager.createHub(hubname);

Publication pub;
String pubname;
SpokeConfig spoke;
Subscription sub;
String subname="SubNameCard";
String tablename="NAMECARD";
String[] tables=new String[]{tablename};

// publish the complete namecard table
pubname="PubNameCard";
pub=hub.newPublication(pubname,dsname,tables);
hub.publish(pub);
```

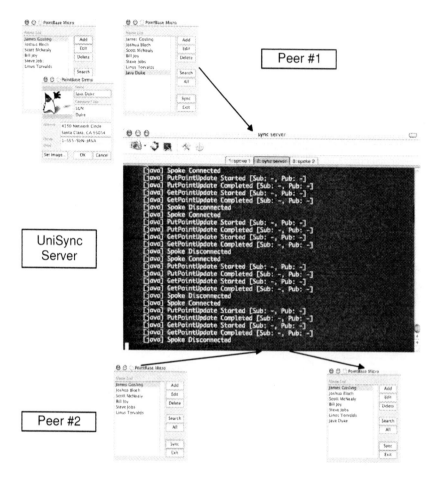

Figure 13.5. Synchronized Contact Manager peers in action.

```
// create two spokes and subscribe
// to this publication
for(int i=1;i<=2;i++) {
  String name="Spoke"+i;
  spoke=hub.createSpokeConfig(name);
  spoke.savePassword("pass"+i);
  sub = spoke.newSubscription(subname, SyncDataSource.DEFAULT,pubname);
  spoke.subscribe(sub);
}

// publish the namecard table; without
```

```
// the picture column

pubname="PubNameCardNoPicture";
pub=hub.newPublication(pubname,dsname,tables);
SyncTable table=pub.getSyncTable(tablename);
table.dropSyncColumns(new String[]{"PICTURE"});
hub.publish(pub);

// create two spokes and subscribe to
// this publication
for(int i=3;i<=4;i++) {
  String name="Spoke"+i;
  spoke=hub.createSpokeConfig(name);
  spoke.savePassword("pass"+i);
  sub = spoke.newSubscription(subname, SyncDataSource.DEFAULT,pubname);
  spoke.subscribe(sub);
}
manager.close();
```

On the client side, since Contact Manager's database access layer is isolated, we mainly need to make changes to the **DBManager** class, and the rest of the application will automatically take advantage of the synchronization features. The following code snippet (Listing 13.7) from **DBManager** demonstrates how to obtain the spoke stub and process the synchronization on the device side. The comments embedded in the code illustrate the differences between the synchronized version and the local version of the application.

Listing 13.7. Refactor the DBManager class in the Contact Manager
example to take advantage of database synchronization

```
// Import proprietary classes for sync
import com.pointbase.me.jdbc.*;

class DBManager {

  // In addition to JDBC connection variables
  // we also need to define variables for sync
  // ... ...
  private Spoke spoke;
  private String spokename;
  private int spoke_id;
  private int spoke_range_start,spoke_range_end;
  final static int ROWS_PER_SPOKE=1<<16;
```

```java
private String syncurl;
private String syncpassword;


private DBManager() {

  // get DB connection parameters
  // ... ...

  // get sync parameters
  syncurl = properties.getProperty("syncurl",
                              "http://localhost:8124");
  String spokeid = properties.getProperty("spokeid", "1");
  spokename = properties.getProperty("spoke", "Spoke"+spokeid);
  syncpassword = properties.getProperty("syncpassword",
                                    "pass"+spokeid);
  url = properties.getProperty("url",
            "jdbc:pointbase:micro:pbdemo"+spokeid);

  connect();
}

// The complete connect method using
// synchronization server
private void connect() {
  try {
    // Connecting to the database...

    Class.forName(driver);

    // If the database doesn't exist,
    // create a new database.
    connection = DriverManager.getConnection(url, user, password);
    statement = connection.createStatement();

    // Check sync metadata and create tables
    loadMeta();

    // Creating prepared statements
    createStatement();

  } catch (Exception e) {
    e.printStackTrace();
    System.exit(1);
  }
```

```
}

// The complete newID method using the sync server
private int getNewID() {
  try {
    ResultSet rs = statement.executeQuery(
      "SELECT MAX(ID)+1 FROM NameCard WHERE "+
      "ID>=" + spoke_range_start +
      " AND ID<"+spoke_range_end);
    rs.next();
    int id=rs.getInt(1);
    if(rs.wasNull()) {
      return spoke_range_start;
    } else {
      return id;
    }

  } catch (Exception e) {
    e.printStackTrace();
  }
  return 0;
}

// Create table and load metadata
// from the sync hub
void loadMeta() {
  try {
    SyncManager manager = SyncManager.getInstance(connection);
    spoke=manager.getSpoke(spokename);
    if(spoke==null) {
      System.out.println(
          "Loading MetaData from url "+syncurl+
          " for spoke "+spokename+
          " using password "+syncpassword);
      spoke=manager.createSpoke(spokename);
      spoke.savePassword(syncpassword);
      spoke.saveHubURL(syncurl);
      spoke.loadConfig();
      spoke.getSnapshot();
    }
    spoke_id = spoke.getSpokeId();
    System.out.println("SpokeID is "+spoke_id);
    spoke_range_start = ROWS_PER_SPOKE * spoke_id;
    spoke_range_end = spoke_range_start + ROWS_PER_SPOKE - 1;
  } catch (SyncException e) {
```

```
      e.printStackTrace();
    }
  }

  // Synchronize spoke databases (mobile databases)
  // with the hub and backend databases
  void sync() {
    try {
      spoke.sync();
    } catch (SyncException e) {
      e.printStackTrace();
    }
  }

  // Other data access methods are the same as the
  // non-synced version.
}
```

13.7 Summary

In this chapter, we introduced a new mobile application architecture: offline but synchronized applications. Synchronization is probably the most used technique to connect wireless devices to corporate networks today. It will continue to be important in the future. We went through tools offered by leading mobile database vendors. The code examples and mini tutorials should get you started on those tools. For detailed information and comprehensive example applications, you can refer to vendor-specific documentation. As database synchronization becomes mainstream, the protocols are likely to be standardized—just as SyncML has done to PIM synchronization today. However, the underlying concepts and technology we discussed in this chapter will remain the same. Near the end of this chapter, we discussed how to refactor synchronization support into the Contact Manager application (Chapter 11).

Resources

[1] The PointBase UniSync server JavaDoc.
http://www.pointbase.com/support/docs/javadoc/UniSync/index.html

[2] The PointBase UniSync JDBC client API.
http://www.pointbase.com/support/docs/javadoc/UniSyncMicroJDBC/index.html

[3] The PointBase UniSync Lite client API.
     http://www.pointbase.com/support/docs/javadoc/UniSyncMicroLite/index.html

[4] IBM DB2 Everyplace Sync Server.
     http://www-3.ibm.com/software/data/db2/everyplace/syncserver.html

[5] The Sybase SQL Anywhere Studio, including MobiLink.
     http://www.ianywhere.com/products/sql_anywhere.html

[6] iAnywhere MobiLink tutorial.
     http://www.ianywhere.com/whitepapers/oracle_asa.html

[7] The Oracle9i Lite, including the Mobile Server.
     http://otn.oracle.com/products/lite/htdocs/o9ilite_datasheet.htm

Chapter 14

Access Backend Databases

CHAPTER OVERVIEW

- Why Remote Database?

- Remote Database Access Schemes

- The Oracle J2ME SQL SDK

- Legacy Applications

- Using Simplicity for Legacy Databases

In Chapter 13, we discussed how mobile applications keep themselves updated via synchronization with backend databases. However, synchronization is not efficient when we deal with frequent (real-time) updates. For many applications, we also need ways to access the remote back end directly. Direct access and synchronization functionalities can coexist in the same application and complement each other. On the CDC or PersonalJava platforms, we can rely on the standard JDBC APIs. But on the CLDC/MIDP platforms, the only option is HTTP proxy servers. In this chapter, we use the Oracle J2ME SDK to demonstrate how to expose simple SQL services via an HTTP gateway.

To migrate existing enterprise applications to the mobile commerce, we need to build mobile clients that can access not only relational databases but legacy databases as well. This chapter explains how to build mobile clients for legacy systems using screen scraping tools provided with the Simplicity IDE tools.

14.1   Direct Access to Remote Databases

In the previous three chapters, we discussed the application architecture of the disconnected but synchronized mobile databases. Although that architecture is adequate for most mobile application scenarios, in some cases, direct connections to remote databases are still preferred or even required:

- Some applications depend on real-time backend data to function correctly. In theory, we can synchronize the databases as frequently as we wish to catch up with the real-time changes, but that would soon become too inefficient. For example, a salesperson might only need to look up the current availability of a specific product. There is no need to synchronize the entire product catalog. It is much better and more flexible to allow the application to query the backend database directly.

- Some devices, especially MIDP devices, do not have enough resources to support large on-device data sets.

- Legacy data on mainframe applications is available only remotely.

Fortunately, the wireless network intermittency and latency, which make always-connected applications impossible in consumer markets, are less a problem in the enterprise markets: Many enterprise users reside on company campus and have always-on, low latency connectivity through WiFi or other company-provided networks. Now, let's have a look at remote database access schemes.

14.1.1   Application-Specific Middleware

In many cases, direct database access only happens inside the middleware layer. The database component is invisible from the client side. The mobile client only needs to know how to integrate with the specific middleware application. This is the approach used in the iFeedBack (see Chapter 3) and Smart Ticket (see Chapter 5) examples. Since this approach is application specific, I suggest interested readers consult those examples to study how it is implemented.

14.1.2   Using JDBC

The JDBC API is a generic way to access relational databases over the network. Some J2ME JDBC implementations allow you to obtain a remote database connection object by supplying a remote URL to the connection factory method. IBM DB2 and Oracle JDBC drivers provide such remote access functionalities. Since JDBC is a well-documented technology, we will not discuss it in detail here. For a quick tutorial on JDBC, please refer to Chapter 11.

14.1.3   Gateway Servlet

Mobile clients, especially MIDP clients that do not support JDBC, can rely on gateway servlets to access backend databases. A gateway servlet takes in a request from the client, queries the remote database, and then sends the data back to the client via HTTP. Commercial products that implement gateway servlets include Oracle9i J2ME SDK and Data Representation Simplicity XML transaction engine. In the rest of this chapter, we discuss how to use those two products to access generic SQL databases and legacy databases.

14.2   The Oracle J2ME SQL SDK

The Oracle J2ME SDK (beta) enables mobile clients to access backend databases through the Oracle9i Mobile Application Server. It works on all J2ME profiles. There are only four classes in the oracle.wireless.me.sql package: DriverManager, Connection, Statement, and ResultSet. Their use is very similar to that of their JDBC counterparts. Those classes contain only very simple and lightweight methods. For example the query results can be retrieved only as string objects.

The SDK connects to a special gateway servlet, J2MEJDBC. The backend database URL and authentication information are stored in the gateway servlet's configuration file. Oracle runs a demo servlet for public testing. A simple example of database query using the SDK is shown in Listing 14.1.

Listing 14.1. Usage of the Oracle J2ME SDK

```
// The example is adopted from the
// Oracle SDK example

// The Oracle test gateway servlet URL.
// The backend DB is configured in the servlet.
DriverManager.init("http://iasw.oracle.com/ptg/j2mejdbc");

// Obtain a connection
Connection con = DriverManager.getConnection();

String sql = "select table_name from user_tables";
// Create a new Statement object
Statement stmt = con.createStatement();
// Get the ResultSet from the sql query
ResultSet rs = stmt.executeQuery(sql);
// Go to the next record
rs.next();
// Get a field in the record
System.out.println(rs.getString(1));
```

14.3   Legacy Applications

For companies with a lot of data on legacy mainframe systems, any mobile commerce strategy requires remote access to the mainframes from either the mobile clients or mobile middleware. However, neither SQL nor JDBC works with mainframe systems. Legacy applications use proprietary wire protocols over TCP/IP raw sockets or even serial lines. We need to hire developers who understand the proprietary protocols and ask them to code the protocol library manually in Java. That is an expensive and slow process.

14.3.1   Screen Scraping

A relatively simple way to access legacy systems without messing with the proprietary wire protocols is to use a technique called *screen scraping*. It works as follows: A *recorder* (or a screen scraper) is a software agent that records every keystroke and all screen displays from a terminal during a period of time. With the recorder turned on, a mainframe user is asked to perform a certain task during an interactive session. The recorder then generates Java code to replicate the same process.

Now, let's have a look at the process the user goes through to search computer inventory in a legacy system. In the first screen (Figure 14.1), the system prompts the user for authentication credentials. In the second screen (Figure 14.2), the user enters the text string *computer* and the systems displays search results. You can use predefined keys (Ctrl-N, in this case) to scroll between pages.

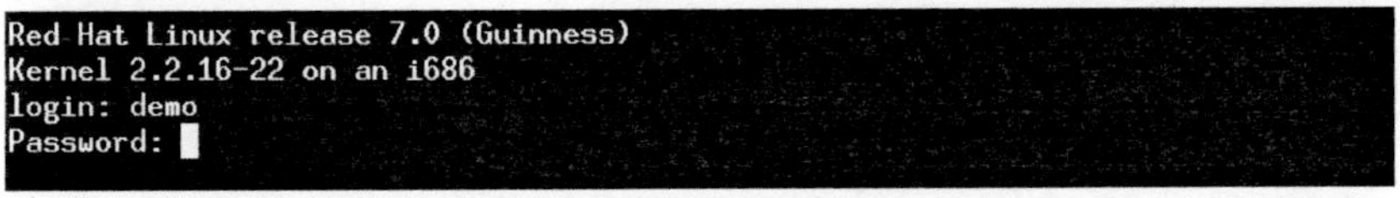

```
Red Hat Linux release 7.0 (Guinness)
Kernel 2.2.16-22 on an i686
login: demo
Password: █
```

Figure 14.1. Search inventory on a mainframe, screen 1.

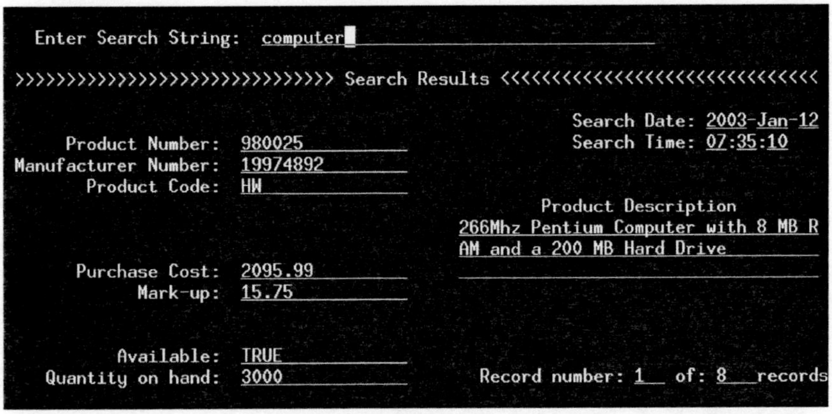

```
   Enter Search String:  computer█

>>>>>>>>>>>>>>>>>>>>>>>>>>>> Search Results <<<<<<<<<<<<<<<<<<<<<<<<<<<<<<<<<

                                              Search Date: 2003-Jan-12
      Product Number:  980025                 Search Time: 07:35:10
  Manufacturer Number:  19974892
        Product Code:  HW
                                                 Product Description
                                           266Mhz Pentium Computer with 8 MB R
                                           AM and a 200 MB Hard Drive

       Purchase Cost:  2095.99
             Mark-up:  15.75


           Available:  TRUE
    Quantity on hand:  3000              Record number: 1   of: 8   records
```

Figure 14.2. Search inventory on a mainframe, screen 2.

The recorder records when and how to connect the server, send out the username/password combo, send out the query string, scroll result pages, and parse needed information from the formatted display screen. Then, it generates a Java stub method that returns search results when invoked with a query string and user credentials. In mobile applications, the stub can reside inside a gateway servlet that interacts with mobile clients through standard HTTP remote procedure call (RPC; for more information, please refer to Chapters 5 and 16). We discuss this scenario in the next section.

14.4 Using Simplicity for Legacy Databases

Screen scraping relies on the recorder tool and code generator. Now, let's take a detour to check out the tool we are going to use: the Simplicity IDE (v1.5) from Data Representations.

The Simplicity IDE is an all-visual Rapid Application Development (RAD) tool. Many IDEs have visual builders for UI components, but Simplicity allows you to build application logic components through the drag-and-drop model as well. Simplicity is written entirely in Java and supports application development for both J2ME and part of J2EE (mostly gateway servlets for mobile clients). We use the Simplicity IDE to demonstrate how to integrate legacy back ends in your mobile enterprise solutions.

Note

This book is not intended to be a comprehensive Simplicity IDE tutorial. The Simplicity software is distributed with sample applications and step-by-step tutorial books.

14.4.1 Simplicity Mobile

The central part of the Simplicity IDE is its visual composer. Figure 14.3 illustrates a fully assembled MIDP application in the Simplicity for Mobile Devices IDE. Besides nodes representing normal MIDlet life cycle methods, you should pay attention to two nodes Transactions and Display. Modules under those two nodes are dragged and dropped from modules palettes, which are also shown on the figure. One strength of the Simplicity IDE is that it provides a lot of preconfigured modules that we can directly use. There are roughly two kinds of modules.

- Modules such as TextBox and Form take care of the view logic. In this composer, Form presents application information to users using MIDP UI components; TextBox maps user input to internal variables. The view modules have functionalities similar to visual UI components found in other IDE RAD tools.

- The Transactions module is part of the business logic. It contains a micro XML parser and can talk with Simplicity Enterprise server via a proprietary XML protocol. It also has a built-in, configurable RMS cache for transactional data. The business logic modules are linked to the view logic modules through internal variables.

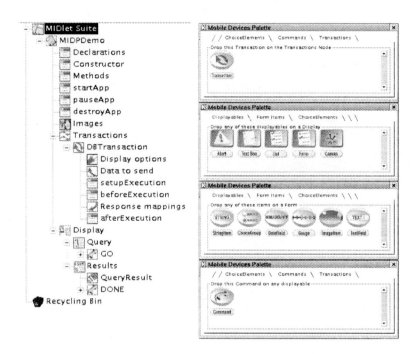

Figure 14.3. An example Simplicity project.

Now, we can use the Simplicity Enterprise IDE to build the gateway servlet for a demo legacy mainframe application. The gateway servlet contains a module that is designed to talk with the MIDlet's Transaction module.

Note

Simplicity Enterprise also allows you to construct JDBC gateway servlets that bridge mobile clients to JDBC remote databases using the same MIDP Transaction module.

14.4.2 Simplicity Enterprise Legacy Rejuvenation

Simplicity Enterprise is a separate IDE from Simplicity for Mobile Devices. Simplicity Enterprise runs its own built-in HTTP server and servlet engine for development. It also bundles a PointBase embedded database for internal use. The application composer in the Simplicity Enterprise IDE looks very

similar to the one in Simplicity for Mobile Devices. Legacy Rejuvenation
is a palette of enterprise modules that help us write legacy gateways. The
legacy palette is shown in Figure 14.4.

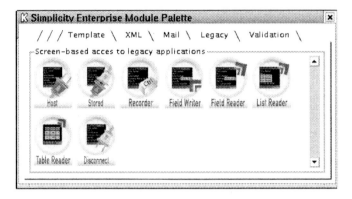

Figure 14.4. The legacy palette in Simplicity Enterprise.

Figure 14.5 shows the structure of a legacy gateway servlet. The modules
are the following.

- The **Form** module processes HTTP requests from clients. It holds references to all the important interval variables.

- The **XML Exporter** module exports interval variables to an XML stream
  that is understood and parsed by the MIDlet side **Transaction** module.

- We use the **HostConnection** module to specify the IP address and connection port of the legacy server. We should also specify the serial
  terminal type that the legacy server supports.

- The **Recorder** module is the user interaction recorder of the screen
  scraper. It contains an emulated serial terminal that connects to the
  server according to parameters set in the **HostConnection** module. Figure 14.6 shows such a screen. The row of buttons above the emulator
  window specify emulated user interactions. For example, we need to
  wait for the *Enter Search String* text to appear on a certain screen position before we send in the search string. We can highlight the Enter
  Search String text in the emulator, click the Wait button, and then
  assign the appropriate wait action (Figure 14.7). Then, we can use the
  Send Text button to send in the search string from an internal variable
  in the **Form** module.

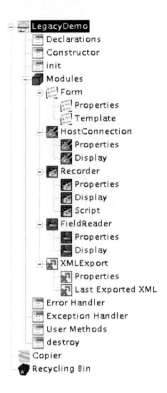

Figure 14.5. Structure of the Simplicity legacy gateway servlet.

- The **Field Reader** module reads information from the emulated screen. For example, if we need to read out the product number, we can highlight the Product Number text; it becomes a textbox, and we assign it a variable name *varProdNum* (Figure 14.8) for use in other modules (e.g., the **XML Exporter** module).

Your legacy gateway servlet is now ready.

Code Generation from Simplicity

The Simplicity IDE generates the source code for you. If you study the source code, you can find out how the modules in Simplicity libraries are used. Then, you can separate the code segments for screen scraping and mobile client interaction. This way, you might be able to use Simplicity Legacy Rejuvenation technology outside of the Simplicity IDE.

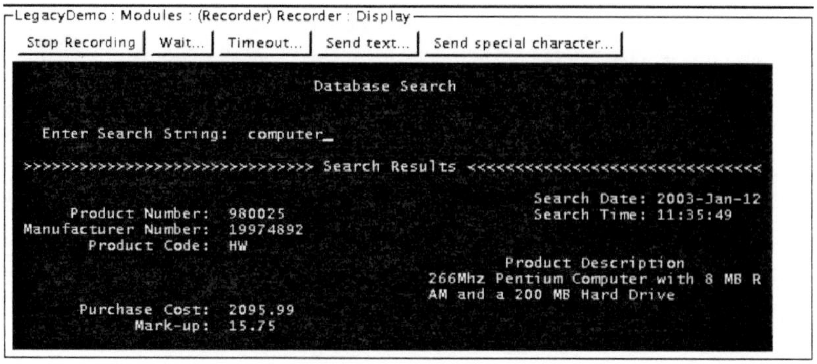

┌─LegacyDemo : Modules : (Recorder) Recorder : Display ─────────────────
│ Stop Recording │ Wait... │ Timeout... │ Send text... │ Send special character... │

```
                        Database Search

   Enter Search String:  computer_

>>>>>>>>>>>>>>>>>>>>>>>>>>> Search Results <<<<<<<<<<<<<<<<<<<<<<<<<<<

                                           Search Date: 2003-Jan-12
       Product Number:  980025             Search Time: 11:35:49
  Manufacturer Number:  19974892
        Product Code:   HW
                                              Product Description
                                     266Mhz Pentium Computer with 8 MB R
                                     AM and a 200 MB Hard Drive

        Purchase Cost:  2095.99
              Mark-up:  15.75
```

Figure 14.6. The legacy recorder, screen 1.

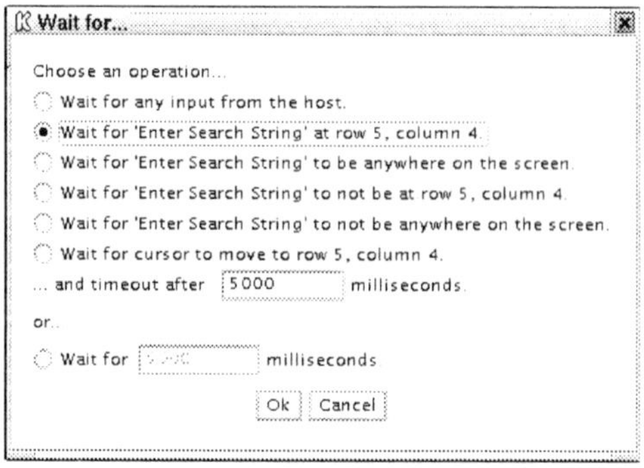

┌─ ⫰ Wait for... ─── ⊠ ─┐
│   │
│ Choose an operation...   │
│ ○ Wait for any input from the host.   │
│ ● Wait for 'Enter Search String' at row 5, column 4.   │
│ ○ Wait for 'Enter Search String' to be anywhere on the screen.│
│ ○ Wait for 'Enter Search String' to not be at row 5, column 4.│
│ ○ Wait for 'Enter Search String' to not be anywhere on the screen.│
│ ○ Wait for cursor to move to row 5, column 4.   │
│ ... and timeout after │ 5000   │ milliseconds.   │
│ or..   │
│ ○ Wait for │   │ milliseconds   │
│   │ Ok │ │ Cancel │   │
└──┘

Figure 14.7. The legacy recorder, screen 2.

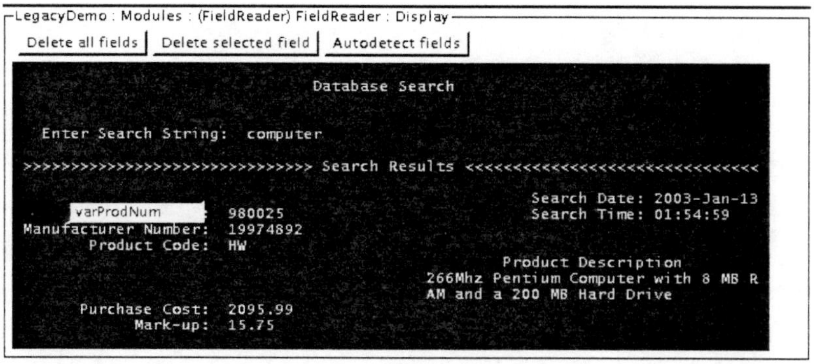

┌─LegacyDemo : Modules : (FieldReader) FieldReader : Display ─────────────
│ Delete all fields │ Delete selected field │ Autodetect fields │

```
                        Database Search

   Enter Search String:  computer

>>>>>>>>>>>>>>>>>>>>>>>>>>> Search Results <<<<<<<<<<<<<<<<<<<<<<<<<<<

                                           Search Date: 2003-Jan-13
     │ varProdNum │     980025             Search Time: 01:54:59
  Manufacturer Number:  19974892
        Product Code:   HW
                                              Product Description
                                     266Mhz Pentium Computer with 8 MB R
                                     AM and a 200 MB Hard Drive

        Purchase Cost:  2095.99
              Mark-up:  15.75
```

Figure 14.8. The screen reader.

14.5   Summary

Direct integration between mobile devices and backend databases enables real-time data access over the air. It is essential for time-sensitive data and is complementary to the synchronization architecture. In this chapter, we discussed several approaches to access backend databases from J2ME devices. In particular, we focused on the end-to-end solution provided by Data Representations' Simplicity IDE. The IDE provides tools to integrate J2ME clients with mainframe applications as well as normal relational databases.

Resources

[1] The Oracle J2ME SDK (including the SQL Web Services module).
     http://studio.oraclemobile.com/studio/sites/otn/j2me.html

[2] The Simplicity IDE from Data Representations.
     http://www.datarepresentations.com/

Part V

XML and Mobile Web Services

Chapter 15

XML for Small Devices

CHAPTER OVERVIEW

- What Is XML?

- Challenges for Small Devices

- XML Parsing Models

- Introducing Amazon XML Services

- Amazon Services via XmlPull

- Amazon Services via kDOM

- A Mobile RSS client

XML is the foundation of componentized and interoperable Web Services. Java and XML are perfectly suited for each other, since Java provides code mobility while XML provides data mobility. In this chapter, we discuss why XML is so important, and we explore common XML parsing APIs on the Java platform and XML support on the J2ME platform. An example of Amazon XML Web Services demonstrates how to process real-world XML messages using different APIs. Finally, we learn about an RSS XML client, and the important concept of XML-based data aggregation is introduced.

15.1   What Is XML?

XML is the acronym of the eXtensible Markup Language. Like any other markup language, it uses nested text tags to enclose content and represent data structure. XML itself does not define a specific set of tags and structures to use. You can define any tags to use in your XML document as long as your applications and other communication parties understand them. Hence, XML is extensible. For example, you can use the following XML document to describe a small computer parts inventory.

Listing 15.1. A sample XML document

```
<product category="CPU">
  <description>Athlon 1.5GHz</description>
  <maker>AMD</maker>
  <UnitPrice>100.0</UnitPrice>
  <Availability>10000</Availability>
</product>
<product category="printer">
  <description>Inkjet color printer</description>
  <maker>HP</maker>
  <UnitPrice>120.0</UnitPrice>
  <Availability>1000</Availability>
</product>
```

Markup data languages have been around since the 1970s. In fact, the HTML itself is a markup language. What makes XML so special? Well, there are several reasons.

- XML has rich expression power. Nested tag elements allow us to easily express hierarchical data structures. More importantly, together with technologies such as XML Schema, XML supports strong data typing.

Strong typed data are fundamental to object-oriented systems (i.e., Java applications). Please see Chapter 16 for more on XML Schema and XML data types.

- XML is both machine and human friendly. Unlike HTML, XML has strict syntax requirements for easy and fast parsing. For example, every XML start tag must have a matching end tag, and they must be properly nested. Since an XML document contains descriptive tag information, it is easy for humans to read and understand.

- XML promotes open standard. XML's extensibility and flexibility allows it to be adopted across many industries. To become a ubiquitous data exchange format, XML must be standardized. XML namespaces and schema are already standardized by W3C. Many industry-specific and application-specific XML formats are also being standardized. Today, XML is the most interoperable data format across many platforms.

XML is quickly becoming the technology of choice for enterprise data exchange and integration. To develop mobile enterprise applications, our mobile clients must talk to XML-powered backend systems.

15.2 Challenges for Small Devices

XML and Java champion similar ideas such as open interface, platform independence, and object-oriented data. XML support on the Java platform is traditionally very strong. All popular XML standards are supported on the J2SE and J2EE platforms. However, XML support on the J2ME platform, especially CLDC/MIDP platform, is still in development. XML-compatible mobile clients are slow to emerge because of the additional processing time and bandwidth required by XML tags. For example, the sample applications in Chapters 3 and 5 opted for tightly packed binary streams for data exchange. But eventually, XML will become the ubiquitous data format for mobile applications. Throughout this and the following several chapters, we will see several real-world examples that showcase capabilities of mobile XML clients.

Note

J2ME Web Services Specification (JSR 172) will provide a standard set of XML parsing APIs on the J2ME platform. Please refer to Chapter 17.

Since CDC and PersonalJava have full support of core Java libraries such as IO and String, we can port J2SE and J2EE XML libraries to those platforms or even run compiled J2SE XML libraries directly. Having said that, specially optimized, fast, and lightweight XML parsers are still preferred on the mobile platform.

On the CLDC platform, we need specially written lightweight XML parsers. There are several different CLDC-compatible XML parsers available from various commercial and open source projects. In this chapter, we focus on the open source kXML package. For more parsers, please refer to the "Resources" section. CLDC parsers provide only the most basic functionalities, and none of them validates XML messages against document type definitions (DTDs) or schemas.

Alternative Lightweight XML Exchange Formats

XML is often considered bandwidth expensive in mobile applications because of the extra tags. There are various ways to minimize the bandwidth impact. In the JXME project (Chapter 9), an XML-like binary format is used for compact data storage; In the WAP world, a standard XML compression scheme called WBXML is widely used. However, neither technology is widely used by enterprise backend applications.

15.3 XML Parsing Models

The XML parser converts text-based XML documents to memory objects accessible to computer programs. There are several ways to parse an XML document.

15.3.1 SAX

SAX (Simple API for XML) is an event-based parsing model. The parser goes through the entire document in a linear pass. When the parser encounters an XML entity—such as a tag, a piece of enclosed text, or an attribute—it emits an *event*. The events are captured and processed by an event-handler method. The application developer implements the event handler to do application-specific tasks with those events. The kXML v1.2 supports SAX. Figure 15.1 illustrates the SAX parsing process.

A simple SAX application looks like the following (Listing 15.2).

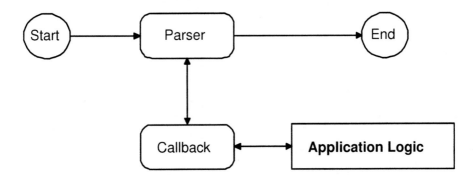

Figure 15.1. SAX parsing process.

Listing 15.2. A simple SAX program

```
// Create a SAX parser.
// This is implementation specific.
Parser p = new SAXParser ();

// "handler" is the callback object that processes SAX events.
p.setDocumentHandler( handler );
p.parse();
```

Although SAX is simple to implement and very popular, it is outdated by the newer pull-based parsing APIs. For more examples using SAX, please refer to Section 17.2.

15.3.2   XMLPull

One big problem the SAX model has is that it is push based: Once the parsing is started, parsing events are pushed in continuously. The parser runs through the entire XML document in one pass. Developers have no control over the flow of the parsing process. For example, let's suppose that you are looking for a specific piece of information located in the middle of an XML document. Under the SAX model, you cannot stop parsing after you retrieve the data. The parse keeps going until it finishes the entire document. This is ineffective, especially for mobile clients.

XmlPull API gives developers more control over the parsing flow. Since the parser is pull based, the application can pause the parsing to take care of other things and come back later, or it can even stop the parsing before the end of the document is researched. The kXML v2.0 supports the XmlPull v1.0 API. Figure 15.2 illustrates the XMLPull parsing process.

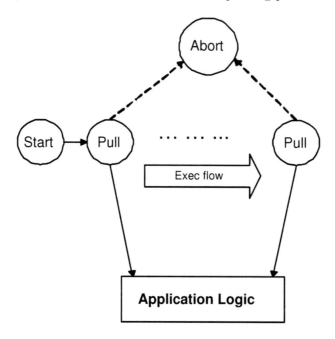

Figure 15.2. XMLPull parsing process.

The heart of the XmlPull API is the XmlPullParser interface. XmlPull providers supply their own XmlPullParser implementation through the XmlPull-ParserFactory factory class. XmlPullParser defines a number of event types (e.g., the START_TAG event) and data access methods (e.g., the getAttribute-Value() method). Core methods to control the parsing flow are next() and nextToken().

- The next() method advances the parser to the next event. Event types seen by the next() method are START_TAG, TEXT, END_TAG, and END_DOCUMENT.

- The nextToken() method gives developers a finer control. It sees all the events the next() method sees. In addition, it sees and reports the following events: COMMENT, CDSECT, DOCDECL, ENTITY_REF, PROCESSING_INSTRUCTION, and IGNORABLE_WHITESPACE.

The use of an XmlPull parser is illustrated in Section 15.5.

15.3.3   Document Model

Both SAX and XmlPull treats the hierarchical XML data structure as a linear flow. To reconstruct data into a logical tree structure requires the developer to control the event handler carefully with flags and case statements. This kind of code is hard to write and hard to debug. Also, SAX and XmlPull support only serial access. We do not have random access to any node in the document. The document model parsers come to the rescue.

A document model parser is essentially a SAX or XmlPull parser with a predefined event handler that stores XML information into an in-memory tree. The application can then access and manipulate any data in the tree model using a set of API methods. Figure 15.3 illustrates the DOM (Document Object Model) parsing process.

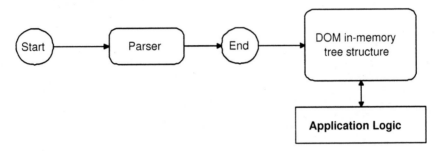

Figure 15.3. DOM parsing.

The building block of any document model is the **Node** object. The **Node** class defines methods that allows multiple **Node** objects to be linked into a tree structure. The XML document is represented by such a tree. Objects representing other XML entities, such as elements, attributes, and text, inherit from **Node**.

A standard XML document model API is DOM, which is defined by the W3C. However, the standard DOM is quite complex. There are several easy-to-use DOM-like APIs, such as the JDOM API, in the Java world. For mobile devices, full support for DOM has proven too expensive. A particularly interesting lightweight XML object model is kDOM, supported by both kXML v1.2 and v2.0. Code examples for kDOM are given in Section 15.6.

15.4   Introducing Amazon XML Services

The Amazon Web Services interface (v2.0) is designed to provide Amazon associates programmatic access to Amazon catalog data and search functionalities. Amazon Web Services is available in two flavors.

An Extremely Small and Tolerant Parser

We often construct "simple and dirty" XML documents to pass information quickly. Those documents often have only elements and attributes. They are not even necessarily well formed (i.e., missing tags or incorrectly nested tags). In fact, most HTML files on the Internet are "broken" XML documents. Standard XML parsers might balk at the broken XML structures. Even if they do parse, standard XML parsers have many features that are *not* needed for simple documents. The XmlReader class in the open source Utils4ME project is an extremely small pull parser that has only a 5 KB memory footprint. It does not handle namespace, comment, or processing instructions, and is tolerant of broken XML structures.

- A standard SOAP Web Service. The application architecture here is SOAP RPC. Query and response data are all enclosed in SOAP messages. We will discuss SOAP in more detail in Chapters 16 and 17.

- A literal XML service. In this model, the query is encoded as parameters in the request URL. The Amazon server returns an XML document containing the response data. The tags and structure of the returned document are defined in DTD files provided by Amazon.

A RESTful Web Service

The Amazon literal XML service turns out to be much more popular than the SOAP service among Amazon associates. A problem with the SOAP model is that it does not take advantage of existing HTTP infrastructure at all. It merely uses the HTTP POST as a convenient transport channel. In the SOAP model, the URLs are never self-contained. They have to be combined with the POST content to describe a certain RPC exchange (see Chapter 16). Since the SOAP Web Service is out of sync with HTTP, it has been difficult for many Web developers to comprehend and use. To reconcile this problem, Roy Fielding proposed a new XML Web Services model that makes use of HTTP's intrinsic semantic structure. It is called the RESTful (Representational State Transfer) Web Service (see "Resources"). The Amazon literal service is a RESTful Web Service. It makes URLs real pointers to unique resources and makes sensible use of HTTP operations such as GET and POST. As a result, the literal service is a lot more intuitive to Web developers and easier to use.

The Amazon service can operate in lite or heavy mode. A lite mode response is smaller but contains less information. Due to the bandwidth and processing power limits of mobile clients, we use the lite mode in this chapter. To use the Amazon service, you have to first obtain an authentication token from the Amazon Web site. Then, you encode query parameters into a URL string. For example, the following URL (without line breaks)

```
http://xml.amazon.com/onca/xml?v=1.0
&t=webservices-20&dev-t=ABCD123456
&KeywordSearch=mobile%20java
&mode=books&type=lite&page=1&f=xml
```

specifies that a user identified by token ABCD123456 asks to search keywords mobile java in books store. Note that the space between keywords is encoded using %20 per URL encoding rules. The first page result is returned as a lite version, literal XML document. Listing 15.3 demonstrates the returned XML document. I have added some white spaces and replaced long strings with ellipses (...) to make it more readable.

Listing 15.3. A sample Amazon search response message

```
<ProductInfo
xmlns:xsi="http://www.w3.org/2001/XMLSchema-instance"
xsi:noNamespaceSchemaLocation=
  "http://xml.amazon.com/schemas/dev-lite.xsd">

  <Details
  url="http://www.amazon.com/exec/obidos/...">
    <Asin>0471034657</Asin>
    <ProductName>
      Mobile Information Device Profile for Java 2
      Micro Edition (J2ME): Professional
      Developer's Guide
    </ProductName>
    <Catalog>Book</Catalog>
    <Authors>
      <Author>C. Enrique Ortiz</Author>
      <Author>Eric Giguere</Author>
    </Authors>
    <ReleaseDate>15 January, 2001</ReleaseDate>
    <Manufacturer>
      John Wiley &amp; Sons
    </Manufacturer>
```

```
<ImageUrlSmall>
  http://images.amazon.com/...THUMBZZZ.jpg
</ImageUrlSmall>
<ImageUrlMedium>
  http://images.amazon.com/...MZZZZZZZ.jpg
</ImageUrlMedium>
<ImageUrlLarge>
  http://images.amazon.com/...LZZZZZZZ.jpg
</ImageUrlLarge>
<ListPrice>\$49.99</ListPrice>
<OurPrice>\$49.99</OurPrice>
<UsedPrice>\$28.99</UsedPrice>
</Details>

<Details url="...">
  ... ...
</Details>

  ... ...


</ProductInfo>
```

Our sample MIDlet **AmazonLite** demonstrates how to parse the Amazon lite document. **AmazonLite** first prompts the user for the keywords to search. Then, the user clicks which XML parsing mode she would like to test. Button **Pull** is for XmlPull, and button **kDOM** is for a document model mode. MIDlet then sends out the query, receives data, parses the response document, and then displays extracted data in a new form. Figure 15.4 shows the program in action.

XML parsing in **AmazonLite** is done by the kXML parser. kXML is an open source XML parser that is compatible with all J2ME platforms. It is developed under the Endrya ME project and released under the CPL license. kXML v2.0 supports the XmlPull interfaces as well as the kDOM document model.

15.5   Amazon Services via XmlPull

Using XmlPull, we parse the document linearly. The application has to remember the state information to retrieve XML contents based on the context. The code is listed in Listings 15.4 and 15.5. The logic flow is the following:

1. When method **getBooksViaPull()** encounters a **Details** start tag, it passes the parser control to method **getBookDetailsViaPull()**.

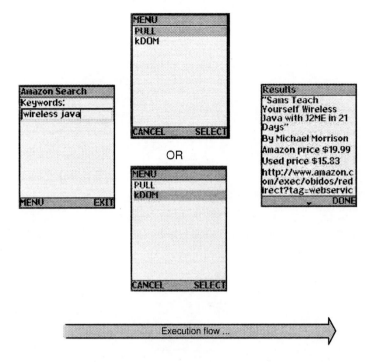

Figure 15.4. Mobile access to Amazon XML search interface.

2. Method getBookDetailsViaPull() instantiates a new BookDetails object and stores the value of the url attribute in it.

3. When method getBookDetailsViaPull() encounters ProducteName, Authors, OurPrice, and UsedPrice tags, it stores their text values into appropriate fields in the BookDetails object.

4. At the Details close tag, method getBookDetailsViaPull() returns the populated BookDetails object. Method getBooksViaPull() stores the BookDetails object into a Vector Books and moves forward to the next Details start tag.

After the parsing is done, all useful data is extracted and stored in the Books Vector.

Listing 15.4. The AmazonLite.getBooksViaPull() method

```
Vector getBooksViaPull (InputStream is) throws Exception {
```

```
Vector books = new Vector ();

InputStreamReader reader =  new InputStreamReader(is);
KXmlParser parser = new KXmlParser();
parser.setInput(reader);
int eventType = parser.getEventType();
while (eventType != parser.END_DOCUMENT) {
  // Only respond to the <Details> start tag
  if (eventType == parser.START_TAG) {
    if ( parser.getName().equals("Details") ) {
      BookDetails bd = getBookDetailsViaPull(parser);
      books.addElement( bd );
    }
  }
  eventType = parser.next();
}
return books;
}
```

Listing 15.5. The AmazonLite.getBookDetailsViaPull() method

```
BookDetails getBookDetailsViaPull (XmlPullParser parser)
                                  throws Exception {
  BookDetails bd = new BookDetails ();
  // get attribute value from the <Details>
  // start tag
  bd.url = parser.getAttributeValue(null, "url");
  int eventType = parser.next();
  while ( true ) {
    // Break out the loop at </Details> end tag
    if ( eventType == parser.END_TAG ) {
      if ( parser.getName().equals("Details") ) {
        break;
      }
    }

    if ( eventType == parser.START_TAG ) {
      String tagname = parser.getName();
      if ( tagname.equals("ProductName") ) {
        // Proceed to the enclosed Text node
        parser.next();
        bd.title = parser.getText().trim();
      }
```

```
    if ( tagname.equals("Authors") ) {
      // First <Author> start tag
      parser.next();
      // White space between tags
      parser.next();
      // Proceed to the enclosed Text node
      parser.next();
      bd.firstAuthor = parser.getText().trim();
    }
    if ( tagname.equals("OurPrice") ) {
      // Proceed to the enclosed Text node
      parser.next();
      bd.newPrice = parser.getText().trim();
    }
    if ( tagname.equals("UsedPrice") ) {
      // Proceed to the enclosed Text node
      parser.next();
      bd.usedPrice = parser.getText().trim();
    }
  }
  eventType = parser.next();
}
return bd;
}
```

Note

In this particular example, all we do is extract information from XML document into a string for display. For this purpose, we do not need intermediate objects such as Books and BookDetails. The extra storage objects are introduced to illustrate how the parser is used in general-purpose applications.

15.6 Amazon Services via kDOM

Using the kDOM document model, parsing is very simple. Just a few lines of code builds the kDOM tree in a Document type object doc from the input XML stream.

```
InputStreamReader reader = new InputStreamReader(is);
KXmlParser parser = new KXmlParser();
parser.setInput(reader);
```

```
Document doc = new Document ();
doc.parse (parser);
```

The rest of the methods, **getBooksViaDOM()** (Listing 15.6) and **get-BookDetailsViaDOM()** (Listing 15.7), in the **AmazonLite** class demonstrate how to traverse the tree to retrieve useful information. All ignorable white spaces are built into **Text** nodes by default. We have to be careful not to mistake them with real **Element** nodes. Since the tree object is already in memory, you can access any random node at anytime. You can even change the content of any node and have kDOM write out the new tree to an I/O stream.

Listing 15.6. The AmazonLite.getBooksViaDOM() method

```
Vector getBooksViaDOM (InputStream is) throws Exception {
  Vector books = new Vector ();

  InputStreamReader reader = new InputStreamReader(is);
  KXmlParser parser = new KXmlParser();
  parser.setInput(reader);
  Document doc = new Document ();
  doc.parse (parser);

  // Use the following code to write
  // in memory doc object to a stream
  // KXmlSerializer serializer = new KXmlSerializer ();
  // serializer.setOutput (System.out, null);
  // doc.write (serializer);
  // serializer.flush ();

  // The <ProductInfo> element
  Element prods = doc.getRootElement();

  int numOfEntries = prods.getChildCount ();
  for (int i = 0; i < numOfEntries; i++) {
    if ( prods.isText(i) ) {
      // Text here are all insignificant white spaces.
      // We are only interested in children elements
    } else {
      // Not text, must be a <Details> element
      Element e = prods.getElement (i);
      BookDetails bd = getBookDetailsViaDOM( e );
      books.addElement( bd );
    }
```

```
  }
  return books;
}
```

> **Listing 15.7.** The AmazonLite.getBooDetailsViaDOM() method

```
BookDetails getBookDetailsViaDOM (Element e) throws Exception {
  BookDetails bd = new BookDetails ();
  // get attribute value from the <Details> start tag
  bd.url = e.getAttributeValue(null, "url");
  int numOfChildren = e.getChildCount ();
  for (int i = 0; i < numOfChildren; i++) {
    if ( e.isText(i) ) {
      // Ignore
    } else {
      Element c = e.getElement(i);
      String tagname = c.getName();
      if ( tagname.equals("ProductName") ) {
        // First child is a text node
        bd.title = c.getText(0).trim();
      }
      if ( tagname.equals("Authors") ) {
        // Goes down the tree: The second child
        // is the first <Author> element. Get the
        // first child of that element.
        bd.firstAuthor =
          c.getElement(1).getText(0).trim();
      }
      if ( tagname.equals("OurPrice") ) {
        // First child is a text node
        bd.newPrice = c.getText(0).trim();
      }
      if ( tagname.equals("UsedPrice") ) {
        // First child is a text node
        bd.usedPrice = c.getText(0).trim();
      }
    }
  }
  return bd;
}
```

15.7   A Mobile RSS Client

The last example of XML parser use in this chapter is a mobile Really Simple Syndication (RSS) client. RSS is a widely used XML format for news and blog sites to feed their headline contents to aggregators. For news sites, RSS makes it possible to advertise their headlines and provides links back to their sites; for aggregators, the use of RSS avoids HTML screen scraping and makes it possible to automatically aggregate a large number of sites.

15.7.1   A Simple RSS Example

RSS is designed to be simple. It is readable by humans and can be easily parsed by machines. Listing 15.8 shows a simple RSS feed. The channel element represents a content source, and it can contain multiple item elements. Each item element represents a headline or a story. Under the channel or the item element, the title, link, and description nodes contain the title, URL link, and synopsis of the content. There are many more optional elements defined in the RSS specification (see "Resources" for more information).

Listing 15.8. A real simple RSS feed

```
<rss version="0.91">
<channel>
  <title>My Site Content</title>
  <link>http://www.mysite.com</link>
  <description>Latest Content</description>
  <language>en-us</language>
  <copyright>Copyright 2003 myself</copyright>
  <lastBuildDate>24/02/03 12:34:56</lastBuildDate>

  <image>
    <title>MySite</title>
    <url>http://www.mysite.com/pic.gif</url>
    <link>http://www.DevX.com</link>
  </image>

  <item>
      <title>Good news</title>
      <description>Product shipped</description>
      <link>http://www.mysite.com/shipped</link>
      <author>me@mysite.com</author>
      <pubDate>22/02/03 11:22:33</pubDate>
  </item>
  <item>
      <title> etc  </title>
```

```
         <description> etc  </description>
         <link> etc  </link>
         <pubDate> etc </pubDate>
     </item>
  </channel>
</rss>
```

15.7.2   PeekAndPick

Jonathan Knudsen's PeekAndPick (v2.0) is an MIDP RSS client. It aggregates headlines from a number of news/blog sites specified by the user. The user can read headlines and have the link emailed to him via the mobile phone (see Figure 15.5).

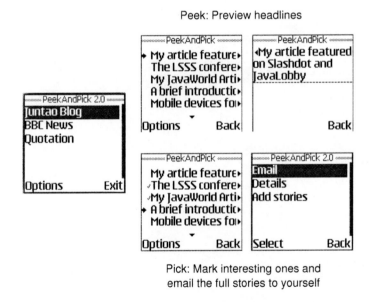

Figure 15.5. PeekAndPick in action.

The complete code and design documentation of PeekAndPick is available (see "Resources"). In the source code package, classes under the rss package provide an RSS parser based on kXML's XmlPull parser and its interface to other programming components. Listing 15.9 shows the code snippet from the kXML12Parser.parse() method which parses the RSS stream. The flow is very simple. The program goes into a channel element, iterates through the item elements, and reads out the contents in the title, link, and description nodes. All other advanced RSS elements are ignored.

Listing 15.9. The kXML12Parser.parse() method

```
public void parse(InputStream in)
                   throws IOException {
  mCancel = false;

  Reader reader = new InputStreamReader(in);
  XmlParser parser = new XmlParser(reader);
  ParseEvent pe = null;

  parser.skip();
  pe = parser.read();
  String root = pe.getName();
  if (root.equals("rss")) {
    parser.skip();
    parser.read(Xml.START_TAG, null, "channel");
  }

  boolean trucking = true;
  boolean first = true;
  while (trucking && mCancel == false) {
    pe = parser.read();
    if (pe.getType() == Xml.START_TAG) {
      String name = pe.getName();
      if (name.equals("item")) {
        String title = null, link = null;
        String description = null;
        while ((pe.getType() != Xml.END_TAG) ||
          (pe.getName().equals(name) == false)) {
          pe = parser.read();
          if (pe.getType() == Xml.START_TAG &&
              pe.getName().equals("title")) {
            pe = parser.read();
            title = pe.getText();
          } else if (pe.getType() == Xml.START_TAG
              && pe.getName().equals("link")) {
            pe = parser.read();
            link = pe.getText();
          } else if (pe.getType() == Xml.START_TAG
          && pe.getName().equals("description")) {
            pe = parser.read();
```

```
        description = pe.getText();
      }
    }
    if (first) {
      if (mCancel == false) fireFirstItem();
      first = false;
    }
    if (mCancel == false)
      fireItemParsed(title, link, description);
  } else {
    while ((pe.getType() != Xml.END_TAG) ||
           (pe.getName().equals(name) == false))
      pe = parser.read();
  }
}
if (pe.getType() == Xml.END_TAG &&
pe.getName().equals(root))
  trucking = false;
}
if (mCancel == false) fireFinished();
mCancel = false;
}
```

The spirit of RSS is very similar to the concept of XML Web Services: offering services through a standard, interoperable interface. In the next chapter, we dive into SOAP XML Web Services.

15.8 Summary

In this chapter, we discussed the importance of XML as an open data exchange format. We explained common models of XML processing and introduced the packages available on the J2ME platform. Using an Amazon XML service browser and an RSS news feed reader as examples, you can learn how to use those J2ME packages to solve real-world problems.

Resources

[1] The SAX specification. http://www.saxproject.org/

[2] The XmlPull specification. http://www.xmlpull.org/

[3] kXML is an Open Source XML parser. http://www.kxml.org/

[4] XmlReader is a minimalist and error-tolerant XML pull parser in the Utils4ME project. http://kobjects.org/utils4me/index.html

[5] Amazon XML Web Services interface. http://www.amazon.com/webservices/

[6] A good introduction to the RESTful Web Service: "Second Generation Web Services," Paul Prescod, February 06, 2002. http://webservices.xml.com/pub/a/ws/2002/02/06/rest.html

[7] The AmazonLite MIDP example. http://www.enterprisej2me.com/book/code/

[8] The RSS specification. http://backend.userland.com/rss

[9] The PeekAndPick mobile RSS reader example. http://wireless.java.sun.com/applications/peekandpick/

Chapter 16

SOAP Web Services on Smart Clients

CHAPTER OVERVIEW

- What Is SOAP Web Services?

- The Web Services Architecture

- Introducing kSOAP

- kSOAP Explained

- Advanced kSOAP

- More kSOAP Examples

- What's in kSOAP v2.0?

- IDE Support for kSOAP

It seems that distributed computing technologies keep reinventing themselves every couple of years. From COBRA to COM to RMI, now XML Web Services is all the rage. Web Services is touted as a platform-independent integration technology that supports loose coupling. It promises universal interoperability and supports advanced messaging protocols. The Simple Object Access Protocol (SOAP) is the foundation for XML Web Services. Smart mobile clients that fit into the corporate Web Services infrastructure could prove crucial for any mobile enterprise solution.

In this chapter, I introduce an open source tool that supports Web Services clients on small wireless devices: the kSOAP parser. Through tutorial examples and source code analysis, we will not only learn how to program in kSOAP but also gain a deeper understanding of Web Services concepts and applications.

16.1   What Is SOAP Web Services?

Standardization is key to the success of XML. Raw XML by itself is just a bunch of tags, attributes, and text that can be used to express almost anything in any format. The flexibility gives XML the power of a universal data language. But in any specific application field, the meaning of XML syntax elements must be standardized to ensure interoperability. In order for XML to carry generic data between object-oriented programming systems, we need a syntax system that expresses complex object and type information in serialized XML format.

16.1.1   The SOAP Advantage

SOAP is the most widely used protocol for XML-based object serialization. It is the technology of choice for future ubiquitous Web Services. Compared with competing technologies, SOAP has the following advantages:

- *Strong type support*: SOAP defines more than 40 standard data types through XML Schema and allows users to custom-define complex data types. Such sophisticated data-type support makes SOAP a powerful and rich language for exchanging information among today's widely deployed object-oriented systems.

- *Flexible and ubiquitous messaging*: In addition to strong data-type support, SOAP also supports various messaging schemes. Those schemes include synchronous RPC, asynchronous messaging, multicast messaging (subscription), and complex message routes with multiple intermediaries.

- *Standardization*: Since SOAP has gained mainstream support as a Web
  Services messaging standard, most other Web Services protocols must
  interoperate or bind with SOAP. For example, WSDL (Web Services
  Description Language), UDDI (Universal Description, Discovery, and
  Integration), and most XML registries support SOAP; XML Digital
  Signature, XML Encryption, SAML (Security Assertion Markup Language), and other secure XML protocols all provide standard binding
  with SOAP. Each binding protocol provides syntax of its own special
  element inside SOAP messages. SOAP's full support for XML namespaces has made it easy to bind with other protocols.

Note

The use of SOAP does present bandwidth and CPU/memory overheads for mobile devices. We have to design our systems carefully
to make judicial use of SOAP Web Services. We should use it only
to interface with external modules or when universal interoperability
is a primary concern.

16.1.2   SOAP Hello World

Listing 16.1 is a Hello World SOAP message. Its body contains a single
xsd:string type of element (as defined in XML Schema) that can be mapped
to a Java **String** object. Of course, XML Schema defines much more than
the string type. Under the xsd namespace, standard XML Schema provides
matching types for all Java basic types, array types, and most Java Collection
types. It even supports Base64 encoded binary content for binary arrays.

> **Serialize Arbitrary Java Objects**
> Arbitrary Java Serializable objects can be serialized to byte arrays and then
> transported by SOAP as a Base64 element. However, this not a recommended
> practice, since it requires the receiving ends to be Java aware too. If we already
> know that both communication parties use Java, Java-only technologies like
> RMI and JMS work better than SOAP. SOAP is designed for serialization (and
> deserialization) based on semantics rather than a simple object wrapper.

Listing 16.1. A simple SOAP message

```
<SOAP-ENV:Envelope
  xmlns:SOAP-ENV="http://www.w3.org/2001/12/soap-envelope"
  xmlns:xsi="http://www.w3.org/2001/XMLSchema-instance"
  xmlns:xsd="http://www.w3.org/2001/XMLSchema">
    <SOAP-ENV:Body>
<message xsi:type="xsd:string">Hello World</message>
    </SOAP-ENV:Body>
</SOAP-ENV:Envelope>
```

SOAP elements can also represent complex custom types. In Listing 16.2, the **message** element has three string children and an integer child. It corresponds to a complex Java object that has those four data member fields. That object's Java type corresponds to the **mytype** XML type in the XML Schema.

Listing 16.2. Another simple SOAP message

```
<SOAP-ENV:Envelope
  xmlns:SOAP-ENV="http://www.w3.org/2001/12/soap-envelope"
  xmlns:xsi="http://www.w3.org/2001/XMLSchema-instance"
  xmlns:xsd="http://www.w3.org/2001/XMLSchema">
    <SOAP-ENV:Body>
<message xsi:type="mytype">
  <from xsi:type="xsd:string">Bob</from>
  <to xsi:type="xsd:string">Alice</to>
  <mesg xsi:type="xsd:string">Hello World</mesg>
  <seqId xsi:type="xsd:int">1</seqId>
</message>
    </SOAP-ENV:Body>
</SOAP-ENV:Envelope>
```

16.1.3   Architecture of SOAP Web Services

As an infrastructure solution, Web Services is touted as self-contained, automatically discovered, and automatically configured reusable software components. Web Services is much more than SOAP—which only serves to provide a platform-independent transport layer. Figure 16.1 illustrates the overall architecture of Web Services.

- Each Web Service makes a description of its service available as a WSDL document. The WSDL describes technical details on how to access the service. Authorized remote clients can download the WSDL file and generate a *stub* that matches the SOAP service interface. Any RPC method in a Java stub can be called from clientside Java applications as if it were a local method. All leading Web Services toolkits provide WSDL-to-stub code generators.

- Web Services register themselves with central registry databases such as the UDDI registry. The client searches the UDDI, finds out the service it needs, fetches the WSDL file, generates the stub, and starts calling remote methods.

Web Services for Wireless Carriers

Wireless carriers also utilize Web Services to communicate with each other and form an integrated carrier network. For example, the 3GPP MM7 specification defines a SOAP RPC protocol for MMSC (Multimedia Messaging Service Center) servers to exchange MMS messages. That allows carrier A users to send MMS messages to carrier B users.

16.2   Introducing kSOAP

To build Web Services clients on J2ME devices, we first need a J2ME-compatible SOAP parser. Most standard Java SOAP libraries (such as the Apache Axis and Java Web SDK) are too heavy for small devices. The open source kSOAP project runs on all J2SE and J2ME platforms, including the MIDP. Built on top of the kXML parser, the entire kSOAP library is only 42 KB. However, as a trade-off for the lightness, kSOAP does not support the entire SOAP specification. It supports the most commonly used SOAP features and is sufficient for most Web Services that are currently available. Currently, almost all major kSOAP applications and tools are based on kSOAP release v1.2, which supports a core subset of SOAP 1.2 features. Although kSOAP v2.0 was released in November 2002, new features are still being developed and debugged. I recommend you use kSOAP v1.2 for important real-world applications but keep an eye on kSOAP v2.0. For developers, kSOAP v2.0 is easy once you understand the key concepts and programming models in v1.2. For the above reasons, we focus on kSOAP v1.2 in this chapter and give a programming tutorial for kSOAP v2.0 in Section 16.6.

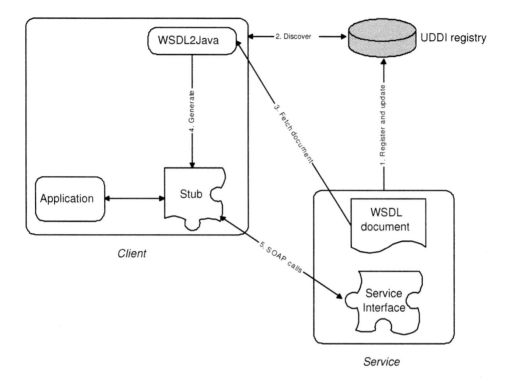

Figure 16.1. Web Services architecture.

16.2.1 What Is SOAP Parsing?

Every generic XML parser with namespace support understands SOAP messages and can extract information from them. In theory, we can always extract text information from a SOAP document using a generic XML parser and then convert those text strings to Java data objects when we need to use them. For example, the statement

```
int i = Integer.parseInt("123");
```

converts a text string "123" to an integer value 123. But such manual conversion burdens application programmers. Extracting Java data objects directly from a SOAP document provides a better approach. Enter the SOAP parser.

A SOAP parser is built on a generic XML parser with special type-mapping and text data-marshaling mechanisms. A SOAP parser understands the data-type information in SOAP messages and automatically converts the SOAP elements to Java data objects. The parser's real value is that it makes SOAP serialization and deserialization—and the entire wire protocol-transparent to object-oriented developers. The programmer just feeds Java objects into a SOAP writer, sends the message, waits for the server response, and then reads Java objects directly from the SOAP parser.

16.2.2   Simple Parsing Example Using kSOAP

Using kSOAP to make simple RPC calls is very easy. Listing 16.3 demonstrates how to make a SOAP call to Google's Web Services interface to obtain the spell suggestion of a phrase. The basic steps are the following:

1. *Prepare the arguments to pass to the remote method.* We instantiate a SoapObject object and add call arguments using the addProperty() method.

2. *Prepare the call transport.* We instantiate a HttpTransport object with the URL to the SOAP interface.

3. *Make the remote method call.* We pass the assembled SoapObject object (from step 1) to the HttpTransport object's call() method. The return value from the remote service is available as the return value of the call() method.

Listing 16.3. Spell check using Google

```
// The URL of the SOAP interface
String endPointURL = "http://api.google.com/search/beta2"
String licenseKey = "Register with Google to get it";

public String spellCheck (String query) throws Exception {
    // Prepare request SOAP message in a memory object
    SoapObject method = new SoapObject("urn:GoogleSearch",
                                      "doSpellingSuggestion");
    method.addProperty("key", licenseKey);
    method.addProperty("phrase", query);

    // Prepare SOAP RPC call object.
    HttpTransport rpc = new HttpTransport(endPointURL, "\"\"");
    // Google uses 1999 SOAP standards.
    ClassMap cm = new ClassMap(Soap.VER10);
    rpc.setClassMap (cm);
```

```
// Conduct RPC call through HTTP and
// directly get results
String spellSugg = (String) rpc.call (method);
return spellSugg;
}
```

16.2.3 How the call() Method Works

The HttpTransport.call() method is local to us. But behind the scenes, it
does a lot of remote work.

1. The call() method first serializes the SoapObject object to a SOAP
   request message with proper namespaces. For the Google spell check
   example, the SOAP request is shown below:

```
<SOAP-ENV:Envelope
 xmlns:xsi="http://www.w3.org/1999/XMLSchema-instance"
 xmlns:xsd="http://www.w3.org/1999/XMLSchema"
 xmlns:SOAP-ENC="http://schemas.xmlsoap.org/soap/encoding/"
 xmlns:SOAP-ENV="http://schemas.xmlsoap.org/soap/envelope/">
  <SOAP-ENV:Body
SOAP-ENV:encodingStyle="http://schemas.xmlsoap.org/soap/encoding/">
    <doSpellingSuggestion xmlns="urn:GoogleSearch"
                  id="o0" SOAP-ENC:root="1">
     <key xmlns="" xsi:type="xsd:string">...</key>
     <phrase xmlns="" xsi:type="xsd:string">
       phon
     </phrase>
    </doSpellingSuggestion>
   </SOAP-ENV:Body>
 </SOAP-ENV:Envelope>
```

2. It submits the request to the endPointURL through normal HTTP.

3. It retrieves the response SOAP message. We show Google's response
   here.

```
<SOAP-ENV:Envelope
 xmlns:SOAP-ENV="http://schemas.xmlsoap.org/soap/envelope/"
 xmlns:xsi="http://www.w3.org/1999/XMLSchema-instance"
 xmlns:xsd="http://www.w3.org/1999/XMLSchema">
  <SOAP-ENV:Body>
```

```
        <ns1:doSpellingSuggestionResponse
          xmlns:ns1="urn:GoogleSearch"
  SOAP-ENV:encodingStyle="http://schemas.xmlsoap.org/soap/encoding/">
          <return xsi:type="xsd:string">phone</return>
        </ns1:doSpellingSuggestionResponse>
      </SOAP-ENV:Body>
    </SOAP-ENV:Envelope>
```

4. At last, it marshals the response to a Java object and returns that
   object. In this case, it is a Java string *phone*.

To fully understand how the call() method works, we need to look at its
source code.

16.2.4   kSOAP Message Transport

Listing 16.4 shows the source code of the HttpTransport class. The Http-
Transport class is currently the only message transport class in kSOAP. It
is based on the very limited MIDP HTTP implementation. If you need
HTTPS, cookie-aware HTTP, authentication-aware HTTP, or support for
other network protocols, you have to plug in your own implementation.

Note

> In kSOAP v1.2, there is no support for SOAP headers. As we can see
> in the HttpTransport class, SoapFault handling is very poor. kSOAP
> v2.0 will provide API to access the header. We can then insert our
> own code to handle SoapFault.

Listing 16.4. The HttpTransport class

```
package org.ksoap.transport;

import java.io.*;
import javax.microedition.io.*;
import org.kxml.*;
import org.kxml.io.*;
import org.kxml.parser.*;
import org.ksoap.*;

public class HttpTransport {

  String url;
```

```
String soapAction = "\"\"";

SoapEnvelope requestEnvelope = new SoapEnvelope ();
SoapEnvelope responseEnvelope = new SoapEnvelope ();

HttpConnection connection;
OutputStream os;
InputStream is;
InputStreamReader reader;

private boolean connected = false;

public HttpTransport () { }

public HttpTransport (String url, String soapAction) {
  this.url = url;
  this.soapAction = soapAction;
}

public void setUrl (String url) {
  this.url = url;
}

public void setSoapAction (String soapAction) {
  this.soapAction = soapAction;
}

public void setClassMap (ClassMap classMap) {
  requestEnvelope.setClassMap (classMap);
  responseEnvelope.setClassMap (classMap);
}

public void call () throws IOException {

  ByteArrayOutputStream bos = new ByteArrayOutputStream ();
  XmlWriter xw =
    new XmlWriter (new OutputStreamWriter (bos));
  requestEnvelope.write (xw);
  xw.flush ();
  bos.write ('\r'); bos.write ('\n');
  byte [] requestData = bos.toByteArray ();
  bos = null; xw = null;

  try {
    connected = true;
```

```
      connection = (HttpConnection) Connector.open (url,
                               Connector.READ_WRITE, true);
      connection.setRequestProperty ("SOAPAction", soapAction);
      connection.setRequestProperty ("Content-Type", "text/xml");
      connection.setRequestProperty (
          "Content-Length", ""+requestData.length);
      connection.setRequestProperty ("User-Agent", "kSOAP/1.0");
      connection.setRequestMethod(HttpConnection.POST);

      os = connection.openOutputStream ();
      os.write (requestData, 0, requestData.length);
      os.close ();

      requestData = null;
      is = connection.openInputStream ();
      reader = new InputStreamReader (is);
      XmlParser xp = new XmlParser (reader);
      responseEnvelope.parse (xp);
  } finally {
    if (!connected) throw
      new InterruptedIOException ();
    reset ();
  }
}

public Object call (SoapObject method) throws IOException {
  requestEnvelope.setBody (method);
  call ();

  if (responseEnvelope.getBody () instanceof SoapFault)
    throw((SoapFault)responseEnvelope.getBody ());

  return responseEnvelope.getResult ();
}

public void call (XmlIO request, XmlIO result)
                           throws IOException {
  requestEnvelope.setBody (request);
  responseEnvelope.setBody (result);

  if (responseEnvelope.getBody () instanceof SoapFault)
    throw((SoapFault)responseEnvelope.getBody ());
}

public void reset () {
```

```
    connected = false;
    if (reader != null) {
      try { reader.close (); }
      catch (Throwable e) { }
      reader = null;
    }
    if (is != null) {
      try { is.close (); }
      catch (Throwable e) { }
      is = null;
    }
    if (connection != null) {
      try { connection.close (); }
      catch (Throwable e) { }
      connection = null;
    }
  }
}
```

16.2.5 kSOAP Stub Generators

The Google spell check example is very easy to code by hand. But things
get complex quickly when the remote service returns complex data objects.
It is a pain to sort through a long WSDL document and figure out the exact
SOAP interface. For complex services, automatically generated client stubs
from WSDL files prove useful. For example, both Apache Axis and Sun Java
Web Services Developer Pack offer WSDL2Java tools.

However, kSOAP is a small footprint library, not a complete Web Services toolkit. It lacks the tools to automatically generate client stubs. Fortunately, several J2ME IDEs provide such tools. kSOAP is adopted by
IBM WebSphere Studio Device Developer (WSDD, a J2ME IDE based on
Eclipse), SunONE Studio and CodeWarrior Wireless Studio as their default
mobile Web Services client library. All of them offer GUI wizards that ask
you the URL to the WSDL file and automatically generate the stubs into
your current project source directory.

Note

The kSOAP client generator in SunONE Studio is only available
through a module for the enterprise edition.

16.3   kSOAP Explained

In this section, we look under the hood to understand exactly how kSOAP v1.2 works. We also learn how to customize kSOAP for our special needs. For the impatient readers, a summary of the kSOAP API is available in Table 16.2 in Section 16.3.5. Now, let's start by examining how kSOAP maps SOAP data structures to Java objects.

16.3.1   The Default Mapping

By default, kSOAP understands the mappings described in Table 16.1. Notice that xsd:float is not supported due to the lack of Float support in CLDC v1.0.

Table 16.1.   Default Type Mapping in kSOAP

SOAP type	Java type
xsd:int	java.lang.Integer
xsd:long	java.lang.Long
xsd:string	java.lang.String
xsd:Boolean	java.lang.Boolean

When a simple kSOAP parser encounters a SOAP element, the parser reads the XML element into a Java object according to the following rules:

- If the SOAP element is one of the default primitive types in the table above, it converts to a Java object of a matching type.

- If the SOAP element has no children (a primitive element) but is *not* a default type, it converts to a SoapPrimitive object. We can retrieve the element's original SOAP type information from the SoapPrimitive.getNamespace() and SoapPrimitive.getName() methods. We can access the element's string value from the SoapPrimitive.toString() method.

- If the SOAP element has children (a complex element), it converts to a KvmSerializable object. KvmSerializable is an interface; the kSOAP package provides the interface's convenience implementation: SoapObject. Similar to SoapPrimitive objects, you can retrieve the element's original SOAP type information from the SoapObject.getNamespace() and SoapObject.getName() methods.

- A complex element's children convert to properties inside the parent SoapObject according to the above three rules in this list. Each property also has an associated PropertyInfo object containing information such as the SOAP element name and the property's Java object type. The PropertyInfo class supports element namespace in kSOAP v2.0 beta.

16.3.2 Object Structure

Since a SoapObject can take other SoapObjects as properties, we can use SoapObject to express complex hierarchical structures. An analogy to the XML DOM can be drawn here: The SoapObject resembles the parent node, and the property and PropertyInfo pairs resemble child nodes.

In simple cases, like the Google spell check example where the document contains only one primitive SOAP element, we can directly retrieve the mapped Java object or SoapPrimitive object through the SoapEnvelope.getBody() or SoapEnvelope.getResult() methods. If the SOAP message contains more information, the above two get methods return a root SoapObject, which contains the entire hierarchy of Java objects mapped from the SOAP elements according to the above rules.

---

getBody() **versus** getResult()

The getBody() method gets the first child element of the SOAP-ENV:Body element. The getResult() method gets the first grandchild of the body element. Method getResult() is used in HttpTransport class to parse the RPC response message because the return value is always embedded in a result element under the SOAP body element.

Figure 16.2 shows such a structure. Each node on the tree represents a SOAP element in the parsed document. The original SOAP element name is stored in the PropertyInfo object, and the SOAP type attribute name/namespace is stored in the property object. Arrows represent property relationships. You can find the Java data objects' original SOAP type information by searching the mappings in the ClassMap object, which contains the information in the above table (more on ClassMap later). As we can see, the root SoapObject lacks a pairing PropertyInfo. Therefore, we lose the root element's name after parsing. However, that is not an issue when we read SOAP documents, since element names normally serve only as indexes for accessing Java data objects, and we do not need an index to access the root element.

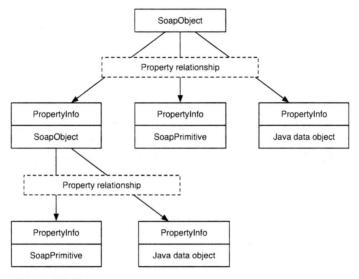

Object contents:
1. PropertyInfo: XML element namespace and name. e.g. **\<myns:mytag** ... **/\>**
2. Java data object: Plain object with its Java type specified in ClassMap.
3. SoapPrimitive: Soap type and the serialized data content.
   e.g. \<... **xsi:type="xsd:float"** ...\>**12.34**\</...\>
4. SoapObject: Soap type and references to properties.
   e.g. \<myns:mytag **xsi:type="xsd:mytype"** ...\>**\<...\>**\</myns:mytag\>

Figure 16.2. Structure of a parsed SOAP document.

16.3.3   Custom Mapping Through Data Marshal

To further automate the marshaling process to handle custom-defined types, we must prepare the parser for two tasks:

- The parser must know the mapping relationship between custom SOAP types to custom Java types. We complete custom mapping by adding matching type pairs to the current parser's **ClassMap** object.

- Since all SOAP data are presented in plain text strings, the parser must know how to convert the string to a desired Java object. The parser converts the string through a **Marshal** object, which is registered with the parser's corresponding custom SOAP and Java type pair in the **ClassMap** object.

SOAP Writing

To compose a SOAP message, we reverse the process. We first build the SoapObject hierarchy in memory. All leaf properties must be either SoapPrimitive or one of the four default type Java objects. Then, we use a kSOAP writer object to serialize the memory object to an XML stream. However, as you might already see, the root element presents a serialization problem. When we construct the structure according to the figure, the root SoapObject contains only the SOAP type name and namespace. No XML element name is available for the root element due to the pairing PropertyInfo's absence. We cannot write an XML element without an element name. The kSOAP v1.2 writer sidesteps this problem by making a notable exception to the parsing rule: When we serialize a root SoapObject, its name and namespace are used as element name/namespace rather than the SOAP type name/namespace (see the Google spell check example).

---

kSOAP provides a standard way to add custom type mapping and marshaling capabilities through the implementation of interface Marshal. The source code for the Marshal interface is shown in Listing 16.5. It declares a method to register itself with ClassMap and two call back methods.

Listing 16.5. The Marshal interface

```
public interface Marshal {
  public Object readInstance (SoapParser parser,
              String namespace, String name,
        ElementType expected) throws IOException;

  public void writeInstance (SoapWriter writer,
              Object instance) throws IOException;

  public void register (ClassMap cm);
}
```

The kSOAP download package provides three Marshal implementations as both convenience tools and programming examples. Let's look at the MarshalDate class, which marshals xsd:dateTime type elements, for an example. Method Marshal.readInstance() actually reads the text string from the SOAP element and then converts it to a Java object. In the case of the MarshalDate, readInstance()'s source code is shown in Listing 16.6.

Listing 16.6. The readInstance() method in the MarshalDate class

---

```
public Object readInstance (SoapParser parser,
              String namespace, String name,
       ElementType expected) throws IOException {

  parser.parser.read (); // Start tag
  Object result =
    IsoDate.stringToDate (parser.parser.readText (), IsoDate.DATE_TIME);
  parser.parser.read (); // End tag
  return result;
}
```

Similarly, method Marshal.writeInstance() describes how to serialize the Java object to a SOAP text string. In kSOAP writers, the method offers a more elegant alternative to using SoapPrimitive objects to handle unknown types. Interested readers can find the source code for that function from kSOAP source distribution. Method Marshal.register() (Listing 16.7) adds the matching custom SOAP type and Java type pair, as well as their processing Marshal object, to a ClassMap object.

Listing 16.7. The register() method for MarshalDate

```
public void register (ClassMap cm) {
   cm.addMapping (cm.xsd, "dateTime", MarshalDate.DATE_CLASS, this);
}
```

Now, let's look at a more complex example that demonstrates the use of SoapObject and Marshal.

16.3.4   A More Complex Example

The example scenario is a response from a stock trade SOAP service. The message is shown in Listing 16.8.

Listing 16.8. Demo stock trade response message

```
<SOAP-ENV:Envelope
 xmlns:SOAP-ENV="http://www.w3.org/2001/12/soap-envelope"
 xmlns:xsi="http://www.w3.org/2001/XMLSchema-instance"
```

```
xmlns:xsd="http://www.w3.org/2001/XMLSchema"
xmlns:n="http://www.javaworld.com/ksoap/test">
 <SOAP-ENV:Body>
   <result>
     <OrderStatus xsi:type="n:orderStatus">
       <CustomerName xsi:type="xsd:string">
         Michael Yuan
       </CustomerName>
       <Transaction xsi:type="n:transaction">
         <Symbol xsi:type="xsd:string">XYZ</Symbol>
         <Share xsi:type="xsd:int">1000</Share>
         <Buy xsi:type="xsd:boolean">true</Buy>
         <Price xsi:type="xsd:float">123.45</Price>
       </Transaction>
       <ExecTime xsi:type="xsd:dateTime">
         2003-03-05T23:20:50.52Z
       </ExecTime>
     </OrderStatus>
   </result>
 </SOAP-ENV:Body>
</SOAP-ENV:Envelope>
```

Listing 16.9 illustrates how to parse and retrieve information from the complex structure. Notice that the Price element is wrapped in a SoapPrimitive because xsd:float is not supported; the ExecTime element is correctly marshaled into a Java Date object because of the use of the MarshalDate.

Listing 16.9. Parsing the stock trade response

```
// Feed the response message into a
// reader object
XmlParser xp = new XmlParser (reader);

// Register Marshal for "xsd:dateTime" type
ClassMap cm = new ClassMap (Soap.VER12);
Marshal md = new MarshalDate ();
md.register (cm);
SoapEnvelope envelope = new SoapEnvelope (cm);
envelope.parse (xp);

// Get the parsed structure
SoapObject orderStatus = (SoapObject) envelope.getResult();

String customerName = (String)orderStatus.getProperty("CustomerName");
```

```
// Second layer of SoapObject
SoapObject transaction =
  (SoapObject)orderStatus.getProperty("Transaction");
String symbol = (String) transaction.getProperty ("Symbol");
Integer share = (Integer) transaction.getProperty ("Share");
Boolean buy = (Boolean) transaction.getProperty ("Buy");
SoapPrimitive price = (SoapPrimitive)transaction.getProperty("Price");
Date execTime = (Date) orderStatus.getProperty ("ExecTime");
```

In addition to the MarshalDate class, kSOAP provides two other Marshal implementations: MarshalBase64 and MarshalHashtable. Base64 is a method for encoding a binary stream into an ASCII string so that it can transport through email or XML/SOAP. MarshalBase64 marshals an xsd:based64Binary element into a Java byte array. kSOAP does not support SOAP attachments, but MarshalBase64 should allow users to send/receive binary data chunks. MarshalHashtable marshals a SOAP Map element into a Java hashtable.

16.3.5   Recap: The kSOAP API

We have covered almost all public classes and interfaces in the org.ksoap and org.kobjects.serialization packages. In recap, the classes and their descriptions are shown in Table 16.2.

16.4   Advanced kSOAP

Now we have seen the basic features of kSOAP. In addition, kSOAP offers limited support for SOAP arrays and document validation. We discuss these two features in this section.

16.4.1   Arrays

One of the important data types in any programming language is the array. kSOAP reads a SOAP array into a Java java.util.Vector object. Method Vector.elementAt(i) extracts the array's nth object. Depending on the arrayType, this object could be a SoapObject, a SoapPrimitive, a default Java type, or a marshaled Java object.

16.4.2   Validate Documents Using SoapTemplate

In the above examples, we take in only SOAP documents and parse them into SoapObjects as they are. However, in many cases, we require the response

Table 16.2. The kSOAP API Classes

kSOAP class	Description
ClassMap	Provides access to customizable properties for SOAP parsing and writing.
Soap	Contains basic variables such as SOAP versions and namespaces.
SoapEnvelope	Provides an envelope to hold the entire SOAP document. We access all SOAP data from this class.
SoapPrimitive	This is a wrapper around unknown SOAP types or SOAP types that do not have J2ME counterparts (e.g., float in MIDP).
SoapObject	Contains the structure of a SOAP node with children. It is a convenience implementation of the general KvmSerializable interface in the org.kobjects.serialization package.
PropertyInfo	This is a class from the org.kobjects.serialization package. It contains the name and namespace of an XML element. Each XML node in a SOAP document is represented by a PropertyInfo object with either a SoapPrimitive or a SoapObject object.
SoapParser	Reads and parses the SOAP stream.
SoapWriter	Writes SoapObjects and other kSOAP memory structures into a SOAP stream.
SoapFault	Represents a SOAP fault message.
Marshal	Allows users to define and register custom type-mapping behaviors.

message to follow certain formats and wish the parser to validate it during the parsing. For example, we might require that the n:transaction-type SOAP elements in the stock trade response (Listing 16.8) contain an xsd:string value Symbol, an xsd:int value Share, an xsd:boolean value Buy, and an xsd:float value Price.

Our old friend, the ClassMap class, can validate the message. We must add into the ClassMap object a SoapObject template associated with the current parser. The SoapObject template is an empty SoapObject with information about the parent SOAP type, children (properties) element names, and their Java types. Again, the children can be templates themselves, which allows us to construct arbitrarily complex templates.

We add the SoapObject template by calling the ClassMap.addTemplate() method (Listing 16.10).

Listing 16.10. Validate and parse the stock trade response

```
XmlParser xp = new XmlParser (reader);

ClassMap cm = new ClassMap (Soap.VER12);

// Register Marshal for "xsd:dateTime" type
Marshal md = new MarshalDate ();
md.register (cm);

// Register the template for validation
SoapObject so = new SoapObject ("http://myns", "transaction");
so.addProperty ("Symbol", new String (""));
so.addProperty ("Share", new Integer (0));
so.addProperty ("Buy", new Boolean (true));
so.addProperty ("Price", new SoapPrimitive ("xsd", "float", ""));
cm.addTemplate (so);

SoapEnvelope envelope = new SoapEnvelope (cm);
envelope.parse (xp);

SoapObject orderStatus = (SoapObject) envelope.getResult();
// ... ...
```

If the parsing succeeds, we can proceed to extract data from orderStatus, as illustrated in Listing 16.9. If the SOAP message's n:transaction element fails to conform to the corresponding SoapObject template, the parser throws an exception and stops.

16.5   More kSOAP Examples

In this section, let's check out two kSOAP applications for real-world services.

16.5.1   The Google Web Services API Demo

In the previous sections, we demonstrated how to invoke a simple Google spell check Web Service. In fact, Google offers much more than the sim-

ple service. With a proper Google ID (free registration), we can use the
Google Web Services interface to search the Web and get any Web site's
Google cache. I developed a complete Google API toolkit based on kSOAP.
The toolkit and its MIDP UI driver are available for download from this
book's Web site (see "Resources"). The Web search service has the most
complex interface. The response SOAP document has three arrays of equal
length: They contain the search result sites' URLs, titles, and cache sizes
respectively. We can use a Java data object **SearchResults** to encapsulate the
Google search results (see Listing 16.11).

Listing 16.11. Class SearchResults encapsulates the Google search results

```
public class SearchResults {

  public Vector urls, titles, sizes;
  public int estimatedTotalResultsCount;
  public String searchTime;

  public SearchResults () {
    urls = new Vector ();
    titles = new Vector ();
    sizes = new Vector ();
    estimatedTotalResultsCount = 0;
    searchTime = "0.0";
  }

  public int getSize () {
    return urls.size();
  }
}
```

Listing 16.12 demonstrates how to send out a search query and marshal
the response to a **SearchResults** object.

Listing 16.12. Google search

```
// The remote search method cannot return
// all the search results -- there could be
// tens of thousands of web sites.
//
// The "start" parameter specifies the index of
// the first entry to return.
```

```
public SearchResults search (String query,
                int start) throws Exception {
  // Prepare request SOAP message in a memory object
  SoapObject method = new SoapObject("urn:GoogleSearch",
                                     "doGoogleSearch");
  // The free license key
  method.addProperty("key", licenseKey);
  // The query string to search
  method.addProperty("q", query);
  // The start index to return
  method.addProperty("start", new Integer(start));
  // Number of results to return
  // from the start index
  method.addProperty("maxResults", new Integer(10));
  method.addProperty("filter", new Boolean(true));
  method.addProperty("restrict", "");
  method.addProperty("safeSearch", new Boolean(false));
  method.addProperty("lr", "");
  method.addProperty("ie", "latin1");
  method.addProperty("oe", "latin1");

  // Prepare SOAP RPC call object.
  HttpTransport rpc = new HttpTransport(endPointURL, "\"\"");
  // Google uses 1999 SOAP standards.
  ClassMap cm = new ClassMap(Soap.VER10);
  rpc.setClassMap (cm);
  // Conduct RPC call through HTTP and get results
  SoapObject so = (SoapObject) rpc.call (method);
  SearchResults sr = new SearchResults ();
  sr.estimatedTotalResultsCount = ((Integer) so.getProperty(
        "estimatedTotalResultsCount")).intValue ();
  sr.searchTime = ((SoapPrimitive) so.getProperty(
                        "searchTime")).toString ();

  Vector items =
    (Vector) so.getProperty("resultElements");
  for (int i = 0; i < items.size(); i++) {
    SoapObject item = (SoapObject) items.elementAt (i);
    sr.sizes.addElement (item.getProperty ("cachedSize"));
    sr.urls.addElement (item.getProperty ("URL"));
    sr.titles.addElement (item.getProperty ("title"));
  }
  return sr;
}
```

16.5.2 SmartPhrases

SmartPhrases is a mobile dictionary and thesaurus, smart spelling checker, and real-world usage checker. It is an award-winning application developed by Ju Long and Michael Yuan. Its source code is freely available from this book's Web site.

To be able to access dictionaries from devices, SmartPhrases includes a SOAP dictionary gateway. The gateway connects to free Internet dictionary servers using the TCP/IP-based DICT protocol. It then exposes dictionary query services through a simple SOAP interface using Apache Axis. Any mobile or desktop SOAP client can access the backend dictionary from the gateway service.

SmartPhrases utilizes Google Web Services to go beyond simple dictionaries: Google allows the user to check the usage of a phrase in real-world scenarios; it has a modern vocabulary list and makes spell suggestions for the entire phrase. The architecture of the application is shown in Figure 16.3.

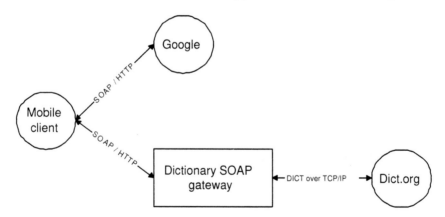

Figure 16.3. The architecture of the SmartPhrases application.

For a complete demo and implementation documentation of SmartPhrases, please download its source package.

16.6 What's in kSOAP v2.0?

The kSOAP v2.0 is based on the improved kXML pull parser. The pull parser could significantly improve the performance in some cases. Other important improvements of kSOAP v2.0 include the following:

- *Access to SOAP headers*: The SoapEnvelope object makes incoming and outgoing SOAP headers available in kDOM Element arrays.

- *Better support for untyped SOAP servers*: Some SOAP servers (notably, Microsoft .NET servers) do not bother to add the xsi:type= "xsd:string" attribute in string type elements. The kSOAP v2.0 SoapSerializationEnvelope provides a dotnet flag to turn on or off support for untyped elements.

- *Better structure and packaging*: Compared with kSOAP v1.0, the kSOAP v2.0 internal structure is more sensible and easier to use.

  - Necessary classes, such as PropertyInfo and KvmSerializable, are moved from org.kobjects to org.ksoap2 so that the kSOAP package is self-contained.
  - SOAP Serialization support is now optional and contained in a separate org.ksoap2.serialization package.
  - Several separate classes (e.g., ClassMap) have been integrated into the class SoapSerializationEnvelope, providing SOAP serialization support. The SoapSerializationEnvelope class extends the base class SoapEnvelope.

16.6.1   Programming for kSOAP v2.0

From the developer point of view, the object models for SoapObject, PropertyInfo and Marshal in kSOAP v2.0 are the same as those in kSOAP v1.2. However, the call model is slightly different. In kSOAP v2.0, the call arguments and return values are passed as follows.

- The HttpTransport.call() method takes in a SoapEnvelope object but does not return any value.

- The bodyIn data member in the SoapEnvelope object is a SoapObject containing the RPC input argument.

- The marshaled result of the RPC return value is stored in SoapEnvelope.bodyOut. Depending on the return type and available Marshal, this could be a Java value object, an array or a SoapObject object.

Listing 16.13 shows how to invoke the Google Web Service to get a spell suggestion using kSOAP v2.0. Please note the use of bodyIn and bodyOut variables.

Listing 16.13. Get Google spell suggestion using kSOAP 2

```
public String spellCheck (String query) throws Exception {
  // Prepare request SOAP message in a memory object
  SoapObject method = new SoapObject("urn:GoogleSearch",
                             "doSpellingSuggestion");
  method.addProperty("key", licenseKey);
  method.addProperty("phrase", query);

  // Google uses 1999 SOAP standards.
  SoapEnvelope envelope =
     new SoapSerializationEnvelope(SoapEnvelope.VER10);
  // Set the request object
  envelope.bodyOut = method;
  // Prepare SOAP RPC call object.
  HttpTransport rpc = new HttpTransport(endPointURL);
  // Make the method call (SoapAction is not needed)
  rpc.call(null, envelope);
  // Retrieve marshaled return value
  SoapObject ret = (SoapObject) envelope.bodyIn;
  String spellSugg = (String) ret.getProperty("return");
  return spellSugg;
}
```

The use of custom data marshal in kSOAP v2.0 is the same as that in kSOAP v1.2. Listing 16.14 shows how to get a site's Google cache using custom Base64 marshaling.

Listing 16.14. Get Google cache using kSOAP 2

```
import org.ksoap2.*;
import org.ksoap2.serialization.*;
import org.ksoap2.transport.*;

public class GoogleSearch {

  // other methods ...

  public byte [] getCache (String url) throws Exception {
    // Prepare request SOAP message in a memory object
    SoapObject method = new SoapObject("urn:GoogleSearch",
                                "doGetCachedPage");
```

```
    method.addProperty("key", licenseKey);
    method.addProperty("url", url);

    // Google uses 1999 SOAP standards.
    SoapEnvelope envelope =
      new SoapSerializationEnvelope(SoapEnvelope.VER10);
    // Set the request object
    envelope.bodyOut = method;
    // Add Base64 marshal.
    // It is for both request and response data.
    Marshal mb = new MarshalBase64 ();
    mb.register((SoapSerializationEnvelope)envelope);
    // Prepare SOAP RPC call object.
    HttpTransport rpc = new HttpTransport(endPointURL);
    // Make the method call (SoapAction is not needed)
    rpc.call(null, envelope);
    // Retrieve marshaled return value
    SoapObject ret = (SoapObject) envelope.bodyIn;
    byte [] cache = (byte []) ret.getProperty("return");
    return cache;
  }
}
```

Listing 16.15 shows the implementation of the kSOAP v2.0 Marshal-
Base64 class using the XmlPull API.

Listing 16.15. The `MarshalBase64` implementation in kSOAP 2

```
public class MarshalBase64 implements Marshal {

  static byte [] BA_WORKAROUND = new byte [0];
  public static Class BYTE_ARRAY_CLASS =
                    BA_WORKAROUND.getClass ();

  public Object readInstance (XmlPullParser parser,
                    String namespace, String name,
                              PropertyInfo expected)
          throws IOException, XmlPullParserException {

    Object result = Base64.decode(parser.nextText ());
    return result;
  }

  public void writeInstance (XmlSerializer writer,
```

```
                        Object obj) throws IOException {

    writer.text (Base64.encode ((byte[]) obj));
  }

  public void register (SoapSerializationEnvelope cm) {
    cm.addMapping (cm.xsd, "base64Binary",
            MarshalBase64.BYTE_ARRAY_CLASS, this);

    cm.addMapping (SoapEnvelope.ENC, "base64",
            MarshalBase64.BYTE_ARRAY_CLASS, this);

  }
}
```

16.7   Summary

In this chapter, we discussed the concepts behind SOAP Web Services and
why it is a big deal. The open source kSOAP library allows us to build
SOAP clients on J2ME devices. Throughout this chapter, we used many
examples to illustrate the use, and more importantly, what's under the hood,
of kSOAP, and we examined kSOAP v2.0.

In addition to kSOAP, the J2ME Web Services API is a JSR community
effort to standardize J2ME APIs for SOAP Web Services. We will discuss
the new standard and its relation with kSOAP in the next chapter.

Resources

[1] The kSOAP project (v1.2). http://ksoap.enhydra.org/

[2] kSOAP v2.0. http://www.ksoap.org/

[3] Google Web Services API. http://www.google.com/apis/

[4] The kSOAP Google API demo and the SmartPhrases application are
    available from the book's web site.
    http://www.enterprisej2me.com/book/code/

Chapter 17

The J2ME Web Services
Optional Package

CHAPTER OVERVIEW

- The J2ME Web Services Specification

- The XML Processing API

- The JAX-RPC API

- Use the Client Stubs

- The Service Provider Interface (SPI) for OP Vendors

- Compare with kXML and kSOAP

A major strength of the J2ME platform comes from the separation between the specification and implementation processes. J2ME API specifications are industry consensuses developed by the JCP. The standardized APIs allow developers to avoid expensive vendor lock-ins because applications written against those APIs run on a wide range of devices.

JSR 172, the J2ME Web Services Specification, defines a standard set of APIs for XML processing, and SOAP Web Service clients on the J2ME platform. Any J2ME vendor can implement JSR 172 to enable Web Services on its device platforms. In this chapter, we discuss the JSR 172 and its relationship to the corresponding J2SE/J2EE specifications. The discussions here are based on the JSR 172 proposed final draft 2 released in July 2003.

17.1   A Little History

When the MIDP v1.0 specification was released in 2000, it was a good compromise between the small footprint required by small devices at that time and features necessary to support simple mobile applications. Since then, capabilities of mobile devices and sophistication levels of mobile clients have increased drastically. MIDP v1.0 is showing its limitations. One such limitation is the lack of support to access structured data. To address this problem, a major design goal for the MIDP v2.0 specification was to add a set of XML and Web Services XML. However, during the development of MIDP v2.0, the expert group could not agree on the exact format, features, and footprint of the XML API. Considering that a large portion of MIDP v2.0 devices will be used for gaming applications and may never consume Web Services, the MIDP v2.0 expert group decided that the XML API should be offered as a standard Optional Package for both CLDC-based and CDC-based profiles. The specification development is delegated to a new expert group in Java Specification Request 172 (JSR 172, "J2ME Web Services Specification").

The JSR 172 expert group consists of 30 industry-leading corporations and individuals. It includes all the big handset manufacturers (e.g., Nokia, Motorola, Sony/Ericsson, LG, Siemens, Sharp, and RIM), system software vendors (e.g., Symbian, IBM, Borland, BEA, and Sun Microsystems) and several leading wireless carriers (e.g., NTT and Cingular). The specifications have been unanimously approved by the JCP J2ME executive committee. An implementation of the J2ME Web Services Optional Package is already available from IBM's Web Services Tool Kit for Mobile Devices. This toolkit integrates with the WebSphere Studio Device Developer IDE. Now, let's have a look at the APIs proposed by JSR 172.

17.2   The XML Processing API

The XML processing API of the J2ME Web Services Optional Package is a
strict subset of JAXP v1.2. Implementations of the optional package must
support the SAX v2.0 API (also see Section 15.3.1). They must support XML
namespace and UTF-8 and UTF-16 encodings. DTD validation support is
optional. However, if a nonvalidating parser encounters a DTD, it must
throw an exception. JAXP features that are not supported include DOM
and XSLT. The target runtime size for the API is about 25 KB.

17.2.1   The API

Table 17.1 lists the JAXP subset API supported by the J2ME Web Services
Optional Package.

A simple example of the use of the JAXP SAX API is illustrated in
Listing 17.1. The example program parses the XML file specified by the first
line argument and prints out every start tag and attribute.

Listing 17.1. A JAXP SAX API example

```
import java.io.*;
import javax.xml.parsers.*;
import org.xml.sax.*;
import org.xml.sax.helpers.*;

// Parse the XML file specified by the first
// line argument and print out every start tag
// and attributes
public class SAXExample {

  public static void main(String[] args) {

    SAXParser parser;
    try {
     SAXParserFactory factory =
       SAXParserFactory.newInstance();
     parser = factory.newSAXParser();

     MyHandler handler = new MyHandler ();

     InputStream fis = new FileInputStream(args[0]);
     InputSource is = new InputSource (fis);
     parser.parse(is, handler);
```

```
    } catch (Exception e) {
      e.printStackTrace();
    }
  }
}

// Define a custom callback handler
class MyHandler extends DefaultHandler {

  public void startElement(String uri,
      String localName, String qName,
      Attributes attributes) throws SAXException {

    System.out.println(qName);
    for (int i=0; i<attributes.getLength(); i++) {
      System.out.println("   "
                          + attributes.getValue(i));
    }
  }
}
```

17.3   The JAX-RPC API

The J2ME Web Services Optional Package also defines a strict subset of the JAX-RPC v1.0 API that runs on both CLDC and CDC devices. JAX-RPC allows Java developers to use their familiar RMI-like APIs to invoke remote SOAP services without caring about the underlying transport or marshaling mechanisms. This is a Java-centric approach in which the developer never sees SOAP messages. All remote procedure calls are simply mapped to local calls to stub objects. Figure 17.1 illustrates the architecture of the JAX-RPC package for J2ME.

17.3.1   Features

The J2ME Web Services Optional Package is required to implement the following JAX-RPC v1.0 features.

- Support for SOAP v1.2.

- HTTP Basic Authentication and session support in the underlying message transport. HTTPS support is optional.

Table 17.1. XML API in J2ME Web Services Optional Package

Class	Description
Package javax.xml.parsers	See classes below
SAXParser	The main class that controls the parsing flow and handles events via callback methods.
SAXParserFactory	The factory class that instantiates SAXParser objects.
FactoryConfigurationError	Configuration error.
ParserConfigurationException	Configuration error.
Package org.xml.sax.helpers	See classes below.
DefaultHandler	The class that the application can extend to provide custom callback handlers for parsing, validation and error events. It can be passed as a parameter to the SAXParser.parse() method.
Package org.xml.sax	See classes below.
Attributes	The interface that represents a list of XML attributes.
Locator	The interface that provides support for associating a SAX event with a document location.
InputSource	The class that encapsulates an input source in a single object. The input source can be an Input-Stream, a Reader or a String object.
SAXException	Runtime error.
SAXNotRecognizedException	Runtime error.
SAXNotSupportedException	Runtime error.
SAXParseException	Runtime error.

- Simple SOAP type mappings defined in Table 17.2. XML structs and complex composite types are supported. This allows passing simple JavaBean objects as RPC parameters and return values. However, extensible type mapping is not supported.

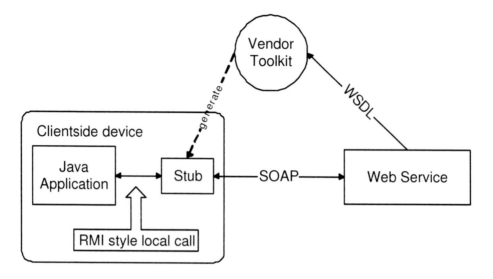

Figure 17.1. Architecture of JAX-RPC for J2ME.

- Mapping SOAP (or WSDL) Fault messages to the appropriate Java exceptions on the client side.

- Both document and literal styles of SOAP messages.

- Generating J2ME client stubs for remote services from their WSDL documents.

Note

The xsd:float and xsd:double types are mapped to Strings on handsets that do not support float and double data types (i.e. CLDC v1.0 devices).

Serverside APIs and SOAP attachments are not supported.

17.3.2   The API

Table 17.3 lists user APIs defined in the J2ME Web Services Optional Package. All of them are J2SE/J2EE (especially JAX-RPC) classes that are added back to J2ME. The RMI classes are also available from the CDC RMI Optional Package.

Now, let's have a look at exactly how we use the J2ME Web Services Optional Package.

Table 17.2. Supported Java and SOAP Type Mapping

SOAP type	Java type
xsd:string	java.lang.String
xsd:int	int
xsd:long	long
xsd:short	short
xsd:boolean	boolean
xsd:byte	byte
xsd:float	java.lang.String or float
xsd:double	java.lang.String or double
xsd:QName	javax.xml.namespace.QName
xsd:base64Binary	byte []
xsd:hexBinary	byte []
xsd:complexType	JavaBeans with getter and setter methods

17.3.3   A User Scenario

To build a Web Services client using the Optional Package, we need to go through several steps.

1. Fetch the WSDL document from the service provider and generate a javax.xml.rpc.Stub class for each service. The stub class generator is a desktop utility. For example, we can generate a GoogleSearchStub class using the WSDL file fetched from the Google Web site (see Section 16.2.2 for more details).

2. Put the generated class into the project class path and instantiate an instance of the Stub when necessary in the application code.

```
GoogleSearchStub stub = new GoogleSearchStub ();
stub._setProperty(
    Stub.ENDPOINT_ADDRESS_PROPERTY,
    "http://api.google.com/search/beta2");
// Set more properties if authentication is needed
```

Table 17.3. J2ME JAX-RPC User API

Class	Description
Package javax.xml.rpc	See classes below
Stub	This is an interface representing a generated stub (or clientside proxy) for the remote service. An implementation of the stub is generated by the Optional Package for each Web Service. It understands how to handle the underlying SOAP messages.
NamespaceConstants	This class holds static constants for namespace prefixes and URIs.
JAXRPCException	Error from the JAX-RPC runtime.
Package javax.xml.namespace	See classes below.
QName	This class represents a qualified name as defined in the XML Schema specification.
Package java.rmi	See classes below.
Remote	This is a tagging interface that declares no method but acts as an indicator (or tag) for classes/interfaces supporting remote methods.
MarshalException	This exception is thrown when an I/O error occurs during the argument and return value serialization and deserialization.
RemoteException	This exception indicates a communication error during the remote call.
ServerException	This exception indicates an error on the server side.

3. Use the **Stub** object to invoke remote services and get the return value as a Java object.

```
String key = "Google license key";
String query = "badspell";
String suggestion = stub.doSpellingSuggestion(key, query);
// Go on and make use of the suggested word
```

4. When the development work is done, we need to bundle the generated Stub classes with the application before deploying them to devices.

Now, we have seen how to use J2ME Web Services Optional Package from the user point of view. The generated Stub class shields the underlying complexity from us. Since the Stub interface is standardized, we can change the Optional Package vendors without changing the application code. JSR 172 does not stop here. It made further efforts to standardize the operation of the Stub by defining standard Service Provider Interfaces (SPIs).

17.4 The SPI for Implementers

The SPI specifies the interface to pass data between the generated Stub classes and the underlying implementation. The SPI benefits both application developers and the JSR 172 specification implementers.

- Application developers can reuse the generated Stub classes when switching implementation providers. This makes the application more portable.

- Multiple implementation providers can share the same Stub generator and focus on their core business—implementing the communication and marshaling logic.

The SPI classes are defined in package javax.microedition.xml.rpc (Table 17.4). Those classes correspond to elements in the programming model defined in the WSDL document. The JSR 172 specification implementers must implement them.

For more up-to-date documentation and usage examples of the SPI, please refer to the specification documents released by JSR 172.

17.4.1 Support for Gateway-Based Clients

The SPI is just a set of interfaces. There are many innovative ways to implement it. For example, a vendor can implement most of the SOAP parsing methods on a gateway. The SPI implementation on the client device could communicate with the gateway using optimized proprietary protocols (Figure 17.2. This way, we can reduce the device hardware and bandwidth requirements of mobile Web Services clients. Oracle's J2ME Web Services gateway application server is a step toward this direction.

Table 17.4. SPI Classes in the javax.microedition.xml.rpc **package**	

SPI Class	Description
Type	It represents a simple type defined in a WSDL document.
Element	It represents an xsd:element element with a qualified name (QName) and a type.
ComplexType	It represents an xsd:complextype element containing an array of Elements.
Operation	It represents a wsdl:operation element that defines a target endpoint in a WSDL document. This class defines the invoke() method which does the plumbing for the remote call.
FaultDetailHandler	It is an interface implemented by the stubs to handle custom faults.
FaultDetailException	This exception is thrown if the server returns a fault. It returns the fault details and associated QNames to the Stub.

17.5   Compare with kXML and kSOAP

The J2ME Web Services Optional Package does not make kXML and kSOAP obsolete. The kXML and kSOAP libraries work at a lower level and target developers who want more flexibility. In fact, kXML and kSOAP can be used to implement the Optional Package. The major differences between the Optional Package and kXML/kSOAP are as follows:

- *Support for XML processing models*: The Optional Package supports only SAX, while kXML supports SAX, XMLPull, and kDOM.

- *Java-centric versus XML-centric*: A big feature of the Optional Package is its Java-centric design that treats SOAP RPC calls the same way as Java native RMI RPC calls. However, the trade-off is that we do not have any direct control over the underlying SOAP messages. In contrast, kSOAP allows us to peek into the XML structure, add custom headers/attributes, and manipulate arbitrary nodes. The difference between the Optional Package and kSOAP is analogous to the difference between JAX-RPC and Apache Axis.

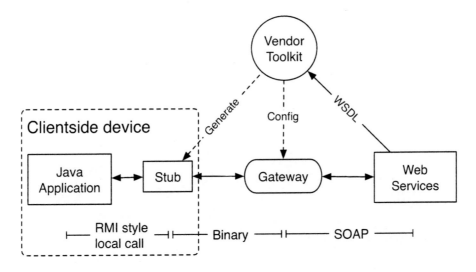

Figure 17.2. Implementing a mobile Web Services gateway using the SPI.

- *Custom type mapping*: Extensible data marshaling that requires access to the underlying SOAP structure is available only in kSOAP.

- *Support for flexible architecture*: The support for Web Services gateways via the SPI is a big plus for the Optional Package.

- *Availability*: kXML and kSOAP packages are available in production quality now on almost all MIDP-based and CDC-based devices. Commercial implementation of the Optional Package is still several months away. In fact, the kXML and kSOAP libraries can be used to implement the Optional Package.

17.6 Summary

The J2ME Web Services Optional Package offers a Java-centric way to build mobile Web Services clients through generated client stubs. It standardizes the SAX XML parsing API and JAX-RPC API subset for both CLDC and CDC devices. The specification also standardizes the generated clientside stub by defining a set of SPIs that the vendors must adhere to. The Optional Package handles JavaBean marshaling and runtime exceptions very well using techniques familiar to Java developers. It is likely to gain widespread support from the industry.

Resources

[1] JSR 172: The J2ME Web Services Specification
     http://www.jcp.org/en/jsr/detail?id=172

[2] Java API for XML Processing (JAXP)
     http://java.sun.com/xml/jaxp/index.html

[3] Java API for XML-based RPC (JAX-RPC)
     http://java.sun.com/xml/jaxrpc/index.html

[4] The SAX API http://www.saxproject.org/

[5] The IBM Web Services Tool Kit for Mobile Devices provides an
     implementation for the J2ME Web Services Optional Package
     http://www.alphaworks.ibm.com/tech/wstkmd

Chapter 18

Case Study: Mobile Clients for Location-Based Services

CHAPTER OVERVIEW

- Location-Based Service

- Microsoft MapPoint Web Services

- The Apache Axis Web Services Facade

- MapPoint J2ME Clients

- Enhancing the Driving Directions Application

- The J2ME Location API

In the previous two chapters, we discussed how to consume Web Services on mobile devices using the kSOAP and J2ME JAX-RPC APIs. In this chapter, we study real-world mobile Web Services in an emerging key mobile application field: Location-Based Services (LBS). After explaining basic LBS concepts, we introduce Microsoft MapPoint Web Service, a leading LBS Web Services provider. Then, we create a concrete example that allows users to look up driving directions on the move. It uses J2ME at the mobile front end, Apache Axis in the middleware gateway, and MapPoint Web Services at the back end. The last two sections of this chapter focus on clientside location technologies, including a brief introduction to the upcoming J2ME Location API.

18.1   Location-Based Services

LBS include all applications that make use of location and geographic data. It is touted as the killer app for mobile commerce because it enables brand new applications not possible in the desktop world. There are several types of LBS applications:

- *Pull-based applications*: The user actively sends out her location information to a server and pulls in location information such as driving maps and nearby stores.

- *Push-based applications*: Service providers detect users in their proximity and push out services such as coupons and advertisements. A central issue in push-based applications is how to protect user privacy. Location information can be highly sensitive. It is extremely important vendors get information from and push services to only opt-in users.

- *A combination of pull and push*: For example, a user can first pull nearby coffee shop locations and make a mobile reservation. Then he can send meeting alerts to peers within certain distances from the shop. The peers will be able to accept or reject the invitation.

Although LBS offers appealing business values, its implementation technologies are sophisticated. The core technology for any LBS solution is Geographic Information System (GIS), which performs important functions such as determining street addresses from coordinates and vice versa; look up yellow pages and landmarks; calculate optimal routes and render custom maps. It is the integration point of many heterogeneous components in the LBS application. This makes XML Web Services a perfect fit here. In the next section, we discuss a leading commercial GIS Web service: Microsoft MapPoint.

18.2   Microsoft MapPoint Web Services

Standalone GIS servers (e.g., Oracle GIS server) that are capable of geocoding, map rendering, and other complex geographic algorithms have been commercially available for a long time. However, running a GIS server by yourself is probably too expensive for most small to mid-sized businesses. The costs include:

- Hiring GIS experts to set up and maintain the system.

- Licensing high-resolution digital maps and business yellow page listings. This could be very expensive if your users roam across many metropolitan areas.

- Aggregating geographic information updates from many sources (e.g., road construction and business address changes) and updating them frequently to the database.

- Ongoing server administration for secure and high availability services.

- Licensing cost of the GIS server software itself.

For most companies, it makes sense to outsource the entire GIS operation to specialized providers. Microsoft's MapPoint Web Service is a managed GIS solution accessible via a set of platform-independent SOAP Web Services APIs. MapPoint also allows users to import their own geocoding data and points-of-interest listings for customized services.

Note

You can pay for MapPoint services based on the number of queries you perform. Or, you can get unlimited queries for a flat subscription fee. Developers can evaluate the service for free for 45 days.

18.2.1   The MapPoint v3.0 SOAP API

MapPoint Web Services expose a very rich set of SOAP APIs. Important remote methods in MapPoint v3.0 are divided into four categories.

- *Common Service* contains utility functions that are common to other services.

- *Find Service* allows the user to do generic geocoding tasks, including finding addresses from latitudes and longitudes, and vice versa. It also allows searching for nearby points of interests.

- *Route Service* calculates routes and directions based on locations and waypoints. It also generates map view representations of the calculated routes. The map view can be used to highlight routes on a map.

- *Render Service* renders the map for the locations or routes. It highlights routes, places pushpins and icons, and supports zoom.

Table 18.1 lists the methods from all categories. The first 5 methods in that table belong to the common service; the next 5 methods belong to the find service; the next 2 methods belong to the route service; and the last 4 methods belong to the render service. The API also defines many composite data types (e.g., Address, MapView, and RouteSpecification) to pass data to or from those service methods. Detailed discussions on how use the MapPoint API is beyond the scope of this book. For interested readers, the Axis gateway example in Section 18.2.3 demonstrates the use of many basic API functions from a Java client.

18.2.2   The Aggregated API

Through the SOAP API, MapPoint Web Service offers fine-grained access to its GIS back end, allowing us to design flexible applications without arbitrary limitations imposed by preset scripts. However, the trade-off is that we have to make separate method calls for each small step to complete a task. For example, in order to retrieve driving directions between two addresses, we have to go through the following steps.

1. Convert the addresses to latitude and longitude coordinates.

2. Calculate the route according to options.

3. Render the overview map with the route and start and end locations highlighted.

4. Retrieve turn-by-turn instructions for each route segment.

5. Render highlighted turn-by-turn maps for each route segment.

The last two steps need to be performed repeatedly for a long route with many segments. Since all those method calls are remote SOAP calls,

Table 18.1. The MapPoint v3.0 SOAP RPC API

Method	Description
GetCountryRegionInfo	Look up country or region information.
GetDataSourceInfo	Return information of a data source (e.g. North America and Europe).
GetEntityTypes	Look up the data source to find information about entities.
GetGreatCircleDistances	Calculate an array of great circle distances for a set of location points.
GetVersionInfo	Return version information of the current MapPoint service.
Find	Find geographic entities based on search options.
FindAddress	Return a list of addresses based on search options.
FindNearby	Find points of interests close to a specified location.
GetLocationInfo	Return address or other information of a specified pair of latitude and longitude.
ParseAddress	Return an Address object from a string representation of an address.
CalculateSimpleRoute	Calculate a route from start/end points specified by their latitude and longitude coordinates using default options.
CalculateRoute	Calculate routes or route segments from route specifications. It allows more options than the CalculateSimpleRoute method.
GetMap	Retrieve the rendered map according to the rendering options and map specifications pass to this method.
GetBestMapView	Get an optimal map view that contains all locations and routes. We can pass this map view as part of the map specifications to the GetMap method to get the actual map.
ConvertToLatLong	Convert pixel coordinates on a map to latitude and longitude coordinates.
ConvertToPoint	Convert latitude and longitude coordinates to pixel coordinates.

those excessive round trips cause long delays over slow wireless networks. To minimize the data transfer over wireless networks, we can place a remote facade between the mobile client and MapPoint. The facade takes in two human-readable addresses in a single SOAP call, queries MapPoint via many API calls over the wired Internet, constructs the resultant driving directions, and returns the results. It provides a coarse-grained, simple interface that aggregates functions of the fine-grained MapPoint API methods for specific applications. Figure 18.1 illustrates the facade architecture.

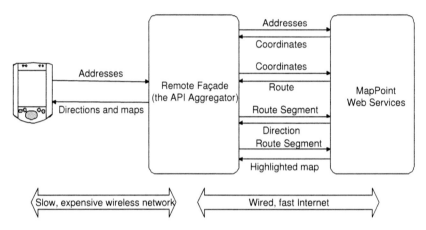

Figure 18.1. The remote facade architecture.

MapPoint Authentication

MapPoint Web Services use HTTP Digest Authentication to authenticate users and keep track of billing. So, any client application must support HTTP Digest headers in the network transport layer. A J2ME example of HTTP Digest-aware connection class is mentioned in Chapter 6, Section 6.5.

Note

As a Microsoft platform, MapPoint was never designed for Java clients. But the use of SOAP Web Services makes it platform-independent. This highlights the power of Web Services.

18.2.3   The Axis Facade

In this section, we introduce a Java-based SOAP facade (gateway) that aggregates generic MapPoint APIs into convenient remote methods for specific tasks to minimize round trips for mobile clients. The gateway is built using Apache Axis (v1.0). It is developed as follows:

1. Generate Java SOAP stub classes for the MapPoint SOAP API using the WSDL2Java tool in Axis.

2. Use those Java stub classes to develop a Java object, MPClient, that contains convenience aggregated methods.

3. Publish the MPClient object as a SOAP Web Service via Axis's server interface. This is the RPC interface for mobile devices. The steps are as follows.

    (a) Configure and run Axis server inside a Tomcat server.
    (b) Copy the JAR file containing the MPClient class to Axis library directory.
    (c) Specify the scope of the service object, methods to expose, and other options via a .wsdd file.
    (d) Deploy the .wsdd file to Axis through its server administration utility.

   Detailed tutorials on how to configure and use Axis are beyond the scope of this book. Please refer to Axis documentations in the "Resources" section. Due to the limited space, I show only the public interfaces of remote methods in the MPClient class here (Listing 18.1). The API usage is embedded in the code comments. The complete code is available in the AxisFacade project, downloadable from this book's Web site. The project archive also contains generated stub classes, Axis libraries, sample .wsdd files, and ANT script to build and deploy the facade gateway.

Listing 18.1. The Axis facade MPClient class

```
public class MPClient {

  // Authentication credentials obtained from
  // MapPoint Web site
  private static String userName = "userid";
```

```
private static String password = "password";

// other variables

// The cached route segments
private Segment[] segments;

// Get the driving directions between
// two human-ready addresses. This method
// also caches the route in the segments array
//
// You have to run this method before you can
// retrieve maps for the entire route or for
// each route segment.
public String [] getDirections (
 String fromStreet, String fromCity,
 String fromState, String fromZip,
 String toStreet, String toCity,
 String toState, String toZip
                        ) throws Exception {
  // method body
}


// Return the number of segments of the current
// cached route. The number is available after
// you call the getDirections() method.
public int getSegmentNum () throws Exception {
  // Method body
}


// Get a map from the current cached route.
// The return value is a byte array for
// the GIF image.
//
// index == 0 for the overview map
// index <= segmentNum for a segment map
public byte [] getMap (int index,
        int width, int height) throws Exception {
  // Method body
}
}
```

Note

You have to call the getDirections() method to obtain the route before you can retrieve any map.

The MPClient facade class aggregates driving direction services for illustration purposes only. In real-world, location-based applications that require more functionalities, you should design and implement facade gateways that fit your own application needs.

18.3   MapPoint J2ME Clients

With the Axis facade gateway, we have transformed the MapPoint Web Service to a wireless-friendly service while still preserving the benefits of SOAP Web Services. In fact, we can use any Web Services-compatible client to access MapPoint services through the Axis gateway. Those clients can be developed on almost all Microsoft platforms, all Java editions, script languages such as Perl and AppleScript, as well as many native C/C++ SOAP frameworks. In this section, we demonstrate two simple J2ME clients for driving directions.

18.3.1   CDC/PP and PersonalJava Clients

Figure 18.2 demonstrates the driving directions client in action on a PocketPC device running Jeode PersonalJava VM. Thanks to the standard AWT library, the same client runs on CDC/FP/PP devices (e.g., IBM WebSphere Micro Edition's Personal Profile runtime) and standard J2SE desktops (e.g., Windows, Linux, and Mac OS) without modification.

Key code snippet that queries the Axis gateway service for directions and maps is shown in Listing 18.2.

Listing 18.2. The CDC/PP driving directions client

```
public class AWTMap extends Frame
    implements WindowListener, ActionListener {

  private String endPointURL;

  private TextField fromStreet;
  private TextField fromCity;
  private TextField fromState;
```

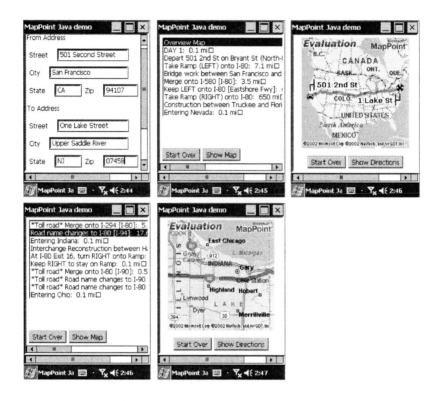

Figure 18.2. The PDA-based driving directions client in action.

```
private TextField fromZip;
private TextField toStreet;
private TextField toCity;
private TextField toState;
private TextField toZip;
private java.awt.List directionsList;

private ClassMap cm;
private Marshal md;

// Other variables

// Lists the driving directions
private void listScreen (boolean newSearch) {
  try {
    if (newSearch) {
      SoapObject method =
```

```
        new SoapObject("", "getDirections");
    // Use the SE version for standard JDK
    // Http methods
    HttpTransportSE rpc =
      new HttpTransportSE(endPointURL, "\"\"");
    rpc.setClassMap(cm);
    method.addProperty("in0", fromStreet.getText());
    method.addProperty("in1", fromCity.getText());
    method.addProperty("in2", fromState.getText());
    method.addProperty("in3", fromZip.getText());
    method.addProperty("in4", toStreet.getText());
    method.addProperty("in5", toCity.getText());
    method.addProperty("in6", toState.getText());
    method.addProperty("in7", toZip.getText());
    Vector v = (Vector) rpc.call (method);

    directionsList = new java.awt.List(10, false);
    directionsList.add("Overview Map");
    for (int i = 0; i < v.size(); i++) {
      directionsList.add((String) v.elementAt(i));
    }
    directionsList.setSize(200, 200);
  }
  Panel top = new Panel ();
  top.setLayout(new FlowLayout(FlowLayout.LEFT));
  top.add(directionsList);
  Panel bottom = new Panel ();
  bottom.setLayout(new FlowLayout(FlowLayout.LEFT));
  bottom.add(startOver);
  bottom.add(showMap);

  scroll.remove(content);
  content = new Panel ();
  content.setLayout(new BorderLayout());
  content.add(top, BorderLayout.CENTER);
  content.add(bottom, BorderLayout.SOUTH);
  scroll.add(content);
  setVisible(true);

  } catch (Exception e) {
    e.printStackTrace();
  }
}

private void mapScreen (int i) {
```

```
      try {
        ImageItem img;
        byte [] imgarray;
        SoapObject method = new SoapObject("", "getMap");
        HttpTransportSE rpc =
          new HttpTransportSE(endPointURL, "\"\"");
        rpc.setClassMap(cm);
        method.addProperty("in0", new Integer(i));
        method.addProperty("in1", new Integer(200));
        method.addProperty("in2", new Integer(200));
        imgarray = (byte []) rpc.call (method);
        img = new ImageItem(imgarray, 200, 200);

        Panel top = new Panel ();
        top.add(img);
        Panel bottom = new Panel ();
        bottom.add(startOver);
        bottom.add(showDirections);

        scroll.remove(content);
        content = new Panel ();
        content.setLayout(new BorderLayout());
        content.add(top, BorderLayout.CENTER);
        content.add(bottom, BorderLayout.SOUTH);
        scroll.add(content);
        setVisible(true);

      } catch (Exception e) {
        e.printStackTrace();
      }
    }

    // Other UI and event handling methods
}
```

18.3.2 MIDP Clients

Figure 18.3 shows the MIDP client in action in a MIDP v2.0 emulator. Since MapPoint supports only GIF image format rendering at this stage, but MIDP requires PNG format, driving maps are not yet available in the MIDP client. A quick fix would be to convert GIF images to PNG images inside the facade using the Java imaging API.

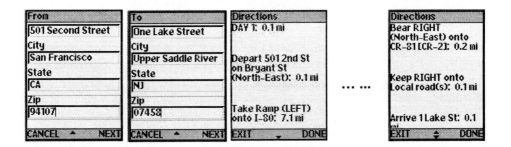

Figure 18.3. The MIDP phone-based driving directions client in action.

Complete source code and build scripts for both Java clients as well as for a .NET Compact Framework client are available for download from this book's Web site.

18.4 Enhancing the Driving Directions Application

The driving directions application we demonstrated above is not particularly easy to use. For example, if we are lost while driving around, we need to find the route from the current location to the destination. To find out the current street address and manually enter it into the device could be a major nuisance. A driving directions application that is aware of the current location context and automatically fills out the From field can be much more valuable to users. In fact, most LBS business models require access to the mobile client's current location.

18.4.1 Location Determination Techniques

There are several ways to obtain the current locations of mobile devices.

- *Terminal-based*: A GPS-equipped device can calculate its coordinates using GPS satellite signals. This method is accurate and straightforward, and it works everywhere in the world. However, GPS modules are expensive, slow, and a drain on batteries.

- *Network-based*: Cellular network operators can determine location of any phone in the network using its signal strength received by three nearby access stations (triangling). On-device smart applications (e.g., the driving directions application) can access the location data via the data network. With user authorization, the location data can also be made available to third parties from the carrier's Web site. This is an excellent approach if we need to track a large number of users from the back end (e.g., push services). However, the drawbacks are that the user must be within the cellular network coverage; the service is not yet available nationally, and the location accuracy is not as good as the GPS approach.

- *Network-assisted GPS*: Of course, we can combine the above two approaches: GPS devices can use network data to determine an approximate position first and then use the GPS module to get accurate corrections. This speeds up the GPS look-up process considerably.

- *Local wireless network-based*: Advances in new technologies will also enable location determination in local wireless networks, such as WiFi and Bluetooth networks, in the future.

- *User-assisted*: As the last resort, we can also ask the user to identify the closest landmark and calculate an approximate coordinate based on the known coordinate of the landmark. This works well in controlled environments like a college or company campus.

Note

The Oracle wireless application server works with wireless carrier location servers to provide SOAP interfaces for network-based location data of all devices in the network.

What Is E911?
The Enhanced 911 (E911) is a government initiative to enable the police and emergency workers to determine the location of any cell phone caller in the United States. It requires all U.S. wireless carriers to install network-based location tracking systems and make the data available to authorized government agencies. Once deployed, E911 will create a universal cell phone location system available to commercial location-based service providers.

The original timetable for E911 was to have the complete deployment by the end of 2004, but it has been delayed significantly in the past several years. The completion time is now estimated to be 2007.

18.4.2   The Location API for J2ME

The J2ME Location API (JSR 179) is a standard Optional Package for both CDC-based and CLDC-based devices. It allows J2ME applications to access location information on any device through standard APIs regardless of the underlying technology and service provider. Table 18.2 shows the entire J2ME Location API defined in the javax.microedition.location package. It is based on the v1.0 final release (September 2003).

Table 18.2.   The javax.microedition.location **Package**

Class	Description
AddressInfo	Contains information about an address, such as building number, street number, city, and state.
Coordinates	Represent three-dimensional geographic coordinate information (i.e., longitude, latitude, and altitude) from GPS devices or network operators.
QualifiedCoordinates	Extend the Coordinates with 1-sigma error bars qualifying the accuracy of the coordinates data.
Orientation	Contains data about the device's three-dimensional orientation. It is up to the device to define its own axes.
Location	Holds information about the device's current location, including the current QualifiedCoordinates, speed, course, coordinates retrieval method, and an optional AddressInfo.
LocationProvider	It is the factory class to retrieve Location from underlying providers (e.g., GPS device interface or network location server).
Criteria	Specifies criteria to select location providers. Those criteria include cost, accuracy, response time, power consumption, and supported features.
LocationListener	It is a listener interface that can be registered with a LocationProvider. It handles events of location and provider state changes.
Landmark	Represents a location with a known address.
LandmarkStore	Represents a collection of Landmark objects.
ProximityListener	This is a listener interface that can be registered with a LocationProvider. It handles events when the device enters the proximity radius of the specified coordinates.

Note

CLDC v1.1 is required for the J2ME Location API because coordinates are expressed in float or double numbers.

Listing 18.3 illustrates how to construct a simple location-based application using the JSR 179 API. For more information about the J2ME Location API and usage examples, please refer to JSR 179 documentation.

Listing 18.3. A simple J2ME Location API application

```
Criteria criteria = new Criteria ();
criteria.setPreferredResponseTime(20);
criteria.seVerticalAccuracy(10);
// set other criteria

LocationProvider provider =
    LocationProvider.getInstance(criteria);

// The StepTracker's locationUpdated() method
// will be called every 1 second until the 100th second.
// The passed location data cannot be more than 2 seconds old.

StepTracker tracker = new StepTracker ();
provider.setLocationListener(tracker, 1, 100, 2);

// Add the collision handling logic. The CollisionHandler's
// proximityEvent() method is called when the device
// enters the 0.5 meter radius of either coord1 or coord2

Coordinates coord1 = new Coordinates(lat1, long1, alt1);
Coordinates coord2 = new Coordinates(lat2, long2, alt2);
CollisionHandler collision = new CollisionHandler ();
provider.addProximityListener(collision, coord1, 0.5);
provider.addProximityListener(collision, coord2, 0.5);

public StepTracker implements LocationListener {

  public StepTracker () {
  }

  // Both threads below must return immediately.
  // So, put long processes in a separate thread.
```

```
    public void locationUpdated (LocationProvider provider,
                                 Location location) {
      // Do something with the new location
      // For example, update the steps on a map.
    }

    public void providerStateChanged(LocationProvider provider,
                                     int newState) {
      // Handle the state change. For example, if the
      // provider becomes unavailable, alert the user.
    }

  }

public CollisionHandler implements ProximityListener {

  public CollisionHandler () {
  }

  public void proximityEvent(Coordinates coordinates,
                             Location location) {
    // Handle the collision here.
    // For example, alert the user and provide a direction
    // to move away from the collision point.
  }

  public void monitoringStateChanged(boolean isActive) {
    // Handle the state change in the provider
  }

}
```

18.5   Summary

In this chapter, we used a driving directions example to illustrate how to build mobile facades and clients for MapPoint Web Services. The techniques we discussed in this chapter could be used to build general location-based applications on MapPoint Web Services. We also explored general topics in location-based services, such as alternative location determination technologies and the J2ME Location API.

Resources

[1] Download the MapPoint facade and mobile clients source code.
http://www.enterprisej2me.com/book/code/

[2] JSR 179: J2ME Location API. http://jcp.org/en/jsr/detail?id=179

[3] Microsoft MapPoint Web Services.
http://www.microsoft.com/mappoint/net/

[4] Enhanced 911 services news.
http://www.wirelessdevnet.com/e911/news.html

Part VI

Advanced Mobile Security

Chapter 19

Mobile Security for Enterprise

CHAPTER OVERVIEW

- Enterprise Security Requirements

- Content-Based Security

- Device Security

- Lightweight Mobile Cryptography Toolkits

- Bouncy Castle Lightweight API

- The IAIK ME JCE

- Phaos Technology Micro Foundation Toolkit

- NTRU jNeo for Java Toolkit

- B3 Security

- Device-Specific APIs

- Standardization of J2ME Security APIs

This is not the first time we discussed security in this book. In Chapter 6, we discussed advanced HTTP techniques, including mobile clients for secure HTTP (HTTPS) and HTTP Basic/Digest Authentication protocols. Although HTTP-based security measures prove sufficient for most of today's Internet commerce applications, future mobile applications demand more flexible, customizable, and better-optimized security schemes. In this chapter, we discuss the security requirements of mobile enterprise applications and how third-party J2ME tools can help developers meet those requirements.

19.1 What Is Advanced Mobile Security?

The three most important aspects of mobile security are data confidentiality, access control and device security.

19.1.1 Content-Based Security

HTTP Authentication headers, HTTPS, SSL (Secure Socket Layer), and TLS (Transaction Layer Security) are connection-based security protocols. The basic idea is to secure communication channels and hence secure everything that passes through those channels. However, this approach has several problems:

- *Direct connection between the client and server must be established:* If our application has multiple intermediaries to provide value-added services, multiple HTTPS connections must be piped together. That not only opens potential security holes at connecting nodes, but also creates a public key certificate management nightmare. Figure 19.1 illustrates a mobile transaction involving multiple intermediaries.

Field agent	**Manager**	**Payment center**	**Factory**
Sign and send an order. The order contains an encrypted account number.	Verify the order signature; attach an approval signature.	Verify the approval signature; decrypt account number; attach a payment status signature; remove the account number.	Verify the payment status signature; verify agent address; send product.

Figure 19.1. A mobile transaction involving multiple intermediaries.

- *All content is encrypted:* In some application scenarios, such as broadcasting stock quotes or getting multilevel approval of a transaction, parts of the communication should be open. Yet we still want to verify the authenticity of those quotes and approval signatures. Connection-based security is of no use here. Unnecessarily encrypting all content also introduces more processing overhead.

- *HTTPS is inflexible for applications that have special security and performance requirements:* It lacks support for custom handshake or key exchange mechanisms. For example, HTTPS does not require clients to authenticate themselves. Another example is that any minor digital certificate-formatting problem causes the entire HTTPS handshake to fail. The developer has no way to specify what errors can be tolerated.

Other connection channel-based security technologies, such as Virtual Private Network (VPN), have similar problems. For future mobile commerce applications, we must secure *content* rather than channels.

19.1.2   Distributed Access Control

Mobile applications often interact with multiple backend servers, pull information from them as needed, and assemble personalized displays for users. Each information service provider might have its own user authentication and authorization system. It is a major inconvenience for mobile users to sign on to each backend server manually.

One way to combat this problem is through the use of single sign-on services. Single sign-on servers manage user profiles and provide time-stamped access tokens, such as Kerberos tickets, to authenticated users. The user presents the token when requesting services. Service providers use the single sign-on servers to validate tokens. Figure 19.2 illustrates that process. Being a one-to-one protocol, HTTPS is unfit in single sign-on schemes.

Note

The iFeedBack application discussed in Chapter 3 utilizes a very simple single sign-on scheme based on SOAP Web Services. The tokens used in iFeedBack are neither encrypted nor signed.

Single sign-on domains can form alliances and federations. Allied domains recognize tokens from each other. Important single sign-on alliances include Microsoft .Net Passport and Sun Microsystems' Liberty Alliance Project. Figure 19.3 illustrates the structure of federated single sign-on domains. To integrate into single sign-on service domains, smart mobile clients

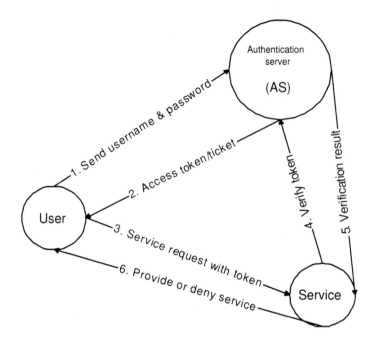

Figure 19.2. Sign-on process involving an authentication server.

must be able to handle security tokens. Those tokens are often cryptographic hashes with attached digital signatures.

19.1.3   Device Security

Mobile devices are easy to steal or lose. We must prevent nonauthorized personnel from accessing a device's sensitive data. For example, your company's financial data or private keys should not be recovered from a stolen mobile device. On-device information security is one of the most important challenges we face today.

HTTPS does not support on-device information security. Mobile clients are responsible for protecting their own data. Strong password-based encryption protects on-device information.

19.2   Lightweight Mobile Cryptography Toolkits

To take advantage of advanced security technologies, mobile developers must have programmatic access to cryptographic algorithms. So, throughout the rest of this chapter, I discuss third-party J2ME cryptography toolkits. Those toolkits let us implement flexible solutions meeting the above requirements.

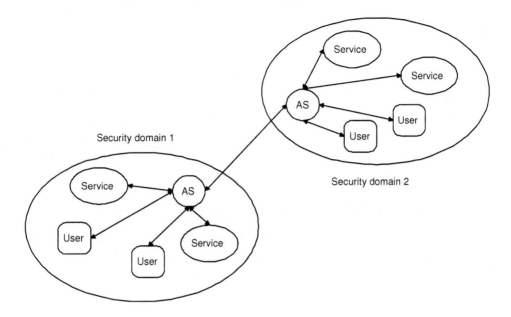

Figure 19.3. Federation of single sign-on domains.

Those toolkits prove crucial to the mobile phone platform, since standard CLDC and MIDP do not provide any cryptography APIs. Higher end J2ME platforms such as profiles based on CDC (or PersonalJava) can optionally support the java.security package in JCA (Java Cryptography Architecture) but not the javax.crypto package. As a result, crucial security APIs such as encryption/decryption ciphers are missing from all these standard profiles. Even for APIs in the java.security package, the bundled JCA provider might not implement the proprietary algorithm we need or might have an inefficient implementation. So, for high-end J2ME devices, lightweight toolkits also prove essential.

19.2.1   General Requirements

A toolkit suitable for mobile commerce must meet some general requirements:

- *Fast:* Mobile devices are personal devices that must be responsive. However, they have slow CPUs, and Java is not known for its raw performance. Handling CPU-intensive cryptography tasks, especially public key algorithms, at an acceptable speed on J2ME devices is a big challenge.

- *Small footprint:* Most modern, comprehensive cryptography packages consume several MBs of storage space. However, a MIDP phone device might have only 100 KBs of storage space. We must balance features with footprint.

- *Comprehensive algorithm support:* A cryptography package's goal is to support flexible security schemes. Such flexibility comes from the ability to choose from a range of algorithms. Important cryptographic algorithms include the following:

  - Symmetric key encryption

  - Password-based encryption

  - Public key encryption

  - Digital signatures

- *Sensible APIs:* To support a wide range of algorithms through a consistent interface, cryptography package APIs often have multiple layers of abstractions and complex inheritance structures. However, a too complex API will hinder its adoption.

- *Easy key identification and serialization:* In a general-purpose cryptography package, keys for different algorithms must be identified and matched properly on both communication ends. The public key pair-generation process is often too slow on devices. So, we must pregenerate keys on the server side and then transport keys to devices. The API should provide the means to ease and secure this process.

- *Good reputation:* A security solution provider must be trustworthy and have a good track record. Also, no algorithm is secure if the implementation is poorly conceived.

- *Timely bug fixes:* Security holes and algorithm weaknesses are discovered frequently around the world. The security solution provider must track this information and provide fixes or patches promptly.

Now let's look at some toolkits available for J2ME. In this chapter, we give only an overview of each toolkit. Code examples for selected toolkits are presented in Chapter 20.

Secure Random Numbers

Cryptographic algorithms rely on truly random numbers to function securely. Most implementations provide quasi-random number generators based on the current time. To leverage truly random events, such as user typing pattern and battery voltage, secure random number generators should come from the device vendor.

19.3   Bouncy Castle Lightweight API

Bouncy Castle (BC) started out as a community effort to implement a free, clean-room, open source JCE provider. BC developers developed their own lightweight API (BC lightweight crypto API) to be wrapped in BC JCE provider classes. The BC lightweight API can also be used standalone, with minimum dependence on other J2SE classes.

The BC (v1.16) J2ME download package contains the implementation of the BC lightweight API as well as two core Java classes not supported in CLDC: java.math.BigInteger and java.security.SecureRandom.

19.3.1   The Power of Open Source

BC's strength comes from its open source development model:

- When security holes or bugs are found, they are fixed quickly.

- BC's flexible API design and community development model allow anyone to contribute new algorithm implementations. BC supports a wide range of well-known cryptographic algorithms.

- The BC community is constantly optimizing existing implementations. For example, BC 1.16 has three AES (Advanced Encryption Standard) implementations that provide a range of compromises between speed and memory usage. From BC 1.11 to 1.16, the BigInteger implementation has improved so much that the time needed for RSA (Rivest-Shamir-Adleman) encryption is only 1/40 of what it used to be.

- Since BC implements an open source JCE provider, you can look at the BC JCE source code to figure out how to use the lightweight API for various tasks. This provides a powerful learning tool for advanced developers.

- It is free.

19.3.2   Things to Watch Out For

However, the ad hoc development model also brings some problems:

- Many BC algorithm implementations come straight from textbooks. There are simply too many algorithms and too few volunteer developers to optimize everything. The lack of optimization results in relatively poor performance, especially for some public key algorithms. As of version 1.16, BC public key performance proves sufficient for only high-end phones or PDAs.

- The BC API design is flexible but quite complex, and beginners find it hard to learn. Some developer-friendly API features are missing. For example, although BC provides full support for ASN.1 (Abstract Syntax Notation.1), it lacks a set of ready-to-use general-key serialization APIs.

- The community support via mailing list often works well. But there is no guarantee that someone will answer your question, much less in your specified timeframe.

To support so many algorithms, BC has a large footprint. The lightweight API jar file itself is nearly 1 MB. However, most mobile applications use only a small subset of BC algorithms. BC's free license terms allow you to pack and redistribute only the classes required in your application. Some J2ME post-processing tools and IDEs (for example, IBM WebSphere Device Developer) can automatically find class dependence and delete unused files from your jar file. Those tools prove handy when you develop with BC.

Tips on How to Run BC Applications

BC provides clean-room implementations of two Java core language classes not supported in J2ME/CLDC. However, the Java code security model dictates that an application should not overload classes in Java core language namespaces. So, if you deploy a BC application directly to a device, it might result in a security exception. A workaround is to obfuscate your byte code. The obfuscation process replaces package, class, variable, and method names to make them shorter and less human readable. The obfuscated package names will not collide with Java core package names.

19.4   The IAIK ME JCE

The Institute for Applied Information Processing and Communications (IAIK) is a leading Java Crypto/Security solution provider based in Austria. It is one of the best known third-party commercial JCE/JCA providers with more than five years of excellent tracking record.

IAIK's J2ME product is its JCE-ME toolkit (v3.0). The single Java binary runs on all J2ME platforms (PersonalJava, CDC, and CLDC) as well as JDK v1.1 or above. It is a free download for evaluation purposes. The IAIK JCE-ME is very small: only 100 KB memory footprint for the fully featured JAR file. The size can be further reduced at packaging/deploy time if you do not need all the features.

The IAIK ME toolkit supports all standard symmetric ciphers (AES, DES, RC2, RC4, and IDEA), message digests (MD and SHA), public key algorithms (RSA and DSA), ASN.1 encoding/decoding, X.509 digital certificates, and key management (key generation, PKCS #8 and #12, and IAIK key stores). However, password-based encryption is only supported through an experimental API as of the v3.0 final release. For J2SE and CDC platforms, IAIK offers alternative OS-native implementations for long integer operations, which could drastically improve performance.

In general, IAIK JCE-ME has good performance. For RSA and DSA algorithms, it outperforms the BC library. However, without native integer enhancements, public key tasks still take seconds on MIDP devices.

19.4.1   Porting Existing JCE Applications

The IAIK API is designed to be similar to the standard JCE but without the complexity of abstract algorithm and abstract provider interfaces. A brief list of IAIK JCE classes and their JDK KCE counterparts are listed in Table 19.1.

For a complete list of IAIK JCE-ME API classes and their corresponding standard JCE classes, please refer to the porting guide distributed with the download package (see "Resources").

19.5   Phaos Technology Micro Foundation Toolkit

Phaos Technology is a Java and XML security solution provider. It offers toolkits for secure XML Java APIs, J2ME lightweight crypto APIs, and one of the first implementations of the SSL protocol on J2ME/CLDC. In this chapter, I focus on the Phaos Micro Foundation (MF, v1.2) lightweight crypto API.

Table 19.1. Comparing IAIK and Standard JDK JCE Classes	
IAIK class	**JDK classes and notes**
iaik.me.security.Cipher	javax.crypto.Cipher
iaik.me.security.CryptoBag	Generic key interfaces such as java.security.Key and javax.crypto.SecretKey.
iaik.me.security.Mac	javax.crypto.Mac
iaik.me.security.MessageDigest	java.security.MessageDigest
iaik.me.security.PrivateKey	Generic private interfaces such as the java.security.PrivateKey as well as specific interfaces for the RSA, DSA, and DH private keys.
iaik.me.security.PublicKey	Generic and RSA, DSA, and DH public key interfaces
iaik.me.security.BigInteger	java.math.BigInteger Note: This is necessary for CLDC devices where the JDK class is not supported. It also allows IAIK to substitute its own high-performance, long integer implementation for other platforms.
iaik.me.security.SecureRandom	java.security.SecureRandom (CLDC-only)
iaik.me.security.Signature	java.security.Signature (CLDC-only)
iaik.me.x509.X509Certificate	Related classes in the java.security.cert package (CLDC-only).

Phaos XML security packages do not currently work with J2ME. However, they are at a leading position to provide future secure Web Services tools for mobile applications. Phaos toolkits are available for free evaluation. You must email the company to get a 30-day license key, which comes with tech support.

Phaos is a reputable security company with a good track record. The technical support staff is also very knowledgeable and responsive. All my support questions were answered via email within 24 hours.

19.5.1　The Phaos Micro Foundation

The Phaos MF runs on both CLDC and CDC. The CDC version also runs under J2SE. The toolkit footprint is 187 KB for the CLDC version and

169 KB for the CDC version. The Phaos API is intuitive and comes with excellent documentation and code examples.

Phaos MF supports a set of frequently used cryptographic algorithms to strike a balance between performance and features. Those algorithms include symmetric ciphers, such as AES, DES (Data Encryption Standard), RC2, and RC4; PKI (Public Key Infrastructure) ciphers and signature schemes, such as DSA (Digital Signature Algorithm) and RSA; and password-based encryption schemes (PBES), such as PKCS #5 and PKCS #12. Phaos MF also supports X.509 certificate parsing, ASN.1 encoding, and efficient memory pooling.

Phaos PBES implementations used in my examples perform worse than their Bouncy Castle and IAIK counterparts. For RSA and DSA algorithms, the Phaos library is better optimized than Bouncy Castle 1.16 and has comparable performance to the IAIK pure Java library.

However, even for IAIK and Phaos, the performance of public algorithms is only barely acceptable for MIDP cell phones. In fact, no matter how much optimization you do, those classic PKI algorithms might just prove too heavy for the smallest devices. Novel algorithms and approaches are needed. NTRU and a startup company called B3 Security provide such solutions.

19.6   NTRU jNeo for Java Toolkit

NTRU PKI algorithms include an encryption algorithm NTRUEncrypt and a signature algorithm NTRUSign, invented and developed by four math professors at Brown University. In my sample programs, NTRU algorithms perform 5 to 30 times faster than other public key algorithms with similar cryptographic strength. NTRU algorithms are published and on their way to becoming IEEE and IETF standards. NTRU patented the algorithms to protect their business interests. NTRU algorithm patents have been licensed by a variety of mobile software, smart card, and DSP (Digital Signal Processor) chip vendors, including Sony and Texas Instruments.

Cryptographic algorithms are scrutinized and improved repeatedly before considered mature and ready for general public adoption. Although NTRU algorithms have been inspected many times by both academic and business worlds, they are still relatively new. Security weaknesses were identified in NTRUEncrypt as late as May 2001. Those weaknesses do not undermine NTRU algorithm fundamentals and have since been fixed. As you should with any critical project, research NTRU security before licensing it.

19.6.1   The jNeo Package

NTRU provides an implementation of its algorithms in a Java package called
NTRU jNeo (v2.2) for Java. You must work out an agreement with NTRU
before you can evaluate the package. In addition to NTRU public key algorithms, jNeo for Java also includes an implementation of the AES Rijndael
symmetric key algorithm. The jNeo package runs on CLDC, CDC, and
J2SE platforms. It has a memory footprint of 37 KB without signature
key-generation classes, which have a footprint of 35 KB.

The jNeo API is simple and easy to use. In fact, it might be too simplistic.
For example, the block encryption method requires users to divide plaintext
data into blocks themselves.

Using jNeo, NTRUEncrypt key pairs can be generated quickly from pass
phrases. The same pass phrase always produces the same key pair. For that
reason, jNeo does not provide a password-based key store facility. NTRUSign
keys, however, are slow to generate and require floating-point support. The
jNeo package provides a floating-point emulation class, which can support
NTRUSign key generation on a CLDC device. But on-device NTRUSign key
pair generation takes a long time to complete. Generating and distributing
NTRUSign keys from a server computer is a better approach. Fortunately,
a signature key can sign thousands of messages before it needs replacement.

19.7   B3 Security

B3 Security is a San Jose, California, startup that specializes in developing
new, lightweight security infrastructures that minimize the current overhead
associated with PKI. Its flagship products are B3 Tamper Detection and
Digital Signature (B3Sig) SDK and B3 End-to-End (B3E2E) Security SDK.
Both are available for J2ME (both CDC and CLDC). The B3E2E SDK (still
in beta) provides features equivalent to SSL in the PKI world, but with a
shorter handshake, faster session key establishment, and less management
overhead, especially for pushed messages.

19.7.1   How Does B3 Work?

The B3 digital signature scheme is based on keyed hash (HMAC, or keyed-
Hashing for Message AuthentiCation) technology, which has been around
for many years and has proven security. B3 uniquely uses HMAC properties
instead of more computationally intensive public key algorithms, such as
large integer factoring, to form a B3 tamper-proof block of bytes and digital
signature. In a mobile enterprise application setting, it works like so:

- In its preferred operation mode, the B3Sig SDK uses two pairs of shared and non-shared secrets. Analogous to the PKI world, a shared secret acts like a public key with targeted distribution scope, and a non-shared secret acts like a private key. Each user knows her own password in an existing enterprise identity management system. The system only stores a hash (e.g., MD5) of the password. No clear text password is stored anywhere. The B3 SDK uses that hash as the first shared secret. The first non-shared secret comes from a different hash (e.g., SHA-1) of the same password.

- B3 software on a device generates a private root key and the corresponding shared secret. They form the second pair of secrets, which ensures stronger authentication. The second shared secret can be used for third-party verification. A B3 protocol can also use the second pair to efficiently reset a forgotten password.

- Non-shared secrets are used together with the message (or transaction) itself and user ID to generate a unique signing key for every message.

- A B3 algorithm then generates a digital signature containing three interrelated parts.

- A B3 algorithm can verify message and user ID integrity with shared secrets. The receiving party can query the password system to verify the sender's authenticity.

19.7.2   Advantages

B3 scheme has the following advantages:

- *Speed:* Cryptographic hash and HMAC algorithms can run 1,000 times faster than public key algorithms.

- *Seamless integration with existing enterprise authentication infrastructure:* Various password-based identity management systems are already widely deployed in enterprises (the simplest example is a password file). Utilizing existing password-based identity management systems avoids the expensive overhead of digital certificate management associated with PKI digital signature.

- *Strong two-factor authentication:* Only the person who has access to the specific device and knows her application password can generate the correct shared and non-shared secrets to sign messages. That also helps to prevent password guessing and dictionary attacks.

- *Tamper detection:* B3Sig SDK has a conservative design: It assumes that no algorithm is permanently secure, including its own. In case of a successful crypto attack on B3 signature and verification algorithms, the sender can still prove that he did not send the forged message. Part of the B3 signature is linked to the non-shared secrets through well-established non-B3 one-way algorithms (HMACs).

B3 solutions do not dictate complete replacement of the current PKI infrastructure. Rather, B3 solutions can coexist and interoperate with the current system. For example, we can use HTTPS as well as B3E2E SDK to pass shared secrets during setup. The application can add delegated PKI signatures on top of the B3 signatures if desired. To use B3 signatures without an existing identity/password management system, we also need to set up a B3 shared secrets store. To learn more technical details about B3 solutions, please contact B3 directly for white papers and evaluation SDKs.

Leading security experts in the financial services industry, such as Larry Suto, FTCS co-chair at Wells Fargo Bank, and Jim Anderson, a VP of information security at Visa, have agreed to be references for the B3 solutions. If B3 does deliver on its promises, it could become one of the most important security solutions for mobile enterprise applications. However, B3 is still a young company, and its approach has not been tested in large-scale, real-world environments. I recommend you investigate the feasibility of B3 solutions yourself.

19.8 Device-Specific APIs

MIDP device vendors (e.g., Motorola iDEN phones) also provide device-specific cryptography API extensions. Those packages utilize device-native cryptography libraries and special hardware features. Thus, they likely have good on-device performance.

However, applications using vendor-specific APIs are no longer portable to other devices. That causes J2ME platform fragmentation and defeats one of Java's greatest advantages. We do not discuss those APIs in detail here. Interested readers can refer to their device manufacturers' developer manuals.

19.9 Standardization of J2ME Security APIs

Vendor-specific security APIs often offer good performance at the cost of application portability. One way to avoid such fragmentation yet still take advantage of native performance is to develop standard J2ME cryptography API specifications and allow device vendors to provide their own implementations.

The upcoming CDC Foundation Profile v1.1 specification (JSR 219) will include a "Security API optional package." The optional package supports subsets of the J2SE v1.4 Java Secure Socket Extension (JSSE), Java Cryptography Extension (JCE), and Java Authentication and Authorization Service (JAAS) APIs. Most algorithms in the javax.crypto package will be supported. It is not clear, however, whether this optional package can be used in conjunction with the CLDC and MIDP.

The "Security and Trust Services API for J2ME" (JSR 177) is an optional package for both the CLDC and CDC. It supports access to embedded security elements, including SIM cards in GSM phones and UICC cards in 3G phones. Those security cards not only store user keys and personal information but also perform certain cryptography algorithms. At the time of this writing, the JSR 177 expert group is still debating whether to include a lightweight cryptography API in this optional package.

19.10   Summary

In this chapter, we discussed the need for advanced mobile security and the toolkits to implement it. All the tools have reasonable feature support and performance on CDC-based devices. However, cryptographic support on MIDP devices is highly vendor-dependent. It is important that we choose the right tools based on our specific application needs. Next, we really dive into those toolkits and give concrete examples of how to implement common security tasks using each of them.

Resources

[1] The Bouncy Castle project. http://www.bouncycastle.org/

[2] The IAIK JCE-ME library.
http://jce.iaik.tugraz.at/products/10_me-jce/index.php

[3] Phaos Technology Micro Security products.
http://www.phaos.com/products/category/micro.html

[4] NTRU toolkits. http://www.ntru.com/products/toolkits.htm

[5] The NTRU algorithms explained.
http://www.ntru.com/cryptolab/algorithms.htm

[6] B3 Security. http://www.b3security.com

[7] You can download the iDEN J2ME SDK, including the cryptography API, from Motorola's iDEN phone developer Web site. http://idenphones.motorola.com/iden/developer/developer_home.jsp

[8] Bruce Schneier's *Applied Cryptography* is a classic book that discusses all the algorithms (except NTRU) mentioned in this chapter. http://www.counterpane.com/applied.html

[9] To learn more about general security challenges and solutions for mobile Java applications, read Michael Yuan and Ju Long's article "Securing Wireless J2ME" (IBM developerWorks, June 2002). http://www-106.ibm.com/developerworks/wireless/library/wi-secj2me.html

[10] J2ME Foundation Profile 1.1 (JSR 219). http://www.jcp.org/en/jsr/detail?id=219

[11] Security and Trust API for J2ME (JSR 177). http://www.jcp.org/en/jsr/detail?id=177

Chapter 20

The J2ME Crypto Recipes

CHAPTER OVERVIEW

- Symmetric Encryption

- Password-Based Encryption

- Public Key Encryption

- Digital Signature

- The Bouncy Castle API

- The IAIK JCE ME API

- The Phaos Micro Foundation API

- NTRU jNeo API

In the previous chapter, we reviewed leading cryptography libraries for J2ME. In this chapter, we use code examples to show how to perform various common cryptographic tasks using those libraries.

20.1 Overview of Recipes

The sample applications in this chapter provide ready-to-use code snippets for symmetric key encryption, password-based encryption, public key encryption, and digital signature tasks. You can use them in your custom J2ME applications. Brief descriptions of those common tasks are given in Table 20.1. For detailed discussions on those tasks, please refer to the relevant sections.

Table 20.1. Common Cryptographic Tasks Covered in This Chapter

Crypto Task	Descriptions and Applications
Symmetric encryption	Very fast algorithms; private key distribution is a big problem.
Password-based encryption	Human-friendly passwords to secure on-device data stores.
Public key encryption	Secure communication via open channels; very slow; helps key exchange when establishing symmetric key sessions; the basis of the widely used public key infrastructure.
Digital signature	Based on public key infrastructure to provide identity and message integrity guarantee.

The source code zip archive, which you can download from this book's Web site (see "Resources"), contains four sample applications, each demonstrating the API use of a crypto package (Bouncy Castle, IAIK, Phaos, and jNeo). Table 20.2 lists the toolkits versions used in this chapter. Inside each sample application, the most important class is **CryptoEngine**, which stores keys and provides thin wrappers over API methods. **CryptoEngine** sports a monolithic single class design not optimized for code reuse. Please do *not* consider it a best-practice example. Instead, the examples are designed to get you started with working code quickly. Each method in the **CryptoEngine** class demonstrates a complete application task (for example, the RSAEncrypt() method encrypts an input byte array using RSA).

Table 20.2. Toolkits Used in This Chapter	

Toolkit	Version
Bouncy Castle for J2ME	1.16
IAIK JCE ME	3.0
Phaos Micro Foundation	1.2
NTRU Neo for Java	2.2

20.1.1 The Package Structure

All the J2ME crypto libraries used in the sample applications run on both CLDC and CDC platforms. To evaluate their performance in the most restricted environment, I provided user interface (UI) for the MIDP. The MIDlets drive the CryptoEngine and measure time spent on each task.

Building and running the sample applications is easy. You simply change the parameters in the build.xml file to reflect your system settings and run ANT tasks package and run. I bundled Bouncy Castle 1.16 in the BC sample. For other toolkit samples, you must contact vendors to obtain their software and evaluation licenses. You should put library JAR files in the lib/ directory.

20.1.2 Key Serialization

Besides basic encryption/decryption operations, key serialization is a core feature demonstrated in the examples. There are two important reasons for key serialization.

- Except for the NTRUEncrypt algorithm, generating public key pairs on mobile devices is extremely time consuming.

- In most applications, the sender and receiver use different devices, which requires keys to be transported over the network.

Note

In our examples, key serialization is used to minimize on-device key generation. All our encrypt/decrypt and sign/verify method pairs in the CryptoEngine class use the same in-memory key objects.

Classes in directory keygensrc pregenerate keys and serialize them to files in directory res/keys before MIDP suite packaging. CryptoEngine's constructor constructs pregenerated keys from files in the JAR's keys/ directory (res/keys directory in the build system). CryptoEngine also has methods to support direct key generation on mobile devices.

20.2 Symmetric Encryption

Symmetric encryption algorithms use randomly generated secret keys to encrypt and decrypt data. The sender and receiver must share the same key. The biggest advantage of symmetric algorithms is their speed. Symmetric algorithms are viable solutions even on small MIDP phones. However, the data security depends on the secrecy of the key. If an attacker somehow intercepted the key, he could easily forge or decrypt the entire communication content. The transportation and storage of secret keys is a big issue over the insecure networks. Our demo MIDlet for symmetric encryption and decryption is shown in Figure 20.1.

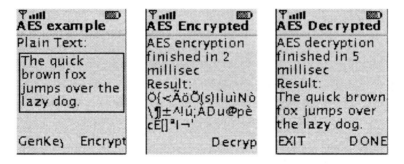

Figure 20.1. AES symmetric encryption using the BC library.

20.2.1 Bouncy Castle

The Bouncy Castle package supports a long list of symmetric algorithms, including AES, Rijndael, DES, triple DES, RC2, and RC4. Each cipher supports multiple buffering, padding, and ECB/CBC modes. The AES implementation is the most optimized. BC has three cipher engine classes for AES: AESLightEngine is an implementation optimized for low memory usage; AESFastEngine is optimized for speed; AESEngine is the compromise of the two.

The AES key and its initial vector (IV) are generated by random number generators in the generateAESKey() method in the CryptoEngine class (Listing 20.1).

Listing 20.1. `Generate AES keys with BC`

```
public void generateAESKey () throws Exception {
  SecureRandom sr = new SecureRandom();
  AESkey = new byte [16];
  sr.nextBytes(AESkey);
  AESinitV = new byte [16];
  sr.nextBytes(AESinitV);
}
```

Listing 20.2 illustrates how to serialize the key and IV to disk files (the **GenerateAllKeys** class). The **CryptoEngine** constructor reads out the serialized keys for later use on the mobile device (Listing 20.3). Since BC's AES keys are simple byte arrays, the serialization and deserialization involve only simple file stream operations.

Listing 20.2. `Serialize AES keys to files offline`

```
out = new FileOutputStream(outdir + "AESkey.dat");
out.write(AESkey);
out.flush(); out.close();

out = new FileOutputStream(outdir+"AESinitV.dat");
out.write(AESinitV);
out.flush(); out.close();
```

Listing 20.3. `Read out AES keys in the CryptoEngine constructor`

```
Class c = this.getClass();
InputStream is;

is = c.getResourceAsStream("/keys/AESkey.dat");
byte [] AESkey = readFromStream(is);
is.close();
is = c.getResourceAsStream("/keys/AESinitV.dat");
byte [] AESinitV = readFromStream(is);
is.close();
```

With keys generated, the AESFastEncrypt() method in the CryptoEngine class uses the AESFastEngine to encrypt a byte array of plain text into cipher text. The AESFastDecrypt() method decrypts the message into a plain text byte array. The code for both methods is shown in Listing 20.4.

Listing 20.4. AES encryption and decryption methods

```
public byte [] AESFastEncrypt (byte [] toEncrypt) throws Exception {
  BufferedBlockCipher cipher =
    new PaddedBufferedBlockCipher(
      new CBCBlockCipher(new AESFastEngine()));
  // If initV is not given, the program will
  // assume all zeros
  ParametersWithIV piv = new ParametersWithIV (
          (new KeyParameter(AESkey)), AESinitV);
  cipher.init(true, piv);
  byte[] result =
   new byte[cipher.getOutputSize(toEncrypt.length)];
  int len = cipher.processBytes(toEncrypt, 0,
                    toEncrypt.length, result, 0);

  try {
    cipher.doFinal(result, len);
  } catch (CryptoException ce) {
    // handles error
  }
  return result;
}

public byte [] AESFastDecrypt (byte [] toDecrypt) throws Exception {
  BufferedBlockCipher cipher =
    new PaddedBufferedBlockCipher(
     new CBCBlockCipher(new AESFastEngine()));
  ParametersWithIV piv = new ParametersWithIV (
     (new KeyParameter(AESkey)), AESinitV);
  cipher.init(false, piv);
  byte[] result = new byte[cipher.getOutputSize(toDecrypt.length)];
  int len = cipher.processBytes(toDecrypt, 0,
                    toDecrypt.length, result, 0);

  try {
    cipher.doFinal(result, len);
  } catch (CryptoException ce) {
    // Handle error
```

```
  }
  return result;
}
```

20.2.2 IAIK JCE-ME

In our IAIK JCE-ME example, the AES key serialization and deserialization part is exactly the same as the Bouncy Castle example. So, we only look at the key generation **generateAESKey()** method (Listing 20.5) in class CryptoEngine.

Listing 20.5. The generateAESKey() method

```
private byte [] AESkey;
private byte [] AESinitV;
// ... ...
public void generateAESKey () throws Exception {
  SecureRandom sr = new SecureRandom();
  AESkey = new byte [16];
  sr.nextBytes(AESkey);
  AESinitV = new byte [16];
  sr.nextBytes(AESinitV);
}
```

The encryption and decryption methods are shown in Listing 20.6.

Listing 20.6. AES encryption and decryption using IAIK JCE-ME

```
public byte [] AESEncrypt (byte [] toEncrypt) throws Exception {
  CryptoBag cipherKey = CryptoBag.makeSecretKey(AESkey);
  CryptoBag ivparam = CryptoBag.makeIV(AESinitV);
  Cipher cipher = Cipher.getInstance("AES/ECB/PKCS5Padding");
  cipher.init(Cipher.ENCRYPT_MODE, cipherKey, ivparam, null);
  return cipher.doFinal(toEncrypt);
}

public byte [] AESDecrypt (byte [] toDecrypt) throws Exception {
  CryptoBag cipherKey = CryptoBag.makeSecretKey(AESkey);
  CryptoBag ivparam = CryptoBag.makeIV(AESinitV);
  Cipher cipher = Cipher.getInstance("AES/ECB/PKCS5Padding");
  cipher.init(Cipher.DECRYPT_MODE, cipherKey, ivparam, null);
```

```
    return cipher.doFinal(toDecrypt);
}
```

20.2.3 Phaos Micro Foundation

In the Phaos MF example, the **generateAESKey()** method (Listing 20.7) generates the AES key and IV.

Phaos Secure Number Generator

The Phaos MF for CLDC package is not shipped with random generator classes. You must supply your own generator, which implements the com.phaos.micro.crypto.RandomBitsSource interface using secure random facilities provided by the device vendor. For testing purposes, I supplied SecureRandom and SecureRBS classes in my Phaos examples. Class SecureRandom is based on the Bouncy Castle implementation of SecureRandom, and SecureRBS implements the RandomBitsSource interface.

Listing 20.7. Generate AES key and IV with Phaos MF

```
RandomBitsSource.setDefault(new SecureRBS());
RandomBitsSource.getDefault().seed();

public void generateAESKey () throws Exception {
  AlgorithmIdentifier algID = AlgIDList.AES_128_CBC;
  SymmetricKeyGenerator generator =
    new SymmetricKeyGenerator(algID,
              RandomBitsSource.getDefault());
  AESkey = generator.generateKey();

  // Create a new cipher, initialize it and then get
  // CBC init vector.
  Cipher cipher = BlockCipher.getInstance(algID,
      AESkey, BlockCipher.PADDING_PKCS5);
  CBCAlgID AESalgID =
    (CBCAlgID) cipher.createAlgID();
  AESinitV = AESalgID.iv;
  return;
}
```

In the Phaos MF package, the key serialization API is slightly different from BC and IAIK. Listings 20.8 and 20.9 illustrate the serialization and deserialization processes.

Listing 20.8. Serialize AES key and IV

```
FileOutputStream out = new FileOutputStream(outdir + "AESkey.der");
out.write(AESkey.keyMaterial);
out.flush(); out.close();

out = new FileOutputStream(outdir + "AESinitV.der");
out.write(AESinitV);
out.flush(); out.close();
```

Listing 20.9. AES key and IV deserialization in the CryptoEngine
             constructor

```
// 192 bit AES key
private SymmetricKey AESkey;
// CBC cipher init vector
private byte [] AESinitV;
// ... ...
Class c = this.getClass();
InputStream is;

// The AES init vector
is = c.getResourceAsStream("/keys/AESinitV.der");
AESinitV = readFromStream(is);

// The AES key
is = c.getResourceAsStream("/keys/AESkey.der");
byte[] keyMaterial = readFromStream(is);
AESkey = new SymmetricKey(keyMaterial, 0, keyMaterial.length);
```

The AESEncrypt() and AESDecrypt() methods demonstrate how to use the cipher (Listing 20.10).

Listing 20.10. The AESEncrypt() and AESDecrypt() methods

```
public byte [] AESEncrypt (byte [] toEncrypt) throws Exception {
  if ( AESkey == null || AESinitV == null )
```

```
      throw new Exception("Generate AES key first!");
  CBCAlgID AESalgID = new CBCAlgID(OIDList.AES_128_CBC, AESinitV);
  Cipher cipher = BlockCipher.getInstance(AESalgID,
        AESkey, BlockCipher.PADDING_PKCS5);
  PooledArray ciphertext =
    ((BlockCipher)cipher).encryptFinal(toEncrypt, 0, toEncrypt.length);
  return ciphertext.toByteArray(true);
}

public byte [] AESDecrypt (byte [] toDecrypt) throws Exception {
  if ( AESkey == null )
    throw new Exception("Generate AES key first!");
  CBCAlgID AESalgID = new CBCAlgID(OIDList.AES_128_CBC, AESinitV);
  Cipher cipher = BlockCipher.getInstance(AESalgID,
                  AESkey, BlockCipher.PADDING_PKCS5);
  PooledArray plaintext =
    ((BlockCipher)cipher).decryptFinal(toDecrypt, 0, toDecrypt.length);
  return plaintext.toByteArray(true);
}
```

20.2.4 NTRU jNeo

Symmetric key encryption is not the core innovation of NTRU but it is
provided for the completeness of the package. AES key and IV are generated
using code in Listing 20.11.

Listing 20.11. Generate AES key and IV with jNeo

```
RandomNumber rn =
  new RandomNumber(NTRUConst.NTRU_SHA1_HASH);

// ... ...

public void generateAESKey () throws Exception {
  AESinitV = new byte [RijndaelKey.BLOCK_SIZE];
  rn.getRandom(AESinitV, 0, AESinitV.length);

  byte [] keydata =
    new byte [RijndaelKey.BLOCK_SIZE];
  rn.getRandom(keydata, 0, keydata.length);
  AESkey = new RijndaelKey(keydata,
                  RijndaelKey.NTRU_SYM_KEYSTRENGTH_128);
```

```
  return;
}
```

The key serialization (Listing 20.12) and deserialization (Listing 20.13) processes are both very simple.

Listing 20.12. AES key and IV serialization

```
out = new FileOutputStream(outdir + "AESinitV.dat");
out.write(AESinitV);
out.flush(); out.close();


out = new FileOutputStream(outdir + "AESkeydata.dat");
out.write(keydata);
out.flush(); out.close();
```

Listing 20.13. AES key and IV deserialization

```
// AES init vector and 128 bit key
private byte [] AESinitV;
private RijndaelKey AESkey;
// ... ...
Class c = this.getClass();
InputStream is;

is = c.getResourceAsStream("/keys/AESkeydata.dat");
byte [] keydata = readFromStream(is);
AESkey = new RijndaelKey(keydata,
                RijndaelKey.NTRU_SYM_KEYSTRENGTH_128);
is.close();

is = c.getResourceAsStream("/keys/AESinitV.dat");
AESinitV = readFromStream(is);
is.close();
```

Now, we can encrypt and decrypt messages (Listing 20.14). However, one thing important to note is that the plain text array to encrypt MUST have a length of a multiple of 16 bytes. If the message does not satisfy this requirement, the caller application must pad it properly. Please refer to the source code of the MIDlets for padding examples.

Listing 20.14. The AES encryption and decryption methods

```
// toEncrypt array length must be a multiple
// of 16 bytes
public byte [] AESEncrypt (byte [] toEncrypt) throws Exception {
  if ( AESkey == null || AESinitV == null )
    throw new Exception("Generate AES key first!");
  if ( toEncrypt.length \% 16 != 0 )
    throw new Exception("Not multiple of 16 bytes");

  int len = AESkey.ciphertextLength(
              RijndaelKey.NTRU_ENC_RIJNDAEL,
              RijndaelKey.NTRU_SYM_MODE_CBC,
              RijndaelKey.NTRU_SYM_KEYSTRENGTH_128,
              toEncrypt.length, false);
  byte [] result = new byte [len];
  AESkey.encrypt(toEncrypt, 0, toEncrypt.length,
                result, 0, RijndaelKey.NTRU_SYM_MODE_CBC,
                AESinitV, 0, false);
  return result;
}

public byte [] AESDecrypt (byte [] toDecrypt) throws Exception {
  if ( AESkey == null || AESinitV == null )
    throw new Exception("Generate AES key first!");

  int len = AESkey.plaintextLength(
              RijndaelKey.NTRU_ENC_RIJNDAEL,
              RijndaelKey.NTRU_SYM_MODE_CBC,
              RijndaelKey.NTRU_SYM_KEYSTRENGTH_128,
              toDecrypt.length, false);
  byte [] result = new byte [len];
  AESkey.decrypt(toDecrypt, 0, toDecrypt.length,
                result, 0, RijndaelKey.NTRU_SYM_MODE_CBC,
                AESinitV, 0, false);
  return result;
}
```

20.3   Password-Based Encryption

One problem with symmetric algorithms is that the users must keep the random keys. Since there is no way users can remember them in their heads, they store the keys in files, and that significantly increases the security risk. Password-based encryption (PBE) schemes use easy-to-remember passwords to generate keys for underlying symmetric parsers. PBE schemes are widely used to protect on-device data. In fact, we can use PBE-protected storages to keep other symmetric or private keys. Now, let's have a look at how PBE works in those libraries. Since the key is generated every time on-the-fly from the password, there is no key serialization process. All operations are contained in the encryption and decryption methods in the CryptoEngine class. For all algorithms, the underlying key generated from the password must be mixed in over and over again with a random "salt" to guarantee security. The iteration number is a programmable parameter and should be at least 1000. Our demo MIDlet for password-based encryption and decryption is shown in Figure 20.2.

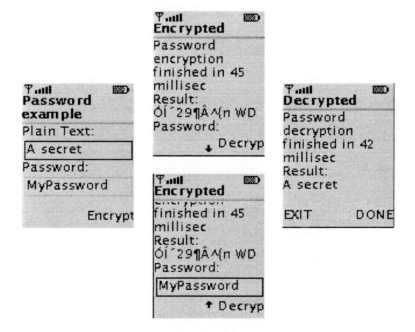

Figure 20.2. Password-based encryption using BC's library

Note

The password is stored in a char array instead of in a byte array or a string object. Each character in the password string is 16 bits. A string object is statically allocated by the JVM and could cause security leaks if someone does a memory dump before it is garbage collected.

20.3.1 Bouncy Castle

Password-based encryption and decryption using the Bouncy Castle package are demonstrated in Listing 20.15.

Listing 20.15. Methods for PBE in the Bouncy Castle CryptoEngine example

---

```
// Generate random salt
private byte [] salt;
SecureRandom sr = new SecureRandom();
salt = new byte [16];
sr.nextBytes(salt);

// Get password to generate symmetric key with
// (or without IV) To be used in
// an AES underlying cipher
private CipherParameters getAESPasswdKey
        (char [] passwd) throws Exception {
  PBEParametersGenerator generator =
     new PKCS12ParametersGenerator(new SHA1Digest());
  generator.init(
PBEParametersGenerator.PKCS12PasswordToBytes(passwd),
       salt, 1024);
  // Generate a 128 bit key w/ 128 bit IV
  ParametersWithIV key =
(ParametersWithIV)generator.generateDerivedParameters(128, 128);
  // Generate a 128 kit key
  // CipherParameters key =
  // generator.generateDerivedParameters(128);
  return key;
}

// Password based encryption using AES
public byte [] AESPasswdEncrypt (byte [] toEncrypt,
```

```
                            char [] passwd)throws Exception {
  ParametersWithIV key =
    (ParametersWithIV) getAESPasswdKey(passwd);
  // The following code uses an AES cipher to
  // encrypt the message
  BufferedBlockCipher cipher = new PaddedBufferedBlockCipher(
                      new CBCBlockCipher(new AESFastEngine()));
  cipher.init(true, key);
  byte[] result = new byte[cipher.getOutputSize(toEncrypt.length)];
  int len = cipher.processBytes(toEncrypt, 0,
                    toEncrypt.length, result, 0);
  try {
    cipher.doFinal(result, len);
  } catch (CryptoException ce) {
    // handle error
  }
  return result;
}


// Password based decryption using AES
public byte [] AESPasswdDecrypt (byte [] toDecrypt,
                  char [] passwd) throws Exception {
  ParametersWithIV key = (ParametersWithIV) getAESPasswdKey(passwd);
  // The following code uses an AES cipher to
  // decrypt the message
  BufferedBlockCipher cipher =
      new PaddedBufferedBlockCipher(
        new CBCBlockCipher(new AESFastEngine()));
  cipher.init(false, key);
  byte[] result =
   new byte[cipher.getOutputSize(toDecrypt.length)];
  int len = cipher.processBytes(toDecrypt, 0,
                    toDecrypt.length, result, 0);
  try {
    cipher.doFinal(result, len);
  } catch (CryptoException ce) {
    // handle error
  }
  return result;
}
```

In the demo code package (see "Resources"), I have also included an example of PBE using underlying triple DES symmetric key. The triple DES key does not have an IV parameter.

20.3.2 IAIK JCE-ME

The use of PBE in IAIK JCE-ME is similar to that in Bouncy Castle but
with a simpler API. I demonstrate the use of RC2 as the underlying cipher
in the IAIK example (Listing 20.16).

Listing 20.16. PBE in the IAIK JCE-ME

```
private byte [] salt;
SecureRandom sr = new SecureRandom();
salt = new byte [16];
sr.nextBytes(salt);
// ... ...
public byte [] PBEEncrypt (byte [] toEncrypt,
            char [] passwd) throws Exception {
  PBE pbe = PBE.getInstance(PBE.OID_PKCS12_RC2_40_SHA);
  Cipher c = pbe.getCipher(Cipher.ENCRYPT_MODE,
                       passwd, salt, 1024, null);
  return c.doFinal(toEncrypt);
}

public byte [] PBEDecrypt (byte [] toDecrypt,
            char [] passwd) throws Exception {
  PBE pbe = PBE.getInstance(PBE.OID_PKCS12_RC2_40_SHA);
  Cipher c = pbe.getCipher(Cipher.DECRYPT_MODE,
                       passwd, salt, 1024, null);
  return c.doFinal(toDecrypt);
}
```

20.3.3 Phaos Micro Foundation

In the Phaos MF example (Listing 20.17), we use the PKCS #5 scheme to
generate the symmetric key. The salt mix-in iteration number is the default
1024 specified by the implementation. In the Phaos MF API, we need to
generate the random IV AESinitV for the AES key ourselves. Also, please
note that although handling PooledArray is tedious, it produces performance
gains on small devices.

Listing 20.17. Password based encryption and decryption using Phaos MF

```
private byte [] salt;
RandomBitsSource.setDefault(new SecureRBS());
```

```
RandomBitsSource.getDefault().seed();
salt = new byte[PBES2AlgID.DEFAULT_SALT_LENGTH];
RandomBitsSource.getDefault().randomBytes(salt);
// ... ...
// PKCS #5 password scheme 2 using
// AES as underlying cipher
public byte [] AESPasswdEncrypt(byte [] toEncrypt,
                String password) throws Exception {
  // Use SHA1 with AES
  AlgorithmIdentifier algID = new PBES2AlgID(salt,
                PBES2AlgID.DEFAULT_ITERATION_COUNT,
                PBES2AlgID.KEY_LENGTH_NOT_PRESENT,
                        AlgIDList.HMAC_WITH_SHA1,
      new CBCAlgID(OIDList.AES_128_CBC, AESinitV));
  ByteArrayInputStream in = new ByteArrayInputStream(toEncrypt);
  PooledArray plaintext = ByteArrayPool.getArray(in.available());
  in.read(plaintext.buffer, 0, plaintext.length);
  in.close();

  // PKCS #5 only uses lower 8 bits of
  // each password char
  PasswordBasedEncryptionScheme pbes =
    PasswordBasedEncryptionScheme.getInstance(algID,
                                password.getBytes());
  PooledArray ciphertext =
      pbes.encryptFinal(plaintext.buffer, 0,
                        plaintext.length);

  ByteArrayOutputStream out = new ByteArrayOutputStream ();
  algID.output(out);
  out.write(ciphertext.buffer, 0,
            ciphertext.length);
  byte [] encrypted = out.toByteArray();
  out.close();

  plaintext.release();
  ciphertext.release();
  return encrypted;
}

// PKCS #5 password scheme 2 decryption
//
// Since the algID is embedded inside the
// encrypted byte array, this method can decrypt
// any Phaos PBES messages with any
```

```
// underlying ciphers.
public byte [] AESPasswdDecrypt(byte [] toDecrypt,
                String password) throws Exception {
  ByteArrayInputStream in = new ByteArrayInputStream(toDecrypt);
  AlgorithmIdentifier algID = new AlgorithmIdentifier(in);
  PooledArray ciphertext = ByteArrayPool.getArray(in.available());
  in.read(ciphertext.buffer, 0, ciphertext.length);
  in.close();

  PasswordBasedEncryptionScheme pbes =
    PasswordBasedEncryptionScheme.getInstance(algID,
                        password.getBytes());
  PooledArray plaintext =
      pbes.decryptFinal(ciphertext.buffer, 0,
                    ciphertext.length);

  ByteArrayOutputStream out = new ByteArrayOutputStream ();
  out.write(plaintext.buffer, 0, plaintext.length);
  byte [] decrypted = out.toByteArray();
  out.close();

  plaintext.release();
  ciphertext.release();
  return decrypted;
}
```

20.4 Public Key Encryption

Public key algorithms eliminate the key exchange problems associated with symmetric algorithms. Basically, each user has a pair of keys. The *public key* is available to anyone, and the *private key* is known only to the user. Public key algorithms are designed to be one-way trapdoor systems where a message encrypted by the public key can only be decrypted by the corresponding private key (see Figure 20.3). So, if Alice wants to send Bob a secret message, she uses Bob's public key to encrypt the data and sends it over any general insecure network. Only Bob himself has the correct private key to decrypt the message. The beauty of this scheme is that no secret key ever needs to be exchanged.

However, without built-in hardware acceleration or native long-integer support, public key encryption can be very slow on mobile devices. In reality, we often use public key algorithms to exchange symmetric keys and use

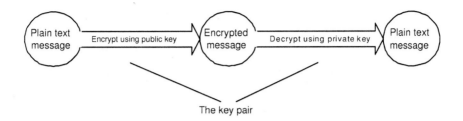

Figure 20.3. Public key algorithms are one-way trapdoors.

symmetric key channels for further communication. Our demo MIDlet for RSA public key encryption and decryption is shown in Figure 20.4.

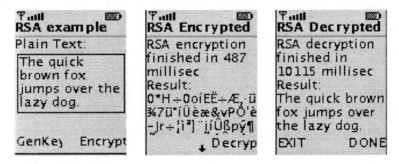

Figure 20.4. RSA public key encryption using the Phaos MF library.

20.4.1 Bouncy Castle

To generate an RSA key pair, BC requires the developer to pick a mathematical parameter called *public exponent*. A common pick is 65537 (Hex 10001) for strong security and fast performance. Listing 20.18 demonstrates how to generate an RSA key pair in the CryptoEngine class.

Listing 20.18. BC RSA key pair generation

```
public void generateRSAKeyPair () throws Exception {
  SecureRandom sr = new SecureRandom();
  BigInteger pubExp = new BigInteger("10001", 16);
  RSAKeyGenerationParameters RSAKeyGenPara =
      new RSAKeyGenerationParameters(pubExp, sr, 1024, 80);
  RSAKeyPairGenerator RSAKeyPairGen = new RSAKeyPairGenerator();
```

```
RSAKeyPairGen.init(RSAKeyGenPara);
AsymmetricCipherKeyPair keyPair = RSAKeyPairGen.generateKeyPair();

RSAprivKey = (RSAPrivateCrtKeyParameters) keyPair.getPrivate();
RSApubKey = (RSAKeyParameters) keyPair.getPublic();
}
```

Listings 20.19 and 20.20 demonstrate how to serialize the key pair offline to disk files and then read them back. Please note that since BC does not support a good key serialization mechanism in its lightweight API package, we have to manually serialize all key parameters, which is tedious.

Listing 20.19. Serialize the key pair to disk files

```
BigInteger mod = RSAprivKey.getModulus();
out = new FileOutputStream(outdir + "RSAmod.dat");
out.write(mod.toByteArray());
out.flush(); out.close();

BigInteger privExp = RSAprivKey.getExponent();
out = new FileOutputStream(outdir + "RSAprivExp.dat");
out.write(privExp.toByteArray());
out.flush(); out.close();

pubExp = RSAprivKey.getPublicExponent();
if ( !pubExp.equals(new BigInteger("10001", 16)) )
  throw new Exception("wrong public exponent");
out = new FileOutputStream(outdir + "RSApubExp.dat");
out.write(pubExp.toByteArray());
out.flush(); out.close();

BigInteger dp = RSAprivKey.getDP();
out = new FileOutputStream(outdir + "RSAdp.dat");
out.write(dp.toByteArray());
out.flush(); out.close();

BigInteger dq = RSAprivKey.getDQ();
out = new FileOutputStream(outdir + "RSAdq.dat");
out.write(dq.toByteArray());
out.flush(); out.close();

BigInteger p = RSAprivKey.getP();
out = new FileOutputStream(outdir + "RSAp.dat");
out.write(p.toByteArray());
```

```
out.flush(); out.close();

BigInteger q = RSAprivKey.getQ();
out = new FileOutputStream(outdir + "RSAq.dat");
out.write(q.toByteArray());
out.flush(); out.close();

BigInteger qInv = RSAprivKey.getQInv();
out = new FileOutputStream(outdir + "RSAqInv.dat");
out.write(qInv.toByteArray());
out.flush(); out.close();
```

Listing 20.20. Deserialize the key pair in CryptoEngine constructor

---

```
Class c = this.getClass();
InputStream is;
is = c.getResourceAsStream("/keys/RSAmod.dat");
BigInteger RSAmod = new BigInteger(readFromStream(is));
is.close();
is = c.getResourceAsStream("/keys/RSAprivExp.dat");
BigInteger RSAprivExp = new BigInteger(readFromStream(is));
is.close();
is = c.getResourceAsStream("/keys/RSApubExp.dat");
BigInteger RSApubExp = new BigInteger(readFromStream(is));
is.close();
is = c.getResourceAsStream("/keys/RSAdp.dat");
BigInteger RSAdp = new BigInteger(readFromStream(is));
is.close();
is = c.getResourceAsStream("/keys/RSAdq.dat");
BigInteger RSAdq = new BigInteger(readFromStream(is));
is.close();
is = c.getResourceAsStream("/keys/RSAp.dat");
BigInteger RSAp = new BigInteger(readFromStream(is));
is.close();
is = c.getResourceAsStream("/keys/RSAq.dat");
BigInteger RSAq = new BigInteger(readFromStream(is));
is.close();
is = c.getResourceAsStream("/keys/RSAqInv.dat");
BigInteger RSAqInv = new BigInteger(readFromStream(is));
is.close();

RSAprivKey = new RSAPrivateCrtKeyParameters(
    RSAmod, RSApubExp, RSAprivExp, RSAp,
```

```
    RSAq, RSAdp, RSAdq, RSAqInv);
RSApubKey = new RSAKeyParameters(false, RSAmod, RSApubExp);
```

Now, we can encrypt and decrypt messages using the public key RSApubKey and private key RSAprivKey respectively (Listing 20.21).

Listing 20.21. RSA encryption and decryption with BC

```
// Public key encrypt using RSA
public byte [] RSAEncrypt (byte [] toEncrypt) throws Exception {
  if (RSApubKey == null)
    throw new Exception("Generate RSA keys first!");

  AsymmetricBlockCipher eng = new RSAEngine();
  eng = new PKCS1Encoding(eng);
  eng.init(true, RSApubKey);
  return eng.processBlock(toEncrypt, 0, toEncrypt.length);
}

// private key decrypt
public byte [] RSADecrypt (byte [] toDecrypt) throws Exception {
  if (RSAprivKey == null)
    throw new Exception("Generate RSA keys first!");

  AsymmetricBlockCipher eng = new RSAEngine();
  eng = new PKCS1Encoding(eng);
  eng.init(false, RSAprivKey);
  return eng.processBlock(toDecrypt, 0, toDecrypt.length);
}
```

20.4.2 IAIK JCE-ME

Listing 20.22 illustrates how to generate an RSA key pair using the IAIK library.

Listing 20.22. Generate RSA keys using the IAIK library

```
public void generateRSAKeyPair () throws Exception {
  RSAKeyPairGenerator rsaKeyPairGenerator = new RSAKeyPairGenerator();
  rsaKeyPairGenerator.initialize(1024, null, null);
  CryptoBag cryptoBag = rsaKeyPairGenerator.generateKeyPair();
```

```
RSApubKey =
    (PublicKey) cryptoBag.getCryptoBag(cryptoBag.V_KEY_PUBLIC);
RSAprivKey =
    (PrivateKey) cryptoBag.getCryptoBag(cryptoBag.V_KEY_PRIVATE);
return;
}
```

Listings 20.23 and 20.24 demonstrate the serialization and deserialization processes in the GenerateAllKeys class and the CryptoEngine constructor.

Listing 20.23. Serialize the keys to a disk file

```
out = new FileOutputStream(outdir + "RSApub.dat");
out.write(RSApubKey.getEncoded());
out.flush(); out.close();

out = new FileOutputStream(outdir + "RSApriv.dat");
out.write(RSAprivKey.getEncoded());
out.flush(); out.close();
```

Listing 20.24. Deserialize the RSA key pair

```
Class c = this.getClass();
InputStream is;

byte [] asnArray;
is = c.getResourceAsStream("/keys/RSApub.dat");
asnArray = readFromStream(is);
is.close();
RSApubKey = new PublicKey(new ASN1(asnArray));

is = c.getResourceAsStream("/keys/RSApriv.dat");
asnArray = readFromStream(is);
is.close();
RSAprivKey = new PrivateKey(new ASN1(asnArray));
```

With the key pair, we can now encrypt and decrypt messages (Listing 20.25). Notice how simple the API is!

Listing 20.25. RSA encryption and decryption

```
// Public key encrypt using RSA
public byte [] RSAEncrypt (byte [] toEncrypt) throws Exception {
  if (RSApubKey == null)
    throw new Exception("Generate RSA keys first!");

  Cipher rsa = Cipher.getInstance("RSA/ECB/PKCS1Padding");
  rsa.init(Cipher.ENCRYPT_MODE, RSApubKey, null, null);
  return rsa.doFinal(toEncrypt);
}

// private key decrypt
public byte [] RSADecrypt (byte [] toDecrypt) throws Exception {
  if (RSAprivKey == null)
    throw new Exception("Generate RSA keys first!");

  Cipher rsa = Cipher.getInstance("RSA/ECB/PKCS1Padding");
  rsa.init(Cipher.DECRYPT_MODE, RSAprivKey, null, null);
  return rsa.doFinal(toDecrypt);
}
```

20.4.3   Phaos Micro Foundation

Using the Phaos MF library, generating an RSA key pair is easy (Listing 20.26).

Listing 20.26. Generate a RSA key pair using Phaos MF

```
public void generateRSAKeyPair () throws Exception {
  RSAKeyGenParams params = new RSAKeyGenParams(1024);
  KeyPairGenerator kpg =
    KeyPairGenerator.getInstance(
            OIDList.RSA_ENCRYPTION, params);
  KeyPair kp = kpg.generateKeyPair();
  RSApubKey = (RSAPublicKey)kp.publicKey;
  RSAprivKey = (RSAPrivateKey)kp.privateKey;
  return;
}
```

Serializing and deserializing keys in the Phaos library are demonstrated in Listings 20.27 and 20.28.

Listing 20.27. Serialize RSA keys to files

```
RSApubKey.output(new FileOutputStream(outdir + "RSApubKey.der"));
RSAprivKey.output(new FileOutputStream(outdir + "RSAprivKey.der"));
```

Listing 20.28. Deserialize keys from the files

```
Class c = this.getClass();
InputStream is;

is = c.getResourceAsStream("/keys/RSApubKey.der");
RSApubKey = new RSAPublicKey(is);
is.close();
is = c.getResourceAsStream("/keys/RSAprivKey.der");
RSAprivKey = new RSAPrivateKey(is);
is.close();
```

Encryption and decryption are demonstrated in Listing 20.29.

Listing 20.29. RSA encryption and decryption

```
public byte [] RSAEncrypt (byte [] toEncrypt) throws Exception {
  if (RSApubKey == null)
    throw new Exception("Generate RSA keys first!");
  byte [] encrypted;

  PooledArray plaintext = ByteArrayPool.getArray(toEncrypt);
  AlgorithmIdentifier algID = new OAEPAlgID();
  Cipher cipher = Cipher.getInstance(algID, RSApubKey);
  PooledArray ciphertext =
    cipher.encrypt(plaintext.buffer, 0, plaintext.length);

  ByteArrayOutputStream out = new ByteArrayOutputStream ();
  algID.output(out);
  out.write(ciphertext.buffer, 0, ciphertext.length);
  encrypted = out.toByteArray();
  out.close();
  plaintext.release();
```

```
  ciphertext.release();
  return encrypted;
}

public byte [] RSADecrypt (byte [] toDecrypt) throws Exception {
  if (RSAprivKey == null)
    throw new Exception("Generate RSA keys first!");
  byte [] decrypted;

  ByteArrayInputStream in = new ByteArrayInputStream(toDecrypt);
  AlgorithmIdentifier algID = new AlgorithmIdentifier(in);
  PooledArray ciphertext = ByteArrayPool.getArray(in.available());
  in.read(ciphertext.buffer, 0, ciphertext.length);
  in.close();

  Cipher cipher = Cipher.getInstance(algID, RSAprivKey);
  PooledArray plaintext =
    cipher.decrypt(ciphertext.buffer, 0, ciphertext.length);
  decrypted = plaintext.toByteArray();

  plaintext.release();
  ciphertext.release();
  return decrypted;
}
```

20.4.4 NTRU jNeo

Generating an NTRU key pair for the NTRUEncrypt algorithm takes only one line of code. The following code snippet generates an NTRU 251-bit encryption key, which has cryptographic strength equivalent to a 1,024-bit RSA key (Listing 20.30).

Listing 20.30. Generate the NTRU encryption key pair

```
private RandomNumber rn =
  new RandomNumber(NTRUConst.NTRU_SHA1_HASH);
private Context ctx = new Context(rn);

// ... ...

public void generateNTRUencKeys () throws Exception {
  NTRUencKeys = new EncKeys(ctx,
      NTRUConst.NTRU_KEYSTRENGTH_251,
```

```
        NTRUConst.NTRU_SHA1_HASH);
  return;
}
```

NTRU jNeo provides its own key serialization methods. Let's see how it is done in the **GenerateAllKeys** class (Listing 20.31) and the **CryptoEngine** (Listing 20.32) constructor.

Listing 20.31. Serialize the key pair to disk files

```
byte [] pubKey = NTRUencKeys.exportPubKey(null, 0, true);
out = new FileOutputStream(outdir + "EncPubKey.dat");
out.write(pubKey); out.flush(); out.close();

byte [] privKey = NTRUencKeys.exportPrivKey(null, 0, true);
out = new FileOutputStream(outdir + "EncPrivKey.dat");
out.write(privKey); out.flush(); out.close();
```

Listing 20.32. Deserialize the key pair from disk files

```
Class c = this.getClass();
InputStream is;

is = c.getResourceAsStream("/keys/EncPubKey.dat");
byte [] encPubKeyData = readFromStream(is);
is.close();
is = c.getResourceAsStream("/keys/EncPrivKey.dat");
byte [] encPrivKeyData = readFromStream(is);
is.close();
NTRUencKeys = new EncKeys (encPubKeyData, 0,
                          encPubKeyData.length,
                          encPrivKeyData, 0,
                          encPrivKeyData.length,
                          true);
```

The encryption and decryption methods are demonstrated in Listing 20.33. Notice that we take care of the proper block handling in our methods.

Listing 20.33. Encryption and decryption using the NTRU algorithm

```
public byte [] NTRUEncrypt (byte [] toEncrypt) throws Exception {
  if ( NTRUencKeys == null )
    throw new Exception("Generate keys first!");

  int cipherBlockSize =
    NTRUencKeys.ciphertextSize(NTRUConst.NTRU_KEYSTRENGTH_251);
  int plainBlockSize =
    NTRUencKeys.blockSize(NTRUConst.NTRU_KEYSTRENGTH_251);

  byte [] cipherBlock = new byte [cipherBlockSize];
  byte [] plainBlock = new byte [plainBlockSize];
  int psize;
  ByteArrayInputStream bais = new ByteArrayInputStream(toEncrypt);
  ByteArrayOutputStream baos = new ByteArrayOutputStream();
  while ( (psize = bais.read(plainBlock)) != -1 ) {
    // resize the last plain text block
    if ( psize < plainBlockSize ) {
      byte tmp [] = new byte [psize];
      for (int i = 0; i < psize; i++) {
        tmp[i] = plainBlock[i];
      }
      plainBlock = tmp;
    }

    NTRUencKeys.blockEncrypt(ctx, plainBlock, 0,
                            plainBlock.length, cipherBlock, 0);
    baos.write(cipherBlock);
  }
  baos.flush();
  byte [] result = baos.toByteArray();
  baos.close(); bais.close();
  return result;
}

public byte [] NTRUDecrypt (byte [] toDecrypt) throws Exception {
  if ( NTRUencKeys == null )
    throw new Exception("Generate keys first!");

  int cipherBlockSize =
    NTRUencKeys.ciphertextSize(NTRUConst.NTRU_KEYSTRENGTH_251);
  int plainBlockSize =
    NTRUencKeys.blockSize(NTRUConst.NTRU_KEYSTRENGTH_251);
```

```
byte [] cipherBlock = new byte [cipherBlockSize];
byte [] plainBlock = new byte [plainBlockSize];
int psize;
ByteArrayInputStream bais = new ByteArrayInputStream(toDecrypt);
ByteArrayOutputStream baos = new ByteArrayOutputStream();
while ( bais.read(cipherBlock) != -1 ) {
  psize = NTRUencKeys.blockDecrypt(ctx,
                   cipherBlock, 0,
                   cipherBlock.length,
                   plainBlock, 0);
  // resize the last plain text block
  if ( psize < plainBlockSize ) {
    byte tmp [] = new byte [psize];
    for (int i = 0; i < psize; i++) {
      tmp[i] = plainBlock[i];
    }
    plainBlock = tmp;
  }
  baos.write(plainBlock);
}
baos.flush();
byte [] result = baos.toByteArray();
baos.close(); bais.close();
return result;
}
```

20.5 Digital Signature

Digital signature can guarantee message integrity and authenticity in an open network environment. To generate a signature, you first calculate a hash (also called *digest*) of your message. Then you encrypt that hash with your private key to generate a signature. The party at the receiving end first decrypts your signature into a hash using your public key. Then she calculates the hash from your message. If the two hashes match, the message is indeed from you and unaltered. The signing and verification processes are demonstrated in Figures 20.5 and 20.6 respectively.

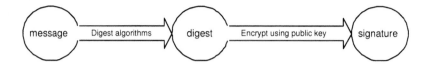

Figure 20.5. Generate a digital signature.

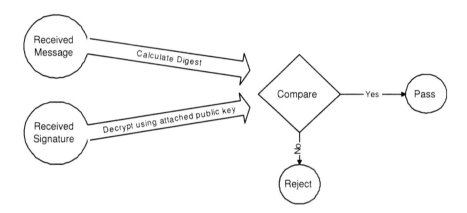

Figure 20.6. Verify a digital signature.

If someone altered the message during its transmission and generated a new hash based on the modified message, public key algorithms guarantee that he cannot produce a matching signature without knowing your private key. The two parties must share four pieces of information: the message itself, its digital signature, the hash and signing algorithms, and the public key. Our demo MIDlet for digital signature is shown in Figure 20.7.

Figure 20.7. NTRUSign signature generation and verification.

Note

> Without infrastructure support, there is no way to guarantee the authenticity of a public key. To make sure that a public key really belongs to its claimed owner, we need the Public Key Infrastructure (PKI) and digital certificates. In PKI, an individual or a company can have its public key digitally signed by a trusted authority. The signed public key and other information constitute the digital certificate. The integrity of the digital signature on the certificate guarantees its authenticity. BC, IAIK, Phaos, as well the standard MIDP v2.0 provide APIs for digital certificate support. For more information on the PKI, please refer to the "Resources" section.

20.5.1   Bouncy Castle

Bouncy Castle supports DSA, RSA, and ECC (Elliptic Curve Cryptography) digital signature algorithms. But only RSA seems to have an acceptable performance on MIDP devices. So, the code example here only shows how to work with RSA signatures. Since the RSA key pair generation and serialization part is already covered by the last section, we go directly to the code for signature generation and verification (Listing 20.34).

Listing 20.34. Sign and verify a message using the RSA algorithm in BC

```
public byte [] RSASign (byte [] toSign) throws Exception {
  if (RSAprivKey == null)
    throw new Exception("Generate RSA keys first!");
  SHA1Digest dig = new SHA1Digest();
  RSAEngine eng = new RSAEngine();

  PSSSigner signer = new PSSSigner(eng, dig, 64);
  signer.init(true, RSAprivKey);
  signer.update(toSign, 0, toSign.length);
  return signer.generateSignature();
}

public boolean RSAVerify (byte [] mesg, byte [] sig)
                            throws Exception {
  if (RSApubKey == null)
    throw new Exception("Generate RSA keys first!");
  SHA1Digest dig = new SHA1Digest();
```

```
    RSAEngine eng = new RSAEngine();

    PSSSigner signer = new PSSSigner(eng, dig, 64);
    signer.init(false, RSApubKey);
    signer.update(mesg, 0, mesg.length);
    return signer.verifySignature(sig);
}
```

20.5.2 IAIK JCE-ME

Our IAIK digital signature example also uses the RSA algorithm. So, again,
we do not show any code for the key generation and serialization. Listing 20.35 demonstrates the signing and verification processes.

> **Listing 20.35.** RSA digital signature sign and verify methods in IAIK

```
// RSA signature
public byte [] RSASign (byte [] toSign) throws Exception {
  if (RSAprivKey == null)
    throw new Exception("Generate RSA keys first!");

  Signature sharsa = Signature.getInstance("SHA1withRSA");
  sharsa.initSign(RSAprivKey, null);
  sharsa.update(toSign);
  return sharsa.sign();
}

// RSA signature verification
public boolean RSAVerify (byte [] mesg, byte [] sig)
                                    throws Exception {
  if (RSApubKey == null)
    throw new Exception("Generate RSA keys first!");

  Signature sharsa = Signature.getInstance("SHA1withRSA");
  sharsa.initVerify(RSApubKey);
  sharsa.update(mesg);
  return sharsa.verify(sig);
}
```

20.5.3   Phaos Micro Foundation

Phaos MF supports DSA and RSA digital signatures. DSA is certainly slower than RSA. But since we already have two RSA examples, we will have a look at a DSA example here. Generating DSA key pairs using the Phaos MF API is illustrated in Listing 20.36. Variable DSApubKeyDer is not the public key itself. Rather, it is a byte array representation of the public key in DER (Distinguished Encoding Rules) format. The public key can be reconstructed from this array using an appropriate algorithm identifier (see Listing 20.38).

Listing 20.36. Phaos MF DSA key pair generation

```
// 1024-bit DSA key
private DSAPrivateKey DSAprivKey;
// This is the DSA public key data you can serialize
private byte [] DSApubKeyDer;

public void generateDSAKeyPair () throws Exception {
  DSAKeyGenParams params =
    new DSAKeyGenParams(1024, RandomBitsSource.getDefault());
  KeyPairGenerator kpg =
     KeyPairGenerator.getInstance(OIDList.DSA, params);
  KeyPair kp = kpg.generateKeyPair();

  DSAprivKey = (DSAPrivateKey)kp.privateKey;

  ByteArrayOutputStream baos = new ByteArrayOutputStream ();
  ((DSAPublicKey)kp.publicKey).output(baos);
  DSApubKeyDer = baos.toByteArray();

  return;
}
```

The Phaos DSA key pair serialization and deserialization processes are illustrated in Listings 20.37 and 20.38.

Listing 20.37. Phaos MF DSA key pair serialization

```
DSAPublicKey pubKey = (DSAPublicKey)kp.publicKey;
DSAPrivateKey privKey = (DSAPrivateKey)kp.privateKey;
pubKey.output(new FileOutputStream(outdir + "DSApubKey.der"));
privKey.output(new FileOutputStream(outdir + "DSAprivKey.der"));
```

```
DSAParams dsaParams =
  new DSAParams(
    new ByteArrayInputStream(
      privKey.createAlgID(true).encodeParameters()));
dsaParams.output(new FileOutputStream(outdir + "DSAparams.der"));
```

Listing 20.38. Phaos MF DSA key pair deserialization

```
// The DSA private key
is = c.getResourceAsStream("/keys/DSAparams.der");
DSAParams params = new DSAParams(is);
AlgorithmIdentifier algID = getDSAalgID(params);
is.close();
is = c.getResourceAsStream("/keys/DSAprivKey.der");
DSAprivKey = new DSAPrivateKey(algID, is);
is.close();

// The DSA public key byte array
is = c.getResourceAsStream("/keys/DSApubKey.der");
baos = new ByteArrayOutputStream();
b = new byte[1];
while ( is.read(b) != -1 ) {
   baos.write(b);
}
is.close();
DSApubKeyDer = baos.toByteArray();
baos.close();
```

The method **getDSAalgID()** (Listing 20.38) retrieves the algorithm identifier from DSA parameters. It is also used in DSA sign and verify examples (Listing 20.39).

Listing 20.39. Phaos MF DSA sign and verify methods

```
private AlgorithmIdentifier getDSAalgID (DSAParams params)
                                        throws Exception {
  ByteArrayOutputStream paramsOut = new ByteArrayOutputStream();
  params.output(paramsOut);
  paramsOut.close();
  return new AlgorithmIdentifier(OIDList.DSA, paramsOut.toByteArray());
}
```

```
public byte [] DSASign (byte [] toSign) throws Exception {
  if (DSAprivKey == null)
    throw new Exception("Generate DSA keys first!");
  Signature signature =
    Signature.getInstance(AlgIDList.SHA1_WITH_DSA, DSAprivKey);
  byte [] result =
    signature.sign(toSign, 0, toSign.length).toByteArray(true);
  DSAParams params = new DSAParams(
    new ByteArrayInputStream(
      DSAprivKey.createAlgID(true).encodeParameters()));
  AlgorithmIdentifier algID = getDSAalgID (params);

  ByteArrayOutputStream baos = new ByteArrayOutputStream ();
  algID.output(baos);
  baos.write(result, 0, result.length);
  baos.flush(); baos.close();

  return baos.toByteArray();
}

public boolean DSAVerify (byte [] mesg, byte [] sig)
                                throws Exception {
  InputStream is = new ByteArrayInputStream(sig);
  AlgorithmIdentifier algID = new AlgorithmIdentifier(is);
  PooledArray sigBytes = ByteArrayPool.getArray(is.available());
  is.read(sigBytes.buffer, 0, sigBytes.length);
  is.close();

  DSAPublicKey DSApubKey = new DSAPublicKey(algID,
          new ByteArrayInputStream(DSApubKeyDer));

  Signature signature =
    Signature.getInstance(AlgIDList.SHA1_WITH_DSA, DSApubKey);

  return signature.verify(mesg, 0, mesg.length,
                  sigBytes.buffer, 0, sigBytes.length);
}
```

20.5.4   NTRU jNeo

The NTRU digital signature algorithm (NTRUSign) uses different keys from
the NTRUEncrypt algorithm. The key generation process is simple (Listing 20.40).

Note

> Unlike RSA and DSA, the public and private keys in the NTRU
> digital signature algorithm are not exchangeable. You can sign only
> with the private key and verify only with the public key.

Listing 20.40. Generate an NTRU signature key pair

```
public void generateNTRUsgnKeys () throws Exception {
  NTRUsgnKeys = new SgnKeys(ctx,
              NTRUConst.NTRU_KEYSTRENGTH_251,
              NTRUConst.NTRU_SHA1_HASH);
  return;
}
```

The serialization and deserialization of the key pair are illustrated in
Listings 20.41 and 20.42.

Listing 20.41. Serialize the NTRUSign key pair

```
byte [] pubKey = NTRUsgnKeys.exportPubKey(null, 0);
out = new FileOutputStream(outdir + "SgnPubKey.dat");
out.write(pubKey);
out.flush(); out.close();

byte [] privKey = NTRUsgnKeys.exportPrivKey(null, 0);
out = new FileOutputStream(outdir + "SgnPrivKey.dat");
out.write(privKey);
out.flush(); out.close();
```

Listing 20.42. Deserialize the NTRUSign key pair

```
is = c.getResourceAsStream("/keys/SgnPubKey.dat");
byte [] sgnPubKeyData = readFromStream(is);
is.close();

is = c.getResourceAsStream("/keys/SgnPrivKey.dat");
byte [] sgnPrivKeyData = readFromStream(is);
is.close();
```

```
NTRUsgnKeys = new SgnKeys (sgnPubKeyData, 0,
                           sgnPubKeyData.length,
                           sgnPrivKeyData, 0,
                           sgnPrivKeyData.length);
```

The NTRU signature generation and verification processes are illustrated in Listing 20.43.

Listing 20.43. NTRUSign signature signing and verification using jNeo

```
public byte [] NTRUSign (byte [] message) throws Exception {
  if ( NTRUsgnKeys == null )
    throw new Exception("Generate keys first!");

  MessageDigest dig = new MessageDigest(NTRUConst.NTRU_SHA160_HASH);
  Signature sig =
    new Signature(NTRUConst.NTRU_KEYSTRENGTH_251,
                  NTRUConst.NTRU_SHA160_HASH);
  dig.updateMessageDigest(message, 0, message.length);
  dig.completeMessageDigest();
  sig.sign(ctx, NTRUsgnKeys, dig);
  return sig.export();
}

public boolean NTRUVerify (byte [] message,
              byte [] sigData) throws Exception {

  Signature sig = new Signature(sigData, 0, sigData.length);
  MessageDigest dig = new MessageDigest(sig.getHashAlg());
  dig.updateMessageDigest(message, 0, message.length);
  dig.completeMessageDigest();

  try {
    sig.verify(ctx, NTRUsgnKeys, dig);
    return true;
  } catch (NTRUException e) {
    return false;
  }
}
```

20.6   Summary

Now we have walked through examples on how to perform symmetric encryption, password-based encryption, public key encryption, and digital signature tasks using the Bouncy Castle, Phaos, NTRU, and IAIK toolkits. I have tried to make those example applications easy to understand. The goal here is to illustrate API usage rather than to provide industry-strength reusable code. Now, it is your turn to develop real-world, highly secure mobile applications!

Resources

[1] The full source code of the cryptography sample applications covered in this chapter. http://www.enterprisej2me.com/book/code/

[2] The Bouncy Castle project. http://www.bouncycastle.org/

[3] The IAIK JCE-ME library.
http://jce.iaik.tugraz.at/products/10_me-jce/index.php

[4] Phaos Technology Micro Security products.
http://www.phaos.com/products/category/micro.html

[5] NTRU toolkits. http://www.ntru.com/products/toolkits.htm

[6] RSA Security's Cryptography FAQ is a good introduction to modern cryptography solutions, including the Public Key Infrastructure.
http://www.rsasecurity.com/rsalabs/faq/

[7] The NTRU algorithms explained.
http://www.ntru.com/cryptolab/algorithms.htm

[8] The National Institute of Standards and Technology (NIST) PKI program home page. http://csrc.nist.gov/pki/

Appendix A

Basics of J2ME Application Development

This book is focused on mobile application architecture, advanced techniques, and power tools. Our target audience is experienced Java developers with some J2ME skills. However, do not panic if you have not worked with J2ME before! This appendix should get you up to speed quickly. As we discussed in Chapter 2, there are two dominant profiles on the J2ME platform:

- *The PersonalJava and J2ME Personal Profile (PP)* run on high-end PDA or set-top box devices. They share the same application structure (e.g., the **main()** method), standard APIs (e.g., I/O and AWT UI APIs) and development tools as the J2SE platform. Any experienced Java developer should easily get started with the PersonalJava/PP development.

- *The J2ME Mobile Information Device Profile (MIDP)* runs on pervasive mobile devices such as smart phones. It is not compatible with the J2SE in bytecode structure and API usage.

In this appendix, we briefly cover the basics of MIDP v1.0 application development through an example.

A.1 Life Cycle Methods

MIDP applications are managed by the Application Management Software (AMS) on devices. The AMS starts, stops, or pauses the MIDP application by calling its main MIDlet class's life cycle methods. The MIDlet can also notify the AMS when its state changes. Any MIDlet class must extend the javax.microedition.midlet.MIDlet class and customize the life cycle methods. The life cycle methods and their descriptions are listed in Table A.1.

Table A.1. MIDlet Life Cycle Methods	
Method	Description
startApp()	Called by the AMS when the MIDlet starts to recover from the pause state.
destroyApp()	Called by the AMS when the MIDlet is terminated.
pauseApp()	Called by the AMS when the MIDlet is paused.
notifyDestroyed()	Called by the MIDlet. It asks the AMS to destroy the MIDlet itself.
notifyPaused()	Called by the MIDlet. It asks the AMS to pause the MIDlet itself.
resumeRequest()	Called by the paused MIDlet (e.g., from a background thread). It notifies the AMS that the MIDlet desires to come out of the paused state and become active again.

A.2   UI Model

After the MIDlet is started, it can retrieve a reference to the current display screen from the Display.getDisplay(this) method. Now, we can add UI widgets in the LCDUI package to the screen. We must also associate an event handler to the screen. The handler listens to and handles UI events generated by the user to this screen. The handler implements the CommandListener interface, which declares one method, commandAction(). Since the commandAction() method is required to return quickly to avoid UI blocking, lengthy event handling actions are processed in separate threads.

A.3   Remote and Local Data

MIDP applications can access remote data via HTTP connections. A connection object can be obtained from the Connector.open() static factory method.

For local data, MIDP provides an API for a linear on-device storage facility: the Record Management System. MIDlets can open and close record stores. Each record store contains a number of records that can hold arbitrary binary content. The MIDP RMS API allows developers to add, iterate through, and manipulate the records.

A.4   Code Walk Through

The sample application in this appendix demonstrates the use of the above MIDP programming model and APIs. The sample application allows the user to enter a URL. When the user clicks the Fetch button, the MIDlet fetches and displays the content from that URL. The MIDlet also stores the URL in RMS for future browsing. Figure A.1 shows the MIDlet in action. Listing A.1 shows the entire source code. Please note that the main MIDlet is also its own UI command listener and handler. The worker threads are inner classes extending the JDK Thread class.

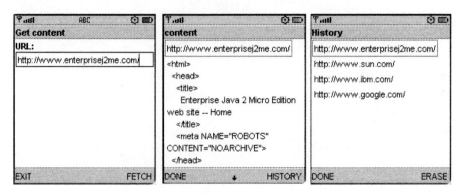

Figure A.1. The sample MIDlet in action.

Listing A.1. The sample MIDlet

```
package com.enterprisej2me.simpledemo;

import java.io.*;
import javax.microedition.midlet.*;
import javax.microedition.lcdui.*;
import javax.microedition.rms.*;
import javax.microedition.io.*;

public class DemoMIDlet extends MIDlet
                implements CommandListener {

  private Display display;
  private Command fetch;
  private Command history;
  private Command erase;
```

```
private Command exit;
private Command done;
private TextField urlField;
private RecordStore store;

public DemoMIDlet () throws Exception {
  display = Display.getDisplay(this);
  fetch = new Command("FETCH", Command.SCREEN, 1);
  history = new Command("HISTORY", Command.SCREEN, 1);
  erase = new Command("ERASE", Command.SCREEN, 1);
  exit  = new Command("EXIT", Command.CANCEL, 1);
  done  = new Command("DONE", Command.CANCEL, 1);
  store = RecordStore.openRecordStore("DataStore", true);
}

public void startApp() {
  startScreen ();
}

public void pauseApp() {
  // Nothing to do ...
}

public void destroyApp(boolean unconditional) {
  try {
    store.closeRecordStore ();
  } catch (Exception exp) {
    exp.printStackTrace ();
  }

}

public void commandAction(Command command,
                          Displayable screen) {
  if (command == exit) {

    destroyApp(false);
    notifyDestroyed();

  } else if (command == fetch) {

    FetchWorker t = new FetchWorker ();
    t.setListener(this);
    t.start();
```

```
    } else if (command == history) {

      HistoryWorker t = new HistoryWorker ();
      t.setListener(this);
      t.start();

    } else if (command == erase) {

      try {
        store.closeRecordStore ();
        RecordStore.deleteRecordStore("DataStore");
        store =
          RecordStore.openRecordStore("DataStore", true);
      } catch (Exception exp) { }

      HistoryWorker t = new HistoryWorker ();
      t.setListener(this);
      t.start();

    } else if (command == done) {
      startScreen();
    }
  }

  private void startScreen () {
    Form f = new Form ("Get content");
    urlField =
      new TextField ("URL: ", "", 30, TextField.ANY);
    f.append (urlField);
    f.addCommand (fetch);
    f.addCommand (exit);
    f.setCommandListener(this);
    display.setCurrent(f);
  }

  class FetchWorker extends Thread {

    private CommandListener listener;

    public void setListener (CommandListener cl) {
      listener = cl;
    }

    public void run () {
      HttpConnection conn = null;
```

```
DataInputStream din = null;
ByteArrayOutputStream bos = null;
try {
  // Get the url
  String url = urlField.getString ();

  // Fetch the remote content to a byte array "buf"
  conn = (HttpConnection) Connector.open(url);
  conn.setRequestMethod(HttpConnection.GET);
  din = conn.openDataInputStream();
  bos = new ByteArrayOutputStream();
  byte[] buf = new byte[256];
  while (true) {
    int rd = din.read(buf, 0, 256);
    if (rd == -1) break;
    bos.write(buf, 0, rd);
  }
  bos.flush();
  buf = bos.toByteArray();

  // Save the history
  store.addRecord(url.getBytes(), 0,
               url.getBytes().length);

  // Display a new screen
  Form f = new Form ("content");
  f.append(url + "\n");
  f.append(new String(buf));
  f.addCommand(history);
  f.addCommand(done);
  f.setCommandListener (listener);
  display.setCurrent(f);

} catch (Exception exp) {
  exp.printStackTrace();
} finally {
  try {
    if (din != null) din.close();
    if (conn != null) conn.close();
    if (bos != null) bos.close();
  } catch (Exception exp) {}
}
}


}
```

```
class HistoryWorker extends Thread {

  private CommandListener listener;

  public void setListener (CommandListener cl) {
    listener = cl;
  }

  public void run () {
    try {
      Form f = new Form ("History");

      RecordEnumeration enu =
              store.enumerateRecords(null, null, false);
      for (; enu.hasNextElement() ;) {
        byte [] data = enu.nextRecord();
        f.append((new String(data)) + "\n");
      }
      enu.destroy();

      f.addCommand(erase);
      f.addCommand(done);
      f.setCommandListener (listener);
      display.setCurrent(f);

    } catch (Exception exp) {
      exp.printStackTrace();
    }
  }

 }
}
```

A.5   Packaging and Building

We can compile MIDP applications using the normal JDK compiler with the
MIDP core classes in the boot classpath. Due to MIDP's lightweight class
verification schemes, we have to pre-verify MIDP classes before deploying
them. The Sun J2ME Wireless ToolKit and vendor MIDP kits provide pre-
verify utilities for many platforms. Those utilities take in compiled MIDP
classes and output pre-verified ones.

Since the AMS cannot take classpath, all MIDP applications must be completely self-contained with all necessary third-party libraries. We can pack all pre-verified application and library classes and all necessary images and other static resource files into the JAR file. The JAR file must contain a manifest file (Listing A.2) that conforms to the MIDP specification.

Listing A.2. The JAR manifest file

```
Manifest-Version: 1.0
MIDlet-1: Demo, ,com.enterprisej2me.simpledemo.DemoMIDlet
MIDlet-Name: Demo
MIDlet-Version: 1.0.0
MIDlet-Vendor: Michael Yuan
MicroEdition-Configuration: CLDC-1.0
MicroEdition-Profile: MIDP-2.0
```

The AMS reads a Java Application Descriptor (JAD) file (Listing A.3) to locate the MIDP JAR file and class names of the MIDlets. The AMS file can also contain custom properties the AMS can pass to the MIDlets at runtime.

Listing A.3. The JAD file

```
Manifest-Version: 1.0
MIDlet-1: Demo, ,com.enterprisej2me.simpledemo.DemoMIDlet
MIDlet-Name: Demo
MIDlet-Version: 1.0.0
MIDlet-Jar-Size: 44405
MIDlet-Jar-URL: SimpleDemo.jar
MIDlet-Vendor: Michael Yuan
MicroEdition-Configuration: CLDC-1.0
MicroEdition-Profile: MIDP-2.0
MIDlet-Install-Notify: http://127.0.0.1:8080/midp/servlet/feedback
MIDlet-Permissions: javax.microedition.io.HttpConnection
```

The build process is illustrated in the ANT script (Listing A.4). The corresponding project directory structure is illustrated in Figure A.2.

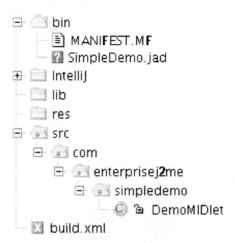

Figure A.2. The project directory structure.

Listing A.4. The ANT build script

```xml
<project name="SimpleDemo" default="all">

  <target name="init">
    <tstamp/>
    <property name="projname" value="SimpleDemo" />
    <property name="WTK" value="C:/Java/WTK20" />
    <property name="midpclasses" value="${WTK}/lib/midpapi.zip" />
    <property name="preverify" value="${WTK}/bin/preverify" />
    <property name="emulator" value="${WTK}/bin/emulator" />
    <property name="tmp" value="anttmp" />
    <property name="tmpclasses" value="${tmp}/tmpclasses" />
    <property name="pvclasses" value="${tmp}/pvclasses" />
  </target>

  <target name="clean" depends="init">
    <delete dir="${tmp}" />
    <delete file="bin/${projname}.jar" />
    <delete file="bin/*.sh" />
  </target>

  <target name="prepare" depends="clean">
    <mkdir dir="${tmp}" />
```

```
    <mkdir dir="${tmpclasses}" />
    <mkdir dir="${pvclasses}" />

    <unzip dest="${tmpclasses}">
      <fileset dir="lib">
        <include name="**/*.zip"/>
        <include name="**/*.jar"/>
      </fileset>
    </unzip>
    <delete dir="${tmpclasses}/META-INF" />
  </target>

  <target name="compile" depends="prepare">
    <javac srcdir="src" destdir="${tmpclasses}"
           bootclasspath="${midpclasses}"
    >
      <classpath>
        <pathelement path="${tmpclasses}"/>
        <pathelement path="${midpclasses}"/>
      </classpath>
    </javac>
  </target>

  <target name="preverify" depends="compile">
    <exec executable="${preverify}">
      <arg line="-classpath ${midpclasses}"/>
      <arg line="-d ${pvclasses}" />
      <arg line="${tmpclasses}" />
    </exec>
  </target>

  <target name="package" depends="preverify">
    <copy todir="${pvclasses}">
      <fileset dir="res" />
    </copy>
    <jar jarfile="bin/${projname}.jar"
         basedir="${pvclasses}"
         manifest="bin/MANIFEST.MF"
    />
  </target>

  <target name="run" depends="init" >
    <exec executable="${emulator}" dir="bin">
      <arg line="-classpath ${projname}.jar" />
      <arg line="-Xdescriptor:${projname}.jad" />
```

```
    </exec>
  </target>

  <target name="all" depends="package" />

</project>
```

A.6   Deployment

MIDP applications can be deployed conveniently Over-the-Air (OTA) to mobile devices. The MIDP v2.0 specification includes a formal OTA specification that defines the exact OTA process. In summary, there are the following steps:

1. *Prepare an OTA server*: The OTA server could be any HTTP Web server with the following correct MIME type setup. Please refer to your server documentation on how to set it up.

   ```
   text/vnd.sun.j2me.app-descriptor    jad
   application/java-archive            jar
   ```

2. *Make the MIDP application available*: You can copy the JAD and JAR files to the server's public directory. You also need to make an HTML or WML file that contains a link to the JAD file.

3. *Start the OTA process on the client side*: On an MIDP-enabled mobile device, you can start the WAP or HTML browser and load the page that contains the JAD link. Click on the link and the JAD MIME type will cause the browser to invoke the MIDP AMS.

4. *Verification and security check*: The AMS downloads the JAR application, verifies its size and manifest with corresponding properties in the JAD file, and checks that it is properly signed and has the correct permissions. If all of those tests pass, the AMS will install the application and notify a server optionally specified in the JAD file.

5. *Application management*: The AMS can also update and uninstall the MIDP application.

A.7   Summary

In this appendix, we discussed the basic programming model, API, and development steps to build and deploy an MIDP smart client application.

Appendix B

Tools and J2ME Runtimes for PDAs

Compared with cell phone devices, Personal Digital Assistants (PDAs) are more powerful. They have larger screen size and more memory, support advanced data entry methods, and are more expandable. Those characteristics make PDAs premium choices for mobile enterprise applications. J2ME runtimes are available for most enterprise-level PDAs, including Palm OS, PocketPC, and embedded Linux (e.g., Sharp Zaurus) devices. However, many devices do not have JVMs preinstalled by the factory. That requires us to install J2ME runtimes ourselves or distribute the JVM as part of the application.

The IBM Pervasive Computing (PvC) division develops J2ME runtimes for a variety of PDA devices. Those JVMs and runtime libraries are distributed as the WebSphere Micro Environment (WME) and WebSphere Custom Environment (WCE) products (also known as the J9 VM). IBM's flagship mobile development tool, the WebSphere Studio Device Developer (WSDD), bundles a powerful Java IDE, the WME/WCE runtimes, and many add-on libraries. The WSDD is freely available for evaluation purposes. In this appendix, I briefly introduce the WSDD v5.5 IDE and cover how to install the WME runtimes onto devices.

Note

The IBM WebSphere Micro Environment for Palm OS is now licensed by Palm and is factory installed in all new Palm Tungsten devices.

B.1   Overview of the WebSphere Studio Device Developer

The IBM WSDD is an Integrated Development Environment (IDE) based on the open source Eclipse platform. Eclipse is a highly regarded IDE framework for advanced Java developers. It has strong support for code-centric tasks such as smart editing, dynamic code completion, refactoring, and collaborative development. Eclipse tightly integrates with the popular open source tools, such as ANT, for custom builds, CVS for versioning control, and JUNIT for unit testing.

In addition to those core IDE features, Eclipse is highly extensible. It features an open architecture for plugins. Through plugins, vendors can add proprietary features to the IDE and sell the enhanced IDE for profits. In fact, this is exactly what IBM did. The IBM WSDD extends the Eclipse IDE with proprietary plugins that handle J2ME-related tasks (see Figure B.1).

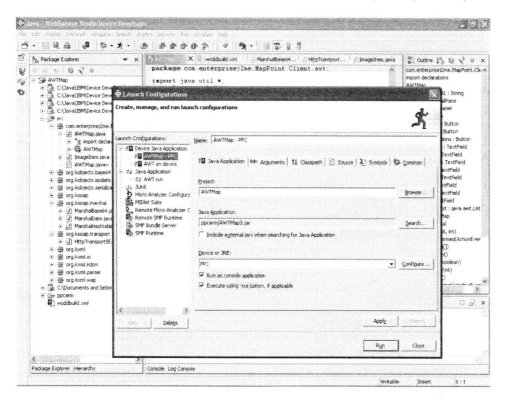

Figure B.1. The WebSphere Studio Device Developer v5.5 IDE.

The WSDD supports wizards and project management tools for J2ME projects. WSDD allows developers to create and test J2ME applications on a desktop computer using WME/WCE for Windows and Linux. Once deployed on the device, the WSDD also supports on-device debugging. You can download the WSDD installer for Windows and Linux from IBM PvC Web site (http://www.ibm.com/software/wireless/wsdd/). The WSDD itself is also extensible. From the Install/Update perspective of the Eclipse workbench, we can select to install a wide variety of runtime libraries, device emulators, wizards, and other add-on tools.

Note

We can use the WSDD to develop standard MIDP and Personal Profile applications. The output binary applications can be deployed to any J2ME-compatible devices, such as MIDP smart phones and Sharp Zaurus PDAs. That makes WSDD a generic J2ME IDE not specifically tied to the IBM runtimes.

In the next two sections, we discuss how to manually install the WebSphere Micro Environment (WME) runtimes on to PocketPC devices. For Palm OS devices that do not have WME preinstalled, the process is similar: Just replace the PocketPC ActiveSync engine with Palm's HotSync engine.

Note

The WME binary packages and deployment licenses are also available from reseller Handango.   Please visit Web site http://www.handango.com/ and do a search on WebSphere to find out more.

B.2   Installing MIDP on PocketPC Devices

To install the WME MIDP runtime on a PocketPC device, you just need to copy a bunch of executable and library files to the device through ActiveSync. The entire JVM and runtime libraries can be installed on the flash card. The detailed steps are as follows:

1. We need to set up a logical directory structure on the device. For example, we can create a top-level installation directory /WSDD. The directory structure under /WSDD is illustrated in Figure B.2.

2. From the IVEHOME/runtimes/pocketpc/arm/ive/bin directory on your development PC (IVEHOME is under the WSDD installation direc-

Figure B.2. The installation directories on the device.

tory), copy the following runtime executable files to the /WSDD/bin directory:

- Console and non-console versions of the JVM: j9.exe and j9w.exe files.
- Dynamically linked runtime libraries for the JVM: j9dyn20.dll, j9prt20.dll, j9thr20.dll, j9vm20.dll, j9zlib20.dll, and iverel20.dll files.
- Debugging libraries: j9dbg20.dll and j9hook20.dll files.
- Native implementations of the CLDC, MIDP, and SWT libraries: j9cldc20.dll, j9midp20.dll, and swt-win32-ce-2023.dll files. The SWT library is the basis for the MIDP LCDUI implementation.

3. Copy the CLDC Java class library file classes.zip from the directory IVEHOME/runtimes/common/ive/lib/jclCldc on the PC to the directory /WSDD/lib/jclCldc on the device.

4. Copy the MIDP Java class library file jclMidp.jxe from the directory IVEHOME/runtimes/pocketpc/arm/ive/lib/jclMidp on the PC to the directory /WSDD/lib/jclMidp on the device.

Note

If you plan to install the runtime on the flash storage card, you can set the top-level directory to /Storage Card/WSDD.

B.3   Installing Personal Profile on PocketPC Devices

To install the CDC, Foundation Profile, and Personal Profile on the PocketPC, we have to expand the installation directory. The new directory structure is illustrated in Figure B.3.

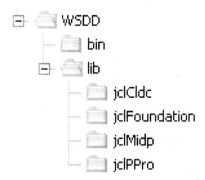

Figure B.3. The installation directories for MIDP and Personal Profile.

Assuming that you already have the J9 VM installed during the MIDP installation process, copy the following additional files from the desktop computer to the device:

1. Copy the Foundation Profile native implementation library j9foun20.dll from the PC directory IVEHOME/runtimes/pocketpc/arm/ive/bin to the device directory /WSDD/bin.

2. Copy the Foundation Profile Java class library classes.zip from PC directory IVEHOME/runtimes/common/ive/lib/jclFoundation to the device directory /WSDD/lib/jclFoundation.

3. Copy the Personal Profile Java class library ppro-ui-win.zip from PC directory IVEHOME/runtimes/pocketpc/common/ive/lib/jclPPro to device directory /WSDD/lib/jclPPro.

Note

The high-level Java UI in the Personal Profile (AWT) and MIDP (LCDUI) share the same underlying native UI library based on IBM SWT.

B.4   Run Java Applications on the PocketPC Device

With the J9 VM and runtime libraries installed, we can now copy Java applications (JAR files or JXE files) to the device. To run Java applications on the PocketPC, follow these three easy steps:

1. *Build a windows link file:* On you desktop PC, use any text editor (e.g., the NotePad) to create a text file with the lnk extension name. The content of the file is a single command line. For example, the following command line (without line break) starts a Personal Profile application from a JAR file myApp.jar.

```
123#"\WSDD\j9.exe" -jcl:foun
"-Xbootclasspath:\WSDD\lib\jclFoundation\classes.zip;
\myApp.jar" "com.enterprisej2me.test" -console "Launch"
```

2. *Copy the link file to the device:* Use ActiveSync to the copy the link file. The link file will have a J9 icon when viewed from the device.

3. *Execute the command in the link file:* Simply tap on the link file to start the VM and execute the command. All log messages will appear in a console window in the background.

Note

PocketPC limits the maximum size of a link file to 255 bytes. A longer file is not recognized as a link even if it has the lnk file extension. The WSDD IDE could help build the link file for your projects.

B.5 Summary

In this appendix, we introduced the IBM WebSphere Studio Device Developer IDE. We also covered the steps on how to install IBM J2ME runtimes on PDA devices.

Index

lightweight cryptography toolkits, 368-
70
security solutions, 368-79
solution providers, 373-75
Mobile Server, 262-63
mobile software platform providers, 12
mobile technology adoption, 7-9, 9f
mobile transaction, 366-67, 366f
mobile Web Services, 48
MobiLink, 260-62
Model-View-Controller pattern. *See* MVC
pattern
ModelFacade class, 93-94
MOM (messaging-oriented middleware),
188, 189, 195, 199
Moore's law, 4
Motorola, 11, 16, 32, 33, 55, 165, 334,
378
MPClient object, 351-53
MQeAdapter class, 204, 204t
MQeCommunicationsAdapter methods, 209
MQeDiskFieldsAdapter class, 204
MQeQueueManager object, 201, 202
MQeTcpipHistoryAdapter methods, 209
MS SQL Server database, 253
msgNumbers vector, 152-53
MSN, 164
Mueller, Thomas, 224
Multimedia Messaging Services. *See* MMS
multiple cookies, 117
multiple devices, 137
Multipurpose Internet Messaging Exten-
sions (MIME), 151, 154
multitiered application models, 54
MVC pattern, 88-92, 132, 141
MVCComponent class, 38-42

N

NAME=VALUE text, 117
NEC, 16
.NET Compact Framework, 25
.Net Passport, 367
New Economy, 4
next() method, 290
NexTel, 6, 16, 32, 33
nextScreen variable, 45
nextToken() method, 290
Nokia, 11, 16, 165, 334

Nokia Mobile Server Services SDK, 177-
78
noLogService() method, 75
notifyIncomingMessage() method, 171
NTRU jNeo, 375-76, 390-92, 406-9, 415-
17
NTRUEncrypt, 375-76, 383, 406
NTRUSign, 375-76, 410f, 415-17
NTT, 334
Numeric Computer Systems, 6

O

Oak, 16
object-oriented language, 17
one-way hashes, 121
open() method, 71, 74
Open Services Gateway initiative. *See*
OSGi
Open Source, 140, 148, 180, 182, 224, 371
openDataInputStream() method, 113
openInputStream() method, 113
Oracle, 55, 132, 357-58
Oracle database, 253, 254
Oracle GIS server, 347
Oracle J2ME SDK, 241-43, 246, 273-74
Oracle9i Application Server, 262
Oracle9i Lite, 228-29, 241
Oracle9i Mobile Server, 262-63
OSGi Alliance, 55
OSGi bundles, 55-59, 64f, 138
OSGi containers, 55-59, 77-78, 78f
OSGi runtime requirements, 59
OSGi Service Platform Release 2, 55, 56,
57t, 60
OSGi Service Platform Release 3, 55, 56,
58t, 60
OSGi services, 52, 56-59, 57t-58t, 78
Otis, 7
OurPrice tag, 295
OUT parameters, 221, 222
Over-the-Air server, 429
Over-the-Air support, 138

P

P2P mobile messaging, 163-86
Palm OS, 12, 158, 199, 228
Palm PDAs, 155
Palm.net, 12